BEHIND THE BURMA ROAD

BEHIND THE BURMA ROAD

The Story of
America's Most Successful Guerrilla Force

by William R. Peers and Dean Brelis

WITH ILLUSTRATIONS

An Atlantic Monthly Press Book

LITTLE, BROWN AND COMPANY • BOSTON • TORONTO

ATLANTIC—LITTLE, BROWN BOOKS
ARE PUBLISHED BY
LITTLE, BROWN AND COMPANY
IN ASSOCIATION WITH
THE ATLANTIC MONTHLY PRESS

Published simultaneously in Canada
by Little, Brown & Company (Canada) Limited

PRINTED IN THE UNITED STATES OF AMERICA

This book is dedicated to the memory of
William J. Donovan
and
Joseph W. Stilwell
and to the Kachin Rangers

Foreword

Lππππππππππππππππππππππππππf

THIS BOOK is the result of an unusual writing collaboration between a commanding officer and one of his men. Colonel W. R. Peers, now attached to SAC, was commander of Detachment 101 of the Office of Strategic Services from December 1943 to July 1945 and, before that, the Operations and Training Officer. Dean Brelis, now a novelist, was a field agent, first as sergeant and then as lieutenant, during 1944 and 1945. Although the story of Detachment 101's guerrilla operations is seen in this book through the eyes of the commanding officer, the actual text is the result of a collaboration between the two men, and we hope that it embodies not only the difficult command problems of a complex guerrilla operation, but the experiences and accomplishments of the men in the field as well.

W.R.P.
D.B.

Contents

Illustrations

(to be found between pages 118 and 119)

General Stilwell and Colonel Peers close to the battle lines in Northern Burma.

Colonel Eifler, first commander of OSS Detachment 101, with *pungyis*.

Lieutenant General Daniel Sultan, Lord Mountbatten, Major General William J. Donovan and Major General Albert C. Wedemeyer.

"A" Group, just before they parachute into Japanese-occupied Burma.

The main building of Detachment 101's base camp at Nazira, Assam.

Burmese and Kachin agents learn how to set up intelligence nets in the field.

Agent Saw Judson instructs future agents in the processes of cryptography

An American field commander inspects Kachin recruits behind enemy lines.

A Kachin muleteer from one of the guerrilla companies, with rifle and *dah*.

Captain Curl and Kachin headman Zhing Htaw Naw.

Supplying guerrillas in remote areas by airdrop.

Three Americans land in a Kachin area behind enemy lines.

Elephants were often the foundation of a guerrilla battalion's transport logistics.

A small detachment of guerrillas moves toward a friendly Kachin village.

Guerrillas' own version of a Bailey Bridge.

A bridge successfully sabotaged by a 101 guerrilla force in Northern Burma.

An American Air Force crew rescued by 101 guerrillas after being shot down behind Japanese lines.

Three Japanese prisoners captured and interrogated by 101 guerrillas.

A wounded American operations leader is evacuated from the field by light plane.

Chin recruits are issued rifles by a Kachin noncommissioned officer.

After the Japanese defeat in Burma the guerrillas are awarded rifles and swords and are discharged.

Maps

PART ONE

A Request

I

The Oath

ᒐᒐᒐᒐᒐᒐᒐᒐᒐᒐᒐᒐᒐᒐᒐᒐᒐᒐᒐᒐᒐᒐᒐᒐᒐᒐᒐᒐᒐᒣ

THE ARMY is always calling people together for a conference; there are many jokes about this, but since many of them are unprintable, it is best to forget them. The meeting that began that day had nothing amusing about it. We were in a bad situation and we came to it not at all certain that the new word would mean less fighting than that which had already taken place.

"You've done a little bit so far. Now I've got the big job for you." He said the words slowly, with the characteristic tightening of his eyes behind the G.I. steel-rimmed spectacles he wore. He walked closer to the map, and looked at the mountain ranges, the rivers, of North Burma. I looked at the red arrows which indicated the enemy. It was a miserable day. There was nothing but rain; the sound of it on the roof, or what passed for a roof, was steady and hard. He was the General, and what he said was more than an order, more than a law. It was conviction. His communication was the sound of history, and you had to accept that if you were to understand Joseph W. Stilwell.

He put a cigarette in his holder, lighted it and pulled noisily, the match burning close to its end before he blew it out. The sweater he wore was khaki-colored with a turned-up collar, and on his desk was the faded campaign hat with the sweaty brim, the five-pointed stars that were neither polished nor new, three stars that said he was a lieutenant general with all the weight that that implied. He bent and adjusted the laces of his canvas leggings, his fingers alert and muscular, the leggings old. He held himself like a piece of leather that cannot crack, that survives time and shows the burn of experience.

From the time we had word that he wanted this talk, I knew that what he would ask would be more than we anticipated, and that this meeting would alter the position of Detachment 101. Maps go together with meetings of this sort and I had brought them along, sensing that new plans were going to cross the maps, and that if we had sweated before, we had best prepare for still more.

Two other men were present besides the General and myself. They were the General's son, Colonel Joseph Stilwell, Jr., who was the Intelligence Officer for the Northern Combat Area Command (NCAC); and Major Chartrand, the Detachment 101 Intelligence Officer.

The meeting place was a command post that stood in a native village in the upper part of the Hukawng Valley. It was cramped for space and looked like a hovel. The structure had been built originally by natives, and now it was protected from rain by the canvas roofing and sides that brought into the space the mildew smell of canvas subjected to torrential rains too long. There was a high wind outside, and whenever it blew open the flap of the tent, it brought a chill.

The General dipped briefly into the aspects and facts of the Burma campaign, reminiscing, in his laconic way, about the long road that he had made out of Burma, when, as he put it, "The Japs beat the hell out of us," in the spring of 1942. The retreat had followed the course of all retreats: extremes of cowardice; the bravery of men who stood and fought rear-guard actions; the hope that the next rise ahead would bring sleep — only to get there and find the Japanese.

Any time Stilwell had a chance to counterattack, he did, knowing all the time it was in a losing game. He had to quit Burma, and what remnants were left after he reached safety in India were reorganized and formed into two so-called divisions (in fact little more than battalions) comprised largely of Chinese who had been sent to Burma to help fight off the expected Japanese invasion.

In his Indian camp, at a place called Ramgarh, Stilwell set about a task that meant starting from zero. He was glad to have that chance, because he was the kind of man who had moved often from zero to altitudes of success. Around him he gathered some highly qualified American officers and noncommissioned officers and they began, with mounting spirits, to reform an Allied Force that would return to Burma; they aimed at remaking the Chinese infantry into an American-style fighting unit, and the training instructions were based entirely on those which governed similar American units.

Their direction was back to Burma, and by the fall of 1943, the Chinese had broken away from Ramgarh and moved to Ledo. They were still in India, but the miles between Burma and India had shortened and the smell of Burma was nearly upon them. Hot and tired, as they camped in Ledo, the chafing of those hours of training, the sweat and shame of defeat, weighed less upon them; they knew they were almost ready for the first strike back. To them and to the commanders of the two Chinese units — one, the 38th Division commanded by General Sun Li Jen, a graduate of Virginia Military Institute; the other, the 22nd Division, commanded by Hakka-born General Liao — there was only one belief, and this they told General Stilwell. They could meet the Japanese and they could win.

The General ordered an advance into North Burma.

Through the Naga Hills, the first natural barrier on the border of Burma, they marched, and showed, upon those few occasions when they met light Japanese infantry scouting detachments, that they were cool under fire, and absolutely desirous of sweeping away token resistance to move on toward the true target, the Japanese Army. The mood of fight was still with them as they came down through the Naga Hills and reached the Hukawng Valley and the Chindwin River. And here came the first test for the Chinese.

They faced an excellent Japanese division — the 18th — and the vigor of this unit had been shown in the jungle blitzkrieg which had won Malaya for the Japanese; the 18th had led the advance. The best of Britain's and Australia's infantry and artillery, prepared to make any kind of sacrifice to hold ground, had fallen before the smooth working actions and plans of the 18th Japanese Division. In short, the 18th was a formidable adversary.

The outlook when the first Chinese advance parties came into engagement with the Japanese in the winter of 1943-1944 was both severe and harrowing. The 18th was solidly dug in. They had shown uncommon aptitude in utilizing the natural terrain as their front line of resistance — and what it was like can best be described as a wall of steel, though in fact, it was bamboo. Since to most of us bamboo suggests something light and fragile, dedicated to the easy way of fishing, it should be explained that this was a variety of bamboo known as *bullaca*; it is from four to eight inches in diameter, and is capable of withstanding light artillery fire. The Japanese had perfected this bamboo into a concrete-strong barricade. Clumps of the bamboo grew ten to fifteen feet in diameter; the enemy had burrowed underground, as if building a tunnel, until they reached the center of the clump. Then, coming up to the center, they had chopped away enough so that they were absolutely surrounded by the natural obstacle, protected against light and heavy rifle fire.

It stopped the Chinese; the barrier took them by surprise. The Chinese advance was held up.

The solution came to General Sun and the 38th Division. After trying easier alternatives, the Chinese decided they would have to go smack into the bamboo fortifications; they would have to dig out the Japanese in the fiercest of hand-to-hand combat.

Everybody on the Allied side was in a state of suspense. The battle would tell whether or not the Chinese could engage the Japanese successfully, would tell whether there was a chance that the Allies could fight their way back into Burma and keep moving until realization of the dream we all wanted; the surrender of the Japanese Army in Burma, the return of Burma to the free world, the raising again of the British, Chinese and American flags that had been torn down in the hellish retreat of 1942. And that day of our 1944 meeting, General Stilwell thought about it again, about that critical time a few months before when, after the Chinese had engaged the Japanese, it had seemed almost over — and in favor of the enemy. The Chinese had moved in attack formations, had almost penetrated the Japanese defenses, had almost reached the belly of the fortifications, when a counterattack smashed through against their oncoming tide, forced a fight on ground that favored the Japanese. The initial attack on the part of the Chinese was made with one thousand men; there were five hundred Japanese opposing them. Seeing their first dead in large numbers, and hearing the banzais of the 18th in full-scale, the Chinese were almost routed in panic. They retreated. Immediately, sensing the situation, General Stilwell picked up the challenge, and suggested to General Sun that a regiment of Chinese should go into the fight, hitting the Japanese left flank. This fresh unit swung into action and drove back the onrushing Japanese, reclaiming at the same time the weary Chinese who had already been in battle — the battle of Yupbang Ga as it was later to be called by historians. When the fighting was done, the Japanese had been clubbed into withdrawing. And for General Stilwell, it proved that he had not asked too much; the Chinese could fight, they could kill, and be killed, and they could force the enemy out of his chosen ground. For the first day since 1942, the Allies in Burma had not been worn down by the enemy. They had won a battle.

The necessity of returning to Burma was strategic, and underlay all our plans for victory in Asia. Before the Japanese invasion of Burma, our supplies had been sent overland from Rangoon across the old Burma Road to China. The Japanese had captured this road, and we had been forced to rely exclusively on airlift over the "Hump." Our new plan demanded a land supply route from India into China across Northern Burma; supplies sent by such a route could keep the Chinese armies fighting in their homeland. The new Chinese advance into Burma from the west made it at last possible to start putting this plan into execution.

American engineers, under the command of Colonel Arrowsmith and later General Pick, had begun building a road from Ledo across the Naga Hills toward the upper reaches of the Hukawng Valley. It was a road-building situation involving the most complicated engineering and extreme hazards; the uncharted road track led through land that had not known anything more than the most tenuous of spoors. Everywhere the topography was a complicated enemy of cliffs, of enormous peaks and hushed forest, of jigsawing rivers and extremes of heat and cold. It was a special kind of road, and its builders were threatened not only by landslides, but by nearly every kind of harmful insect and beast. There were endless threats to the health and well-being of human bodies. Fits of depression and illness were an undercurrent of daily life and yet the mood of the engineer battalions was not as mutinous as might be expected. They made progress in conditions that at any time, other than war, would have been intolerable.

In many of the companies, the soldiers were almost all Negro, and their high morale was emphasized by the sound of their voices, singing with a sense of pride as the hypothetical road slowly became a reality. Anyone who watched them during those days would feel their excitement, their assurance grow as the road took on the shape of a truck route. They were within hearing distance of the battle ahead, and frequently the Japanese infiltrating through the Chinese lines balanced themselves on the high tree branches and sniped at the backs of the sweating men. Even this was not too much. It might put off work for a few hours as our troops flushed out the sniper. When the road crews saw the sniper dead, they turned again with determination to the work. By the time the battle at Yupbang Ga had been won, the engineers were only miles away, continuing their work through the shooting, knowing that the world of the battle was theirs as much as anyone else's. Their progress was also a victory. The Ledo Road had been born, the road that would make it possible to travel overland to China. The road was three lanes wide, gravel, a road for which the miles ahead had still to be won, a road which would virtually be drenched in blood before it had made its way through a country still dominated in large part by a powerful enemy army.

Our advance into Burma had not been extraordinary; yet there was one certainty about it. Infantry were advancing, and directly behind them we were building a road. This was no scouting mission, no moment of flashing strength in the enemy's teeth and then quickly withdrawing. What the road meant was that we were coming to stay and to move on, until at last we had reached the China border.

This was warfare of the most serious kind because in it we had dismissed the notion that we could be defeated for a second time. If there was anything odd about our advance it was that we were staking all we had on a limited number of men.

That first victory at Yupbang Ga had given us an offensive spirit and we were determined to exploit it by continuing to advance, by re-engaging the Japanese Army.

The 38th Chinese Division pushed deeper into the Hukawng Valley with quickness and spontaneity, with orders to contact the enemy. They also made a feint to the south. With the adroitness of a chess player gambling a knight for a queen, General Stilwell sent a regiment of General Liao's 22nd Division on a flanking movement to Taro. Their journey was made difficult because they traveled across country, through remote jungle, where there were no villages. They were supplied by airdrop. They were in luck crossing the Chindwin River undetected, and, when finally they came upon the enemy, they had accomplished complete surprise. At once they attacked and destroyed the enemy force of five hundred men at Taro.

General Stilwell, when he received reports of this success, became sure of what he could do. He could envision his two Chinese divisions driving further south, assured of combat strength through their victories. Because he was aware of the competitive character of the Chinese soldiers, he could prepare a plan which they readily accepted. The two divisions would now go to war together and yet remain in intramural competition with one another. Within thirty days they had advanced another fifty miles into the Hukawng Valley.

By now, General Stilwell had strong attachments to both units; they were advancing across enemy-held territory; they were submitting the Japanese to a little of what our forces had tasted in the retreat. He also had a growing regard for his Chinese commanders. He felt that each in his fashion was in no way second to the other; Sun had perhaps a more instinctive feeling for brilliance of maneuver, while Liao had strength in his personal leadership during actual combat. Such as their talents were, and they were considerable, what made them genuinely excellent in their command was that one was always trying to outdo the other, without jeopardizing their final mission — to cause the Japanese to lose the battles.

The Chinese had been given the characteristics by many of laziness, of quitting, or of being hard to handle; "slopees" they called them. General Stilwell had not accepted any of these notions.

"The two engagements so far," said General Stilwell, "show what can be done with these Chinese outfits if they are properly fed, armed and trained. All you have to do is give them a little combat experience and they are as good as any combat units you will find anywhere, including our American forces. They are accustomed to deprivation and can get along on a few handfuls of rice, peanuts and fish. In this sense they can make out with far less than American troops. Except for ammunition. They are a little jittery and they shoot at the crack of a twig; but this too is being reduced as they get confidence in themselves."

Then he examined the map again, and his finger traced across the vast areas held by the Japanese. A shadow was on his face for a moment, then his eyes twinkled as he looked at me and repeated:

"The big job now, Ray, is for you and 101."

But before we went into that, he wanted us to tell him where our men were, what we were up to; and on that day, he was especially curious about how much success we had had as guerrillas.

"You know," he said, "every time I look at those Jap lines, I realize you've got your people behind them," and then, laughing, "I'm not quite sure . . . "

"Not quite sure?" I said.

"Oh, I've got confidence in you and your boys all right." He smiled to himself. "There's Myitkyina," he said, pointing to the city. His hand made a quick arc over the mountains north of that big and important target of Myitkyina. "We've got people up there. We could be a lot worse off if they weren't up there, Ray. Now, tell me what they're up to."

I stood facing him, seeing the map, realizing that our numbers of people were few. We were guerrillas.

Happily, we were over the first stages of creating a guerrilla unit, and it had gone pretty well considering all things. Guerrillas are

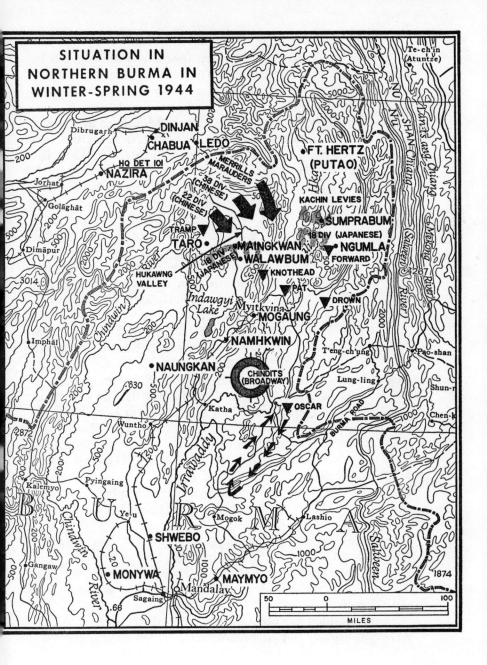

irregulars; they operate not from their own innate strength, but by striking at the enemy's weakness. The guerrilla's first job is to remain anonymous, to live among the enemy in order to discover his weakness.

When the guerrilla learns the weakness, he irritates it. He does not overwhelm it, rather he dodges in and out, in a way that permits him to remain anonymous. A guerrilla fighter is ruthless, has no respect for battle courtesies. He agitates the enemy.

Guerrillas are subordinate to conventional forces. Where conventional forces stake victory or defeat on a plan for battle, guerrillas do not have a legacy of battle conventions. And because of this, guerrilla movements, dispositions, and actions do not follow *any* book. The usual problems of supply, the logistics of troop movement, the recruiting and training of guerrillas are spontaneous acts which, ideally, can swell into unorthodox offensive action, sudden, momentary, but deadly; as quickly as it appears, it can burrow back into a pocket of anonymity.

As a guerrilla becomes more self-sufficient and develops confidence in his ability to conduct effective operations safely behind enemy lines, he begins to double, then treble his force and its scope of operations. His activities, in order to remain guerrilla in nature, must always adhere to the principle that he can never commit himself to action until all the odds favor him. The guerrilla is not concerned with immediate victory. He believes in a slow accumulation of surprises that irritate the enemy. To accomplish this desired end requires infinite patience. The stuff out of which a guerrilla will build his own strength, besides patience, is the equal necessity of wiliness, of invisibility when he travels, and of a courage which is not disturbed by a long period of time behind enemy lines.

I went to the map, put my finger on Myitkyina, then moved it straight north, some fifty miles above that city, up into mountain ranges of over seven thousand feet, following the line of the Irrawaddy River to within its headwaters, to the area of what we called the Triangle.

There I pointed to a place where a party of men were encamped secretly. They had not yet been detected by the enemy, and their code name was FORWARD. So far, they had succeeded in recruiting seven hundred natives as guerrilla fighters, and were just now sending out some individuals on espionage operations. The commander was an American naval officer named Jim Luce. His civilian background was medicine; posted with him was an American lieutenant named Gerry Larsen. They and their men brought a steady flow of information to the Allies about Japanese strength and movements in Northern Burma — it was as if an invisible camp were functioning in the enemy's back yard. Luce and Larsen had been up there for a year with plenty to their credit, including the capture of three Japanese prisoners, alive, who had been brought out of the enemy-occupied area to India for interrogation, and the rescue of several American aircrews shot down flying over the Hump; and, unvaryingly, FORWARD was a refuge for the wounded and lost of the long-range penetration columns led into Burma by General Orde Wingate of the British Army. FORWARD's greatest problem was food. They had managed to cache a small supply against a day when they might be cut off from receiving airdrops; but the increasing numbers of downed aircrews and exhausted British infantrymen staying with them, awaiting evacuation, were diminishing supplies.

Jim Luce had succeeded an Army major named Chris Wilkinson who had been pulled out and sent to develop guerrillas in enemy-held parts of China. Luce's practical experience in medicine was an invaluable asset for a guerrilla leader.

This was the kind of luck that kept us going; Luce's personal presence, his doctor's background, carried great prestige in courting the natives and getting them to join our side. He was popular because he helped sick families, and because he knew how to improvise for jungle surgery under primitive conditions.

The general sat down now, lighting another cigarette. And I saw how small was the command post of our meeting, one cot, one table, one roof, four men and many maps.

Again, his eyes on the map, he said, "Oscar? what about Oscar?"

"Oscar reported by radio as usual last evening at five," I said.

"Where is he now?" asked the General.

The map had the answer. My finger bypassed Myitkyina and

swept south, past mountainous Bhamo, far south, in the direction of Mandalay, a city of cymbals and pagodas, a city occupied by Japanese and unattainable for now, a city for the future.

My finger stopped there, insanely near Mandalay; there wasn't a man in early 1944 who didn't dream of Mandalay, who didn't wish for Mandalay. And mad as it was, I showed the General a contour line atop a hill overlooking Mandalay.

I have seen many reactions of surprise and the General's set a special and private standard.

"There?" he said. "He is there — the damned fool?"

"A month ago, sir," I said. "He went in with apparently no effort, and he is in good health. His intelligence reports make American-British planning safer. We pulled him out a short time ago when it got a bit hot."

"I suppose he's at Firpo's now," said the General, "enjoying Calcutta and all the rest."

"No, he is not at Firpo's; he is not in Calcutta. He's on the border."

"Border?"

"The China-Burma border, sir." My finger moved north on the map, showing where.

"You don't give a man much of a rest, Ray."

"Oscar rests better, General, in his opinion and mine, when he is given complications that he thinks he can manage."

"The man is crazy or brave?"

"Brave, General; he is shrewd, able and he is a bit different."

The General frowned in understanding; but Oscar's exploits were not about to stop him.

He briskly asked about the rest of our secret operations.

I turned to a point not too far away from Oscar's on the Burma-China border, and noted that here too a British officer was in command. His name was George Drown. He had been a captain in the Kachin Levies, one of the traditional native units officered by Englishmen, whose history stretched back to the earliest days of the British raj. Although he was as isolated as a man could be from the amenities of anything approaching civilized life, Captain Drown's habits in the field had an unrelieved fastidiousness. With a degree of ritual and precision, he had trained a native to act as his valet, twice a day laying out those things he needed for shaving and making himself presentable. Without a word being said, the valet knew when to hand over the razor, the towel, the toothbrush in a properly silent manner. In view of Captain Drown's isolation, I sympathized with his living in a manner that made him comfortable.

In matters of espionage, his agents had gone to places thirty and forty miles away from their hideout, returning with information that was radioed to India. The information had been received with gratitude.

Moving the General's attention on, away from the China-Burma border to Myitkyina again, I now found myself describing an operation coded as PAT. This unit was led by two Anglo-Burmese who held second lieutenants' commissions in the Burma Army. Unlike many Burmese during the retreat of 1942, these two men had marched out and then volunteered to go back into Burma. One was named Patrick Quinn, and the other, Dennis Francis. They were young, in their early twenties, and they wanted to fight. They were now located near Myitkyina — and their proximity, only twenty miles from the bulk of the Japanese Army's major base in North Burma, enabled them, as opportunities arose, to attack the enemy truck and rail convoys. They had a small band of about fifty guerrillas and some fine sabotage and espionage agents.

Besides Luce, the other American commander in the field at that time was an Army lieutenant named Vincent Curl. His was the largest camp, located west of Myitkyina, in a range of steep, fortress-like mountains; when the operation was in its planning stage, someone had used the word "knothead" in conversation, and in the ensuing laughter, without further ado, we chose KNOTHEAD for the Curl operation's code name.

Because many varieties of mission were to be asked of Curl, he had two American sergeants with him; Jack Pamplin, a cryptographer, and Fima Haimson, the radio operator. This close partnership, a team in fact, of an American officer and enlisted men working together was to become a fundamental part of our operation. Antagonisms between officers and enlisted men were rare; almost nonexistent.

There were also two Chinese — Skittles and Hefty — under Curl's command. They had been chosen because they both knew Burma as the country of their birth; through many future trials we were to find that their experience and intuition were a great source of wisdom. Skittles, in particular, had been involved before the war in mining engineering, and had traveled over a great part of Burma's remote geography, precisely the kind of terrain that befits guerrilla and espionage operations. Further, Skittles provided KNOTHEAD with an expert linguist; he spoke fluent English, Burmese, Chinese, Hindi, Urdu, Siamese, Kachin and a half dozen obscure dialects of the numerous hill tribes scattered throughout Burma.

We had risked quite a bit in sending KNOTHEAD and all the talents it represented so deep behind the Japanese lines; but it was the only way to launch our operation, and after six months in the field, they were in a zone secure by guerrilla standards, and had quickly made contact with an influential Kachin headman named Zhing Htaw Naw.

Even before KNOTHEAD made contact with him, Zhing Htaw Naw, because of his antipathy to Japanese occupation, had fled to the mountains inaccessible to the enemy and had waged a spontaneous, if modest, guerrilla campaign. When KNOTHEAD and Zhing made contact, the Japanese already had a price on the Kachin's head. It goes without saying that from Zhing's point of view, meeting KNOTHEAD was the fulfillment of a dream. The Kachin and his band were without ammunition and physically weakened, but their spirit was resolute. They asked for ammunition for their guns — weapons so antiquated that they would have seemed at home in a museum.

As for Lieutenant Curl, he immediately requested a drop of modern arms, ammunition, food and medicines. When the drop came, Zhing and his followers needed only the briefest of instructions in handling the carbines and tommy guns.

Precisely because these Kachins were pleased that they had modern weapons and spread the word to other Kachins, KNOTHEAD was besieged with recruits. Curl now wanted more arms, but we had insufficient drop planes.

"Hell," the General interrupted, "you and your pirates stop worrying about drop-plane support."

"Are you saying the matter is settled, General?"

He said it was, and he asked me to continue.

I then described TRAMP, the code name for the third of the British-commanded field units. At the moment, TRAMP was providing the advancing Chinese divisions with the kind of intelligence that assists the movement of any large body of troops about to engage in full-scale battle. TRAMP was commanded by Red Maddox, an English major. He had only a handful of natives with him. We expected no deliberate guerrilla operations from TRAMP at this time. Later, he would expand, but TRAMP's function was the classic one of seeing and hearing as much of the enemy as humanly possible without making itself known.

The plan for each of our operations was to get men placed where their safety was not threatened, where they could keep a knowing eye on the enemy's movements, and where, once they had established themselves with the native people, they could strike the enemy from behind, cutting his lines of communication, hitting him where he thought he was invulnerable. Surprise was essential.

Firepower counted heavily, too, because our men traveled in small units, and therefore when they came upon the enemy a decisive factor was how many they could massacre from ambush. The more they killed — and the goal was *all* — the surer the guerrilla's quick and uncontested escape. Superior firepower means half the battle for a guerrilla, and this we had given our men. And Japanese equipment and firepower in North Burma was a decade behind the times.

"The outcome of what I plan," said Stilwell, "depends a great deal on your men's actions."

The General repeated the names of all the people in the field, needing no prompting from me. He repeated their exact locations, and what they were doing and planning. Our operation was as clear to him as it was to me, and the men were as real. I found that not only had he listened, but he had absorbed it all.

General Stilwell sat back quietly and thought for a minute. Then he said, "This may come as a shock to you and I am sure it will surprise a lot of people, but I fully intend to be in Myitkyina by this summer and that means before the monsoon rains set in."

He was correct; to talk about Myitkyina as ours in a matter of months fell on my ears with an explosive shock. Myitkyina was over two hundred miles away and in between lay the actualities of trackless, heat-ridden jungle as well as the excellent, battle-confident Japanese 18th Division. The monsoon rains could be another cause for agony. Normally, they begin during the first half of June, and it would be of strategic importance to capture Myitkyina by then. At that rate, General Stilwell was saying that we would sit in Myitkyina in only three to four months.

"That's fine, General," I said. "Do you think the two Chinese divisions can do it? It is true, they've done all right against the Japanese so far, but can they take on the whole 18th?" I was beginning to guess, at this point, what he had meant by the big job.

He elaborated upon his plan by stating there were certain things which must be taken into account. First, he had received approval from the War Department to use the 5307th Composite Group (later known as Merrill's Marauders) in Northern Burma as the lead American attacking force. Essential to obtaining Myitkyina were the Chinese 22nd and 38th Divisions. In the general's plan, they were to attack straight through the Hukawng Valley; but at the same time, Merrill's Marauders were to operate as a flanking force, especially in making end runs around the Japanese right, or northern, flank.

Secondly, Stilwell had the 30th Chinese Division in reserve. They were still training at Ramgarh in India, but would be ready to join the battle plan in a matter of weeks. He also expected, if necessary, to receive reinforcements from Generalissimo Chiang Kai-shek.

Thirdly, General Stilwell's plan took into account the diversionary effect of the British plan to employ Wingate's Raiders south of Myitkyina. Wingate's forces, a mixture of English, Burmese and Indian troops, were to strike the Japanese road and rail communication and supply depots, and make every effort to engage Japanese forces generally along a line running east and west through Katha. This diversion would hopefully draw enemy strength away from the true target — Myitkyina — and simultaneously, almost eliminate the possibility of the Allied forces being outflanked.

Fourthly, the Kachin Levies, under the command of British Brigadier Bowerman, had recently come under Stilwell's direct command, and he envisioned them as pinning down the Japanese forces in the area of Sumprabum, north of Myitkyina.

Thus, the plan to liberate Myitkyina involved the arms and men of many nations: frontal attack by the Chinese; flanking movement by the American Marauders; diversion by the British column to the south; and a holding effort by the native Kachins. Stilwell expected to achieve surprise with such an effort. It was to be the first offensive large-scale plan by the Allies against Japanese-occupied southeast Asia. Since General Slim's British 14th Army was still defensively engaged on the Imphal front, Stilwell's stakes were high; he vowed he would fight into the monsoon if necessary to break the Japanese control of North Burma.

The unwritten law for fighting in Burma stated that the monsoons were a time for both sides to establish their positions and stop fighting. Stilwell's idea was to destroy the myth forever. He planned to supply troops by airdrop. He would not let the rains stop the attack. And the enemy, with no airdrop potential, would get into grim trouble trying to keep his motor convoys of supplies rolling over waterlogged roads and trails.

"This attack," said General Stilwell, "is going to be touch-and-go. We will have to utilize every resource at our command. I am convinced that your Kachins can help and I want them on our side. I am going to need intelligence, lots of it.

"Here, now, is the big job for you," he said, and he did not underrate its importance. "I want you to expand your guerrilla force to a strength of about three thousand as quickly as you can. The bulk of the guerrilla forces should be located around about Myitkyina so that when the combined forces of Chinese and American troops get ready to put on their final push, you will be prepared to give them maximum assistance. The other thing I want is intelligence. No matter how difficult, expand your espionage activities; I want to see agents well south of Myitkyina and Mogaung and even further south if you would like; but, above all, make certain we can depend upon their information. Now that is about it. Can you do it? I am not going to try to tell you how to do it, that is your job."

"Yes, we can do it, but we need some things to get it moving on the time schedule you desire. Specifically, we need some qualified personnel, arms and ammunition, a priority for aircraft for parachute drops of personnel, supplies, and equipment — and, finally, we need priority to get some of the backlog of critical people and equipment — particularly signal equipment — we have sitting in the United States, waiting to get here."

He saw this in a favorable light, cursing the red-tape stupidity that held up vital men and supplies from reaching the China-Burma-India (CBI) Theater. But if we needed officers now he could provide them.

I replied that we could get along for the time being with an increase of about six qualified officers.

He said, "Okay, I'll tell you what, you will have eight officers waiting for you tomorrow night in Ledo." With that he scribbled a message to the Commanding Officer of the Replacement Depot at New Malir, outside Karachi, thirty-five-hundred miles away, telling him to "send eight rough, tough and ready lieutenants for guerrilla operations to report to the adjutant general in Ledo tomorrow night."

He then cleared a no-nonsense order for immediate delivery of four hundred carbines and twenty-five 60mm mortars, and sufficient ammunition for our troops. With this done, we got down to the matter of drop airplanes.

I pointed out the difficulties of the weather and Jap Zeros and that we would need more than the two planes we were using for the job he wanted done.

"How many?" he said.

"Initially at least six airplanes," I replied, "on a continuous seven-day-a-week basis."

There was no quibbling. I saw him weigh in a matter of minutes our requirements against the needs of other Allied forces in Northern Burma. It was not just Burma either. He had to think of the Hump aircraft, flying arms and ammunition to the Nationalist Army in China and gasoline to General Chennault's 14th Air

Force. But the powerful reason for his battle plan was to open a secure land route to China. We had to win in Burma if they were going to win battles in China. He gave us the planes we needed.

He terminated the meeting, saying, "If you fellows can do the job that I expect for the Myitkyina campaign, you can automatically plan on increasing the size of your force to ten thousand or whatever it takes to do the job. It may be possible that your outfit will grow into something even bigger than either of us can imagine today. Some day you may have the opportunity to write a chapter on the subject of your — "and smiling, he said — "your form of unconventional warfare.

"Few worse things can happen," he said, "then to lose a battle because we didn't trust the fighting qualities of these people, these Kachins. You've been saying they're anxious to take on the Jap. This is their chance."

PART TWO

Rendezvous with Urgency

11

The Beginning

⎍⎍⎍⎍⎍⎍⎍⎍⎍⎍⎍⎍⎍⎍⎍⎍⎍⎍⎍⎍⎍⎍⎍⎍⎍⎍⎍⎍⎍⎍⎍⎍⎍

WITH THE ORDERS from General Stilwell fresh in my mind, I left and went back to the headquarters of what we were officially called, OSS (Office of Strategic Services) Detachment 101. Naturally, I was excited that Allied forces were about to put on their first comprehensive drive into Burma; and I could not help feeling pride in the role our unit would play.

One can easily imagine resistance movements in Western Europe or the Mediterranean, but southeast Asia was not an area of interest, in traditional terms, to the United States. So our being there at all, and certainly in the capacity of guerrillas, was without precedent. The decision had been carefully made. It was not chance that brought about 101; rather the result of a shrewd decision made by Generals Stilwell and William ("Wild Bill") Donovan.

It grew out of discussions in early 1942, wherein they analyzed some of the reasons for our defeat in the first Burma campaign. Foremost, they reckoned, among these reasons was the factor of Japanese fifth-column activities; ambushes behind our lines, jungle night attacks, demolition work and the all-inclusive roles of the guerrilla: the influence of surprise, the gradual sense of uncertainty, the half-formed thought that all is not safe that arises from unpredictable efforts to stop normal military life — or just to keep it back a step or two.

Such a unit had never been organized within American history. There was nobody trained, qualified or, for that matter, anybody who knew much about carrying on irregular war. Finally, Stilwell from his military tours of duty in Hawaii recalled a man named Carl Eifler, who had been the Deputy Collector of Customs in Honolulu.

Eifler was a reserve officer, had lived for years among the Chinese and Japanese in Hawaii and the Far East, and had spent considerable time with the Border Patrol along the Mexican border.

In checking the whereabouts of Carl Eifler, General Donovan found that he had been called to active duty and was a captain commanding a company in the 35th Infantry Regiment in Hawaii. Obtaining his services from the Army was a simple formality for General Donovan; and the next thing Eifler knew, in March 1942, he was ordered to Washington to report to General Donovan, the Chief, Coordinator of Information (COI), which was later to become the Office of Strategic Services (OSS).

Carl was quite an imposing individual. He stood about six feet two inches and weighed on the order of two hundred and fifty pounds. He was as strong as a young bull, skilled in jujitsu, and even practiced a little yogi. He was intelligent, imaginative, and he had a gambler's insight into understanding how much to leave to chance. He was a natural for the job and in the days before leaving Hawaii for Washington, Carl did a little recruiting.

A fellow officer in the 35th Infantry was Captain John Coughlin, a six-foot-five West Pointer who had been a good baseball pitcher and a heavyweight boxer. Carl knew Coughlin as a keen competitor and a man of vitality, and when he approached him about leaving a rifle company for irregular warfare, John was more than willing to try his hand at it. Carl also enlisted Vincent Curl, his first sergeant in the 35th Infantry; a medical officer named Captain Archie Chun Ming who was also President of the Hawaiian Chapter of the Reserve Officer Association; and Robert Aitken, a captain in the Intelligence Section of the Hawaiian Department. By the time Carl left Hawaii he had recruited a party of men, each, in his curious way, adaptable to the secret operations ahead.

When Carl arrived in Washington, General Donovan issued to him a rather vague and yet singularly unprecedented set of instructions. He told him that his organization would be the first American unit ever assembled and trained to conduct a wide variety of clandestine operations — espionage, sabotage, guerrilla warfare, propaganda, escape and evasion and so on. Furthermore, Carl was to be ready to fight a kind of warfare that knew no rules. His organization might eventually expand, but initially it should remain small, if not obscure, about forty men at the most. General Donovan said the area of operation might be anywhere in the Far East, in jungle country, in ports, in rice fields, in mountains, even in cities as far apart as Rangoon and Djakarta, Kunming and Bangkok. So uncertain was the situation in the Pacific and the Far East that this was about all that could be told to him, this, and that he was to carry out insurrectionary tasks ranging from assassination to bridge-blowing.

On 14 April 1942, Detachment 101 of the Office of the Coordinator of Information was officially activated. Why was it numbered 101? A subtle kind of bravado. Though this was the first United States unit of its kind, a number less than 100 might not have the proper weight of age and experience; 101 seemed the very model of a unit that had been around for a long time.

After his discussion with General Donovan, Carl, a man of practical bent, realized that men of ingenuity and extraordinary enthusiasms were what he wanted. Since he had no idea, no certain knowledge where in the Far East they would begin, ingenuity, to a remarkable degree, must be shown in picking his recruits. He compiled a guide list of the basic talents he needed. He decided that before 101 could engage in successful guerrilla warfare, he would need men who knew military science and tactics, engineering, explosives, radio and other communications, basic medicine, precision machinery, and photography; and men who possessed a language aptitude.

In the 12th Infantry, the "President's Own," at Fort Myer, Virginia, Carl located three young captains, Devlin, Little and Wilkinson, who were willing and eager for an overseas assignment shrouded in secrecy. In a bar one night, Carl struck up a conversation with an officer who just happened to be an engineer — after several hours and several drinks Carl had recruited himself an engineer officer. And so it went. By the time the unit was organized he had recruited four infantry officers, two engineers, three radio technicians, a watchmaker, a court stenographer, a Korean patriot and an American who had been the advisor to Chiang Hsüeh-liang, a powerful Chinese war lord of the mid-twenties known as "The Young Marshal." The initial 101 was a small unit of only twenty-one persons (twelve officers and nine NCO's), but a very well-balanced party that could qualify for whatever schemes were dreamed up for it.

My own admission to this band came about through the inspiration of Captain Coughlin who had joined Carl in Hawaii. I had known him as early as 1937, when I first came on active duty from the University of California in Los Angeles.

In the early months of 1942, just after Pearl Harbor, I was attending a wartime, abbreviated version of the Infantry Officers Advance Course at Fort Benning, Georgia. My family and I were living about twenty-five miles from the post in a rustic lodge which for them was far from comfortable and in winter months, an igloo. Early one Sunday morning on a cool March day, a neighboring farmer, looking bedraggled and damp from his half-mile walk in the rain, informed me that Fort Benning with an urgent message was calling on the telephone.

I thanked the farmer for his courtesy; when I got to the telephone, I learned that the message originated in Washington. It was: "Are you interested in a combat assignment in the southwest Pacific?" Signed, "Captain John G. Coughlin."

Suddenly I knew the answer was yes. The times I had spent with John left no doubt in my mind that whatever was involved would be all right, and possibly, a big show.

By the time the course was completed and I had returned to my home station at Fort Leonard Wood, Missouri, a set of orders was there directing me to report immediately to the Coordinator of Information, Washington, D.C. That afternoon I received a telephone call from Colonel Garland Williams of COI who told me where I was to report. It was fortunate he called because, in those days, so little was known about the COI that one might roam around Washington for days and never find it.

Upon arriving in Washington I checked with Captain Coughlin. He then took me in to meet my new commander, Captain Carl

Eifler. To say I was in for a rude shock would be the understatement of a lifetime. After an exchange of salutes, he offered his hand. I could see it was strong and the way he grabbed my hand was proof. He proceeded to crack every joint, smiling all the time. Back of what he was doing was a message. Danger? The next thing, as if it were entirely habitual, he took a stiletto-type dagger and drove it a good two to three inches into the top of his desk. He looked pleased. I was confused. I had never had anything like this happen before and all I could think was, "What's next?"

It turned out to be a briefing and I have never had one more effective, before or since. He used a standard wall map and his strong hand moved along like a tank, covered nearly all of China and half of Siberia. By way of explaining what we were going to do in the Far East he took me on a few verbal reconnaissance missions and ambuscades. We rode with the pirates on the Yangtze River, on Mongolian ponies with the war lords across the sands of the Gobi Desert, operated with the Dacoits or robbers in the Mekong Valley. The impression was of parachutes, hit-and-run fire fights, resistance movements, sabotage, of missions crisscrossed with danger. My role then, I thought, was shortly to become something I had never expected. I wondered why John had lured me into this. He looked at me pleasantly.

Following this, we went on a short trip through the office. I met Colonel Strong of the Marines and Colonel Garland Williams, the Army officer who had given me directions over the telephone and who was about to leave for parachute training at Fort Benning; and finally I met General Donovan's deputy, Colonel Goodfellow, a reserve officer called to active duty from the *Brooklyn Eagle*; and his secretary, Miss Dockery, who had been with him for years on the newspaper. These were all knowledgeable people, and it seemed totally natural to find them studying books on the terrain features of Japanese-occupied southeast Asia. Then we went in to see General Donovan. I reminded myself that he enjoyed one of the truly fabulous fighting reputations. To see him was to be lifted to the pride of "The Fighting Sixty-ninth." His ribbons commanded my attention: aside from General MacArthur, he was the only soldier who wore our nation's top three awards — the Medal of Honor, the Distinguished Service Cross and the Distinguished Service Medal. The maps on the walls were marked *Secret*. He made us comfortable by pointing out his concern over the Japs pressing India and China and how good guerrillas would be invaluable in slowing up the enemy's progress, in following up every opportunity for information that could eventually mean the defeat of the Japanese. Later, I took John aside and told him how good it was to be part of 101.

In another few days, one part of our unit, consisting of Captain Eifler, Captain Coughlin and the bulk of the officers, went to a British paramilitary indoctrination course in Canada. The other half, of which I was a part, became the first class at the newly established COI School known as B Camp. It was situated in a beautiful location in the Catoctin Mountains of Maryland, a short seventy miles from Washington. It was later taken over for President Roosevelt's use as a mountain retreat and renamed Camp David by President Eisenhower.

The instruction at B Camp lasted for two weeks; it was abnormal to get more than six hours' sleep a day. Our course of training involved skills such as would be useful for our future — methods of agent operations, secret writing, resisting an interrogator, searches for downed aircrews, cryptography, experimenting with a variety of high explosives, learning the difference between blowing a stone or steel bridge. We learned how to use primitive but effective detonators. Sabotage became less of a mystery. Overseeing our course was a precise man named George White who had been a narcotics agent with the Treasury Department. He was short in stature, about as wide as he was high and looked less like an expert saboteur than a harmless grocer.

At our disposal was the whole range of explosives of the day: dynamite, TNT, composition C, and a full line of modern fuses, caps and delaying devices. We were constantly studying and discussing British commando raids on France, Norway and North Africa. A young engineer captain, Charles Parkin, assisted by three lieutenants, Karwaski, Lazarsky and Gleason (nicknamed the Three Skis), were responsible for this phase of our instruction. Though they had no firsthand experience with guerrilla warfare, they were perfectly willing to absorb information from every possible source — and pass it on to us.

The instructor in unarmed combat, on the other hand, bore many visible scars, showing that he was not wanting in gutter-fight experience. His name was Fairbairn, and he was a major in His Majesty's Service. Before the war, he had been chief of police in Shanghai. He was an old hand at killing. He had a distaste for anything that smacked of manners in fighting. He knew all of the dirty tricks and he worked continuously to erase any of our sportsmanlike notions or ideas. To him, there were no rules in staying alive. He taught us to enter a fight with one idea: to kill an opponent quickly and efficiently. He had designed a scalpel-thin, sharp stiletto which would leave hardly any marks or blood, and he could use it with the unerring skill of a surgeon at work. He was equally as effective in his unorthodox method of shooting a pistol at close quarters. He would invariably say, when putting the finishing touches to a would-be victim, "Don't let him lead you up the garden path."

In the final days of our training we were assigned in teams of two the job of destroying a nearby city's industrial plants. We were to move out disguised as Army privates. All possible information on the assigned target was to be obtained, sketches prepared, and plans made to sabotage it. My partner was Nicol Smith, an author who had lived in the Far East, and our target was an aircraft factory in Hagerstown, Maryland. Curiously, we had been supplied with uniforms that were a comic facsimile of those worn during the First World War. They were tattered, dirty and wrinkled, and the general appearance we cut, walking up Main Street in Hagerstown, was pointedly absurd. Yet we could not have been better off. No military policemen bothered to challenge our appearance.

The first move we made was to obtain a copy of the plant directory, and as luck would have it, Nicol was acquainted with one of the executives. After checking into a hotel, Nicol phoned his acquaintance and asked if he could come out and see him; also that he had a close friend with him who had recently been drafted into the Army. Having been cordially invited to come out as soon as possible, it was a simple matter to rent a suit of clothes for Nicol and to get my uniform pressed so that I didn't look so much like a character out of a Charlie Chaplin film. Our host turned out to be most hospitable, and invited us to tour the plant. Obviously, this was a solution to our challenge of discovering how to blow up his plant without being detected.

The tour turned out better than we had expected. To all our questions as to how his factory might be slowed down or damaged, our host provided answers. He showed us plans, how their alarm system worked, where the guards were located. In a matter of a few hours we were presented with all the data we could possibly need for a first-class job of reducing the factory to ruin. None of this was guessed at by our host. Had he known that our purpose was sabotage he would have acted other than hospitably. But one thing was true about our method — an enemy saboteur might cultivate the same kind of friendship for the same ends we had in mind. Naturally, our sabotage plan was not put to a test.

It may appear that the procedures used by Nicol and myself in gaining entry to the plant were not exactly according to the rules and, to a degree, that may be true. However, if an enemy agent were to attempt to case or reconnoiter a plant such as this, he would be extremely fortunate to get himself established within three months and it would probably take him a year to assemble the necessary data. Since we had only a day or a few hours to do the job, it was quite obvious that we had to cut all kinds of corners and take advantage of every situation that presented itself. If we were caught the worst that could happen to us would be to spend a few hours in the local jail until OSS bailed us out. But in the case of an enemy agent, if he were apprehended in time of war, it would probably result in his death.

The schooling was completed and the unit reassembled in Washington toward the end of April, 1942. Shortly thereafter the group received instructions to leave for the Far East in the latter part of May. This posed several major problems. Our knowledge of the Orient was extremely limited; only two members of the group had ever been there. We were slightly better off for our training at B Camp, but that training brought up a lot of questions. How much of each type of explosive should we take with us? What kind of switches or delay fuses should be taken to set off these explosives? What kind of and how many weapons should be obtained? We speculated as to the shape and location of a base camp. We didn't know how big it should be, what kind of transportation we should have, how we would store our supplies. Who was to provide the answers? There was no other outfit quite like ours and we had only six weeks before departure. Not a single item of supply or equipment had been procured for the unit.

Since there were to be about twenty-five Americans in the initial group, twenty-five became our magic number. We procured twenty-five of everything, sleeping bags, jungle gear, mosquito nets, individual sets of equipment and weapons. The specialists drew up lists for their particular areas. Captain Huston and his communications group prepared a detailed request for radio parts and other signal equipment; Captain Chun Ming did likewise for medical supplies; Sergeant Moree for photographic supplies and equipment; Lieutenant Tillquist and Sergeant Hemming for demolitions.

The next problem was to locate, purchase and order the supplies and have them delivered to the port of embarkation, Charleston, South Carolina, not later than 20 May. This meant two weeks to find the equipment.

Captains Little, Devlin, and I had at least had some experience in supply matters so we tried to find the means for getting the job done. However much we did, without Colonel C. P. Townsley of the Army General Staff backing us up, it would have been the old story of soldiers without supplies. And our requests were not easy to fill. Jeeps, for instance, in those days were scarce and in great demand, yet the order of fifteen of them, along with five one-and-one-half-ton trucks, was delivered to us from Detroit on less than two weeks notice.

The procurement of supplies from civilian sources was much more difficult. Most of the purchasing was done from supply catalogs by way of telephone and telegraph to some of the larger suppliers of outdoor equipment, office equipment and radio parts. In order to insure that these items would reach port by the sailing date, it was necessary that a large percentage of it be shipped air freight. It was expensive; however, our second shipment of supplies would not reach us in the China-Burma-India (CBI) Theater until approximately ten months after we reached our destination. Without the supplies we could take with us, Detachment 101 would remain a myth, an expedition that should have stayed home, so it was vitally important, no matter what the cost, that the supplies sail with us.

Meanwhile, during this hectic race for supplies, we purchased books to build up our library on the Far East, and we talked to anyone we could find who knew the geography and the people of the Orient. A number of people gave us a chance to talk about the Far East. Ex-rubber planters from Malaya were one group; wives and relatives of prisoners-of-war still held by the Japanese, another. We saw Dr. Christianson, a professor of history from the University of California who had spent years in Burma and had written several books on the country. He provided much enlightenment on Burma, and later his book became required reading for everyone in the unit.

Carl Eifler, recently promoted to major, left some days ahead of us, taking with him Master Sergeant Curl. When we saw them go, we felt the reality of Asia coming closer, and our training, which had taken us almost to the point of exhaustion, turned now in our minds as something permanent, something that we would never forget.

There was no place for sentiment when our own orders came through. John Coughlin, also recently promoted to major, was designated to head the remainder of the group, first to Charleston, South Carolina, the port of embarkation, and thence to India. A few of the group imbibed a bit too much, but more were comforted by the presence of their families, and one of the young lads got himself married. We went down to Charleston by train, taking along Sergeant Pamplin on a stretcher recovering from an emergency appendectomy. Every mile was kept alive with conversation and the strength we felt from each other.

All our cajoling and telephoning to obtain the supplies seemed useless when we reached the port. Nothing had been loaded aboard ship; and it was obvious from the blank looks we received that no one knew anything at all about Detachment 101. This was our first crisis after the race for the supplies. I believe today, thinking back on it, that the people responsible for the port were bound up in so many labors to get the obvious onto ships that when they came across the 101 materials, the fact that they had no idea about us, no knowledge of where we were going and what we intended to do, gave them a good excuse to put our supplies aside. Fortunately, they made one intelligent decision. They had stacked our boxes together under a single roof, and as we came upon the pile, it seemed a monument to frustration.

But we could not pause to enjoy and curse the irony; now began perhaps our most pressing job, more important than the training itself. Our boxes were in a complicated mess — and we had to pull everything open so that we could learn exactly what was coming with us. None of us had ever worked like that; with the departure time so close, everyone in the group hauled crates around with the pace of stevedores. A harmony developed right there and then.

At all events, we had almost finished the job when there were only five hours remaining until sailing time; and then a new hurdle. Not a single jeep or truck of ours had been loaded when, with a harassment we did not deserve, a new pitfall was laid in our path. We were told that the jeeps and trucks could not be taken aboard. No reason was given except that there wasn't time. All normal arguments failed, and only threats and exhortations of a kind that suited the students of Major Fairbairn's ruthless techniques broke through the barrier. We were told that we could load no jeeps; then, five jeeps; in the end, we managed three more than our quota, the last one still unlashed when our ship cleared the dock. Everyone in our unit in appearance and look and voice was, it seemed, a hundred years older.

We crawled into our bunks, and we knew how tired we were much later when we remembered the events of four days and nights of loading and checked our position to find that we had slept for twenty-six hours.

III

The Waiting Game

 ⎍⎍⎍⎍⎍⎍⎍⎍⎍⎍⎍⎍⎍⎍⎍⎍⎍⎍⎍⎍⎍⎍⎍

IT WAS THE FOURTH of July, 1942, and we celebrated our arrival in the CBI Theater by having a bottle of beer in the newly opened American Officers' Club. There was only a handful of Americans in Karachi at that time and we were the only ones in the club.

Our journey to Karachi had been highly interesting, but uneventful. When our ships' convoy reached Freetown, West Africa, we had disembarked, leaving behind Sergeant Haimson to guard our supplies for the remainder of the trip to India. The rest of the party had flown across Africa and the Near East along the route established for the army by Pan American.

When a person is in the military service, he meets people, makes friends and associations that last for a lifetime. No matter where you go you continually meet old friends, and it simplifies getting the job done. This happened to us throughout the war, as it did at Karachi where the commander of the port of embarkation turned out to be John Coughlin's West Point classmate, Colonel Paul Yount. He arranged everything; the receipt of our supplies when the ship arrived, the rail movement of the unit to New Delhi and a procedure for notifying us to have our supplies unloaded and moved to base camp, wherever it might be.

We were forced by the flooding Indus River to remain almost as if isolated in the airport terminal buildings; and what we heard over the radio and from people who had somehow gotten through to the airport seemed tumultuous. The river had broken its banks, and eyewitness accounts described it as unsuppressable, flooding hundreds of miles of the Sind Desert, and in many places threatening to engulf the railroad embankments, normally a bridge against any flood threat.

Even so, this delay was fascinating because it gave us a closer look at the Moslems, the quiet of morning broken by the call to prayer, the streams of people to the mosques, the minarets like scythes against the sky — and again, as the sun went down, the chorale of voices saying their prayers. After dark, we kept our interest alive by going out to where the camel caravans passed, something endless out of the *Arabian Nights*, the men in their gowns, the camels swaying against the solitude of night, and the lead camel showing the way with a lantern tied around its neck. The caravans, some with scores upon scores of camels, traveled at night because during the day the sun was furnace-hot and intolerable. There were other experiences, with a murmur of Kipling to them. Ever near us were British soldiers, and among their stories they included tales of the Hurs, a troublesome obtrusive set of tough bandits, who haunted the trade routes of northeast India. Camel caravans, passenger trains, motor convoys presented no problem to the Hurs. They were bold and they were not far removed from Jesse James. In one way or another, their henchmen got aboard a train, halted it at a strategic place, and when the main band came aboard, it was easy to rob, pillage, loot and rape. For Europeans they had no sympathy. Not much was said concerning Hur treatment of women, but typical of how they looked upon ruining a man was their practice of cutting off the male organs. It was a foreboding and true picture as we learned from verifying newspaper accounts. Needless to say, when it was dry enough to make our train trip across the Sind we picked our places aboard the car with an eye to its defense. We were armed as if for an attack at any moment.

But the rail journey was safe and peaceful. When we came upon the walled city of Hyderabad with its courtyards and arches, with the smells and noise of traders, the stretch and range of empty desert seemed suddenly picturesque, and through the train windows the ornamented glows of the passing city were a gladdening sight. We managed the unlikely food, simple Indian fare of pieces of chicken, more bone and skin than flesh, and began to feel the trip as a movement closer to the final stop where the enemy waited. Tenaciously chewing on the chicken bones, we ignored the sandy taste of the food, and listened to the engine throb, watched the stars twinkle ceaselessly, and talked of Burma eastward.

We arrived at Lahore, and its markets, which made us think of those at home. We purchased scarves of Kashmir wool, sandal-wood fans and bookends, ivory elephants. Nearly all of us walked through the city, and in its color, its embroidery of turbans on al-most every passing head, we tasted some of the flavors of one world quickly vanishing in favor of another. For here we saw the po-tential conflict between the Moslems and the Hindus and the first fires of nationalism.

When we at last reached New Delhi, no one in the group could conceal his satisfaction. For this was, in one sense of the word, the end of the journey. In New Delhi we hoped to begin the work to prove our belief in guerrilla warfare. We would start to get things done. But as it turned out, New Delhi was to provide frus-tration. The Headquarters Office of the CBI Theater, like many Headquarters, was understaffed. The American staff at New Delhi was small, only fifteen officers, and vastly overworked. In our group alone there were nearly that many officers again, and naturally CBI Headquarters turned its attention to absorbing us into their midst. At every opportunity they tried to exercise means, overt and sub-tle, to propose that we give up this idea of guerrilla warfare and espionage and become a part of their more traditional way for win-ning the war. They had absolutely no appreciation of the potential of resistance forces, espionage, sabotage and other clandestine operations. Their thinking was along conventional military lines, and anything to the contrary was sacrilegious. Diplomacy and tact of the subtlest kind were required to say "no" without giving of-fense. Clearly they could use our manpower, and it was equally as clear that if we became one of them, 101 would cease to be. So as soon as we could, we established our claims.

From the first we made contact with British Intelligence. They treated us in a manner that inspired confidence in ourselves, making available to us maps and reports from their own agents in Burma. There was no report or file they considered too secret for our eyes. In a way, it made our mouths water to learn that it was possible to parachute one's agents behind the Japanese lines and establish communications. Formal and correct though they were, there was an imaginative and witty side to the British Intelligence people. They did not propose that they had a prior claim on Burma, but indeed welcomed a new effort in the profession of irregular warfare. It was their view that the more of us involved in it, the merrier would be the espionage accounts to be filed away in the top-secret files.

Property, even life, in the India of August, 1942, was threatened by the powerful forces of a surging nationalism and by the Japanese preparing to invade India. The combination was potent, and reached the bewildering, bloodthirsty proportions of mob action in the cities. What made it worse was that Gandhi's followers were the chief participants. They were whipped into mob frenzy by Chandra Bose, whose will was for violence. The ulterior purpose of the riots was to create confusion, to plunge India into rebellion to coincide with a Japanese landing on the east coast of India in the area of Madras.

The British discovered the Japanese invasion convoy and, risking all, they achieved surprise and devastatingly bombarded the convoy by air and sea until its threat was destroyed. All the same, the Indian nationalists felt sufficiently strong to try their plan. They created pressure which, for a short and dangerous time, almost got beyond control. In New Delhi alone on the first day the casualties rose into the thousands.

Mobs appeared everywhere, tore down telephone lines, ripped up railway lines, destroyed vehicles, created fires, threw their humanity into desperate acts of ruthless sacking. There were pitched battles in the streets with all sorts of primitive weapons, largely rocks and clubs. But rocks, in the hands of a whole community meaning to kill, were lethally competent in the ensuing massacres. For three days, a mixture of death and fire swept India like a withering plague; gradually the police, backed up by military units, established a shifting semblance of law and order.

We Americans had kept out of the chaos, ready to defend ourselves if attacked; but the sweep of the riots did not carry to our compounds. When we went out into the streets after it was over, we were met by days of funeral atmosphere.

Thousands had died — no one knew quite how many, but the visible evidence was enough to suggest countless numbers. The streets had a lonely, harassed, dismantled air. Close at hand lay the dead. Figures among the bodies removed them to the ghats, stripping whatever belongings could be of use to the living. For days upon days, the air was a cloud of smoke from the fires hurriedly consuming bodies. The British had done well to destroy the Japanese convoy, for the rioters needed an invading army to ensure success. In our own thoughts, British rule in India seemed rather nervous, balanced on a very fine edge.

Understanding the British rule in India was deeply important but difficult. It was not easy to give it thought. The British were our friends and we were fighting together. Yet the nature of imperialism was around us. Poverty and starvation, too, the sort that has no footing anywhere in America. On first impression, the darkness, the unlimited poverty of millions of Indians appeared an unfortunate aspect of the British presence. India was another jewel in Britain's crown, and yet here human decency was wanting. The impression in those first days after reaching India was that British power had a bad side that we had never known. We felt that they had misused the people of India. Not then, but later, as we got to know India, we realized that this was not a sophisticated, nor sufficiently perceptive way, to see the British.

We began to see roads, railroads, communication systems, dams, and industrial capacity. We noticed schools, hospitals and public buildings. We saw huge factories, harbors and transportation centers. These were a British way of life in India for Indians. The results were certainly of economic benefit to British business, but the gains toward an India in line with the twentieth century were also apparent.

There were a few "haves" of the maharajah and marwari (merchant) class and they had much, but there were many "have nots" and they had pitifully little. The "haves" took all they could from the "have nots" in the form of cheap labor, land rentals and simi-

lar forms of exploitation. One may have been somewhat critical
of the manner in which the British landlords treated their laborers,
but it was not comparable to the manner in which the Indian landholders and planters treated their own people. For their part the
British tried to give their laborers and their families decent homes.
In addition, each family was given a plot of land on which to grow
rice and vegetables. Even though their salaries may have amounted
to only four to six annas (ten to twelve cents) a day, it more than
provided the necessities of food, clothing and shelter. A considerable portion of what could have been drained off as profit was, in
fact, returned to the land in the form of benefits to the laborers.
This was not true of the Indian landholders I observed. They returned to their laborers only what they absolutely had to. Most of
their laborers lived in filthy hovels and were dirty and disease-
ridden.

The average life expectancy of the Indian was twenty-seven
years. This appalled the British and they tried to improve the situation by a variety of means. One of the experiments which they
tried was quite interesting. They recognized that a large percentage
of the deaths occurred at birth, so they instigated an extensive
campaign for the development of midwives. This was so successful
that at the end of the second year the population, which had been
increasing at the rate of two million per year, was now growing by
leaps and bounds to almost six million a year. At this rate, India,
which was already seriously short of food, would have been faced
with widespread famine. As a result the midwifery campaign had
to be discarded.

The next month or so in New Delhi was terribly boring to the
entire group, for our only interest was to get started in operations.
We were able to do a few things to earn our keep. After the scare
from the uprisings, CBI Headquarters became concerned about
losing the supplies stored in United States installations through
sabotage by dissident elements or the Japs. Consequently, they
asked us to prepare plans for their demolition or destruction. There
were not many American installations, and it required only three
or four days to complete the job. Lieutenant Dave Tillquist, with
his extensive knowledge of engineering, did the majority of the

work. He knew precisely where the charge of explosive should be placed; how much would be needed for a particular size and type of building; and how to train the demolition teams.

Carl was busy developing contacts with the Indian Army and the Burmese Army. He made a trip to Simla, in Kashmir, to establish liaison with Sir Reginald Dorman Smith, the governor of Burma, from whom he obtained much reliable data concerning the military situation in Burma. He also assembled information concerning refugees from Burma who were in relocation camps in eastern India.

Each day we were in the CBI Headquarters it became increasingly clear Burma would become our principal area of operation. It followed that if we were to work in Burma, we would need all types of people to operate under cover.

Time was on our hands and we knew if we were to get into operations, the sooner we got started the better. It requires a considerable time to recruit, train and infiltrate agents into operational areas. The older officers in CBI kept advising, "Be patient, be patient, General Stilwell should be back in a day or so."

Finally, General Stilwell returned from China, and, as soon as he had settled Headquarters business with his staff, he met with all of the officers and men of 101. He said he was anxious to have us get behind the Japanese lines. Information was scarce, and he believed anything we could reveal about the enemy would influence forthcoming operations. What he wanted was a group eager to knock to pieces the myth that a white man could not survive in the jungle. He thought that we should consider ourselves pioneers in blazing a way back to Burma. Whatever doubts had obscured our destination were now gone, with the result that our depression vanished instantaneously. We had heard the General say it: he had selected Burma as our target. And what until now had been speculation became an order. We readied ourselves for the task, the impotence of waiting forgotten, the sense of mission restored, and the General's calm our blessing.

The written order he gave us to confirm his discussion was typically Stilwell. It said to do these things:

(a) Establish a base camp in northeast India and from there be prepared to (b) conduct operations to deny the Japanese the use of the Myitkyina airport and the roads and railroad leading into it from the south, and (c) closely coordinate operations with the British authorities (XIV Corps) to insure that there would be no mutual interference and that effective liaison be established.

Burma Setting — 1942

WE WERE NOT UNPREPARED for Burma. The months of reading, of interviews, now reaped an agreeable if modest reward. We had one slight advantage in approaching the main target. Everyone knew at least something about Burma. It was the strategic center of the battle. In the landscape of southeast Asia, you could move from Burma into China, into India, into Thailand or into Malaya. Burma had been the goal of the Japanese in consolidating their offensive movement through southeast Asia. Burma was the Allied goal for carrying the fight to the Japanese; and in the meantime, Burma was a key to preventing further Japanese advances.

Geographically, Burma had numerous variations: mountains of disheartening remoteness and height, phosphorescent swamps, unnerving jungle with darkened lairs of powerful animal life, endless coastline, flowering gardens, rivers of unusual terror and wonder, fertile golden plains and limitless rice fields.

It is a country never seriously threatened by famine. Its natural resources abound with opportunities for riches in oil and rubies, gold and tin, teak and copper. Within its frontiers, touching China to the north, India to the west and Siam to the east, there is an atmosphere at once melancholy and happy, where death can be violent one moment, peaceful in another. Six hundred miles wide and twelve hundred miles long, north and south, in square miles it is larger than France, almost equal to Texas. The lower extension of Burma, known as the Tenasserim, extends for over four hundred miles down along the Malay Peninsula.

Upper Burma has a fearsome rib cage of mountains, the shape of a horseshoe, the open end facing the Bay of Bengal. To the west, along the border between India and Burma, are the Naga Hills; to the east lies the formidable Karenni Range bordering on Siam; and to the north are the Himalayas which rise beyond, 20,000 feet high. The drainage from Burma's mountains, bolstered by spring thaws in the Tibetan Himalayas and augmented by monsoon rains, slash across the land as huge, fast-flowing rivers which empty into the Bay of Bengal. Because of its physiography, Burma is known as a "valley state."

The main rivers are the Irrawaddy, the Salween, the Chindwin and the Sittang. When they are in spate from monsoon rains, power equipment is needed to cross them. Other rivers such as the Namtu and Shweli, up to five hundred feet wide form a natural defense line. During the dry season, the Irrawaddy is clear, almost transparent, but with the arrival of the monsoon it rages, taking its toll on lands and villages standing in its way.

There are two large lakes in Burma. To the north in the area of Mogaung is Lake Indawgyi, and south of Mandalay in the Lower Shan States is located Inle Lake. Both of these lakes are approximately five miles wide and twenty miles long and are noted for their beauty.

The climate of Burma is generally tropical. However, because of its length north and south, the climate is considerably varied. During the period of the southwest monsoon, from June through mid-October, all of the lowland areas are hot and humid. The rainfall in these areas exceeds three hundred inches in Southern Burma and recedes to something less than two hundred inches in the area north of Mandalay. During the dry season between the rains, the climate in the northern part of the country becomes increasingly cooler. In January in Myitkyina the days may be warm, 75° to 80° F., but with the setting of the sun and the loss of radiation a chill sets in. The temperature drops 20° or more in an hour, and the night becomes cool, then cold, often only a few degrees above freezing.

To the east and south of Mandalay the land slopes upward into a huge plateau encompassing the Northern and Southern Shan States. Here the average annual rainfall is less than thirty inches and the weather is generally mild throughout the year.

Originally, nearly all of Burma was covered by tropical rain forests and grasses. The trees of the forest are hardwood and difficult to extract. Most of them are so heavy that they cannot be floated down rivers to sawmills until after prolonged, continuous drying. The practice is to lash huge sections of bamboo to the logs as buoys. The grasses are coarse, ten to fifteen feet in height, with edges so sharp they are capable of cutting into flesh with the ease of a razor. The climate in the Shan Plateau creates some unexpected vegetation. Here the light rainfall and mild climate produce low-order conifers and deciduous trees quite similar to those found in American highlands. Since the arrival of the early migrants, large portions of the more readily accessible areas of Burma have been cut away and developed into farmland, principally for the cultivation of rice. Despite the encroachments of man, today 75 to 85 per cent of the country is still primitive forest.

Throughout lower Burma and up to the twenty-second parallel, between Myitkyina and Bhamo, there is efficient and extensive extraction of teakwood. Elephants are a necessity: regardless of jungle or weather conditions, they drag and stack logs with the power and accuracy of modern mechanical equipment. The elephants entail expense, costing $3,000 each, and sometimes as much as $8,000.

The jungle foliage is dense and overhead it forms a natural canopy that keeps out sunlight; days are spent in semi-darkness with the whirring sound of mosquitos constant, night or day. The faint, gloomy light prevents the growth of low-order plants and, consequently, the jungle floor, always in shade, is strangely tidy. Where the lacework of growth between sun and earth is fragile, and the sun's rays flow through, the flora are profuse, a constellation of trees, grasses, thorns and vines. Movement through such areas is difficult, a sweating toil that leaves men staggering. These areas naturally suggested themselves for our work; the jungle depths provided the means for our protection and survival. Among the roots, in the unimaginable thickets, in these naturally veiled sanctuaries, there was refuge and there was food: fruits, leaves, sprouts, bamboo shoots and, throughout the surroundings, pheasant, pigeons, peacocks, deer and pigs could be seen and heard.

A guerrilla's way of life is to live off the land — and it would be inappropriate for him not to know the people of the land. Burma's population is on the order of eighteen million, made up of several ethnic groups and further subdivided into local groups often speaking a separate dialect. Of the ethnic groups the Burmese are by far predominant. They represent more than ten million, or over half the total population. For the most part, they occupy the desirable, arable lowlands and dominate all of the political and economic activity of the country. The remaining groups are principally hill tribes who occupy the mountain highlands surrounding the Irrawaddy watershed. The major groups include the Karens (2 million), Shans (2.5 million), Palaung (.3 million), Kachins (.4 million) and the Chins (.4 million). There are numerous lesser groups, so that throughout Burma there are approximately 250 separate dialects.

The early history of Burma is uncertain. Scholars appear to agree that the first migration into Burma took place about 500 A.D. These people migrated from Mongolia, through China, and eventually settled in Central and Southern Burma. These first arrivals are now referred to as the Burmese. Successive migrations from Mongolia took place for the next eight hundred to one thousand years. The movement of these latter groups into the rich lowlands was prevented by the then warlike and powerful Burmese. As a result, all the groups to arrive at a later date were confined to the hills, where they remain to this day.

Some of the Burmese dynasties were very powerful. In the eleventh century King Anawratha put down all resistance and unified the country. He built Pagan, the city of a thousand pagodas. Later Pagan fell to the Mongolian hordes of Kublai Khan but the Mongols maintained no sovereignty over the country. In the sixteenth century Bayinnaung became the ruler of Burma. He eliminated all resistance within Burma and then engaged in a series of wars with Siam. He twice sacked Ayuthia, the Siamese capital, and started the Burmo-Siamese Wars which continued for a hundred years or more after his death. Burma declined until 1750 when Alaungpaya seized control of Northern Burma and began a series of campaigns which, within five years, culminated in the re-unification of Burma. His dynasty ruled the country until the British conquest and the eventual exile of King Thiebaw and Queen Supayalet in 1885.

In the latter part of the eighteenth century Britain and France had ministers at the court of the Burmese king. As the vast natural resources of Burma became known, both France and England developed designs on the country. Beginning in 1824 with the first Anglo-Burmese War, the British East India Company seized the lower portion of Burma. There followed a second Anglo-Burmese War in 1852, brought on by Burmese mistreatment of British sailors, in which the Burmese were soundly defeated. Finally, in 1886 in the third Anglo-Burmese War, the British, irate over French intrigue, annexed Northern Burma. The pacification of Northern or Upper Burma was not simple, however. It required more than five years and over 40,000 troops. As a result of these wars, Burma was incorporated into India as a province and was governed by the viceroy. In 1937 Burma was separated from India and became a separate colony of the British Empire with its own governor general, its own government and its own army and navy. Such was the situation when World War II reached Burma early in 1942.

Taken together, the Burmese people are carefree and winsome, they are capable at once of mischief and of more somber qualities. Their literature has a tendency towards quarrels between jealous lovers, their festivals are full of laughter and a pleasant touch of sensuality. They are ardent gamblers.

The people of the hill tribes vary considerably in their degrees of civilization. Some of them are quite primitive and hardly out of the head-hunting stage. The most primitive are the Nagas, who still take an occasional head today and are located in the hill tract, known as the Naga Hills, between Burma and India.

The Chins are somewhat more advanced, although in some regions full dress is little more than a G string. The Karens and Kachins are roughly comparable to one another in their development. In some sectors they are still quite uncivilized, but in other areas they are reasonably well educated, some of them having attended colleges or universities. In both instances they are creating a culture which is a mixture of their own and that of the Burmese. The Shans, who are closely related to the Siamese, are perhaps the most highly developed of the hill groups. In cultural attainment they parallel the Burmese.

The present-day Burmese and the Shans are not warlike people. Hence, the bulk of the Burma Army before World War II was composed of Karens, Kachins and Chins, in that order. The Karen Rifles and Kachin Rifles were naturally endowed fighting units in every respect superb jungle fighters, but lacking the capacity, in training and equipment, to battle Japanese mechanized infantry and armor. As the Japanese overran Burma the Kachins and Karens warred on until they had no ammunition; in these circumstances, they hid in hills and mountain villages. They were to be the foundation on which we built our guerrilla force.

Over two-thirds of the sophisticated population are Buddhists. The teachings of Buddha flashed through Burma from China although Buddhism had its origin in neighboring India. Nearly every Burmese village contains a Pongyi Chaung, or monastery, as well as pagodas and shrines. These are tended by monks called pongyies who serve without pay and gain their food by begging. Every male Buddhist must serve for a time as a pongyi and, in the larger communities, yellow-robed and shaven-headed pongyies may be seen everywhere.

Other religions in Burma include the Moslems, the Hindus, the Animists and the Christians. The Asiatic Animists have a sprightly form of nature worship; the breeze in the trees, the ripple on the water, the phases of the moon are all omens and there are literally hundreds of them. Each omen is represented by a *nat*. There are good *nats* and there are bad ones. The good *nats* are not given much attention because they cannot do harm, but offerings and other homage are paid to the bad *nats* to ward off their evil spirits. Animism was present in Burma before any of the other religions. Even though an individual may be a Buddhist, a Christian, even a Hindu, he will not entirely part from an awareness of instances when he can do himself harm by ignoring the *nats*.

At the beginning of World War II there were approximately

half a million Christians in Burma. Of these about 65 per cent were Baptist, 25 per cent Roman Catholic and the remainder represented a variety of churches. The Catholic missionaries were the first to arrive, in about 1725. They confined their work primarily to Lower Burma until a few years before the war.

The story of the beginning of the Baptist missionary work in Burma is utterly fantastic; a storybook tale. It is beautifully described in a book, entitled *The Silver Slipper*, which covers the final days of Burmese royalty. In brief, in 1813 Dr. and Mrs. Adoniram Judson, both Baptist missionaries, arrived in Rangoon from the United States. The Burmese judged their work evil and cast them into a dungeon. However, by coincidence, the Karens of the hills to the east and of the Bassein area near Rangoon had a legend which said that one day a white-haired man would come and bring a book. The book, of course, was the Bible, which was immediately outlawed by the Burmese. The myth had its power. The Book was translated, reproduced and smuggled into the Karen Hills, where it was widely read.

As a result of the Bible incident Dr. and Mrs. Judson were taken to Mandalay to the court of the King Thiebaw, where they were strung up by their feet, lashed, and suffered all the cruel tortures the executioner could conjure up. He could not succeed in obtaining a denial of their faith. This so impressed the King that he allowed the Judsons to go into Upper Burma, near Bhamo, to establish a school. Other missionaries followed to establish churches, schools and hospitals and to convert large numbers of Kachins and Karens to Christianity.

The economy of the country is predominantly agrarian. Rice is the main staple. The rich soil of the valleys produces over eight times that required for local consumption. Before the war Burma was exporting on the order of ten million dollars worth of rice to India each year, principally to the highly populated provinces of Bengal and Behar. Other exports included tin from the Tavoy area, tungsten from the Mawchi mines, which fulfilled approximately one-third of the prewar world demands, and teak lumber. The Namtu mines near Lashio were converted to modern methods by Herbert Hoover early in the century to produce a wide variety

of metals; zinc, antimony, nickel, copper, gold, silver and lead.
Burma also has a sizable oil field. In comparison to the total
world production it is quite small — representing less than one
per cent — but its strategic location makes it of great importance.
The Burmese had long been using the areas of Yenangyaung to
extract oil through shallow digging, but in the early part of the
century, American drillers sank deep wells, and since that time
over four thousand wells had been drilled. The petroleum products
made available by these wells fulfilled Burma's needs and provided
additional surplus for export to several countries of southeast Asia.

The Japanese campaign to seize Burma in 1942 had been swift
and efficient. They assembled two of their best divisions, the 33rd
and 55th, which had swept through China, Malaya and Singapore
with sensational effect. In mid-January 1942 these divisions struck
the initial blow against Burma in the area of Moulmein, which
fell with almost negligible resistance on 30 January.

The Allied defense forces in Burma consisted of the 1st Burma
Division and the 17th Indian Division. Both of these units were
understrength and had serious training deficiencies. The total
Allied combat strength in Burma was something less than 25,000.
The bulk of the forces were native Burmese formations of Karens,
Kachins, Chins and others. British units in the Indian and Bur-
mese divisions totaled about 4,000 and there were about 8,000
Indian troops.

The British, Indian and Burmese forces had built their defenses
with hopes of halting the Japanese at the Salween River. The
Japanese supply lines were over-extended; they were using every
means at their disposal to transport the essential supplies for their
forces from Bangkok in Thailand. Meanwhile, they were making
extensive use of their Air Force against Rangoon, Pegu, Toungoo
and other Burmese cities. Japanese naval forces were also active
in the Bay of Bengal and had sunk several freighters and coastal
steamers. The Japanese began probing the Salween River line in
early February and on 9 February effected a crossing in the area
of Martaban. They pushed on and, in the latter part of February,
succeeded in effecting a crossing of the Sittang River. In seizing
this crossing the Japanese cut off several British and Indian units

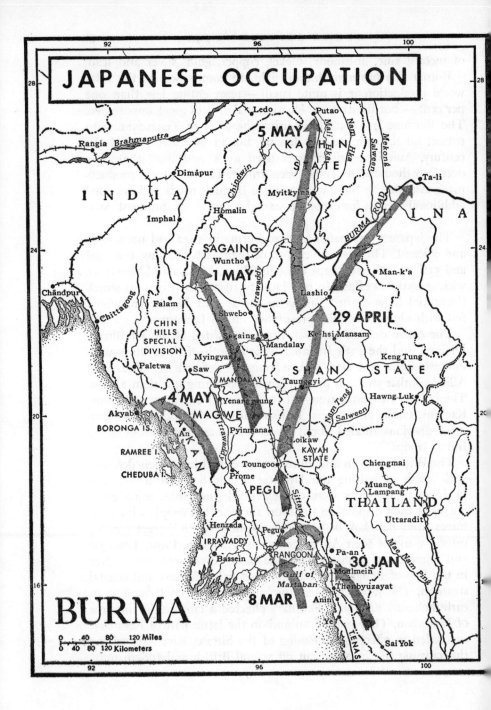

before they could be pulled back across the river. Some of the Indian units were composed of Ghurkas from Nepal. All Allied units gave good accounts of themselves in heavy, close, hand-to-hand fighting, perhaps the bloodiest of the entire campaign for both sides.

Meanwhile, additional British forces, including some light tanks, arrived in Rangoon by ship. They assisted in bolstering the defenses of the Sittang and bitter fighting continued up and down the river line.

Eventually, the Japanese were able to seize Pegu, cut the railroad leading north out of Rangoon, and generally open the way for the occupation of the city. Rangoon was evacuated by the order of the governor and, on 8 March 1942, was occupied by the Imperial Japanese Forces.

Generalissimo Chiang Kai-shek, the President of China, had agreed early in the war to retain General Claire Chennault's American Volunteer Group (AVG's) in Southern Burma to assist in the air defense of Rangoon, the entry port for the Burma Road, the last remaining supply line to China. The British Royal Air Force (RAF) and AVG's combined to inflict heavy losses on the Japanese Air Force. In January and February they shot down over two hundred and fifty known Japanese aircraft at a loss of approximately fifty of their own aircraft. The AVG's, using outdated P-40's, were pitted against the faster and more maneuverable Japanese Zeros; but with the superior air tactics developed by Chennault the P-40's, in fact, outflew the Japanese. Chennault and his airmen were the air-soldiers of fortune. On the ground they were happy-go-lucky, but in the air they became efficient, cool and calculating. As a unit they gained the utmost respect and admiration of the Burmese people.

The Generalissimo had also agreed with General Wavell, the British commander-in-chief in India, to utilize Chinese forces in the defense of Burma and the Burma Road. Of the initial three divisions of the Chinese Fifth Army which were made available in Burma in January and February 1942, only one, the 200th Division, was well-trained. It performed admirably in combat. The remaining units were ill-trained and poorly equipped. Moreover, they had little combat experience. In early March, Major General Joseph

W. Stilwell arrived in Chungking to become Chief of Staff of Allied Forces under the Generalissimo. Shortly thereafter he arrived in Burma, where, for all practical purposes, he was to command the Chinese forces, although his orders were to be issued over the name of the Chinese commander-in-chief.

British General Sir Harold Alexander arrived in early March to replace General Hutton as Commander-In-Chief in Burma. He attempted to consolidate the 1st Burma Division and the 17th Indian Division, but was prevented from doing so by the pressure being applied by the Japanese in the Pegu area. As a result, he was forced to withdraw north in two separate columns: the 17th Indian Division along the road to Prome paralleling the Irrawaddy River, and the 1st Burma Division through Toungoo. General Alexander attempted to consolidate the Allied defenses between Prome and Toungoo, but again Japanese pressure prevented such action.

After the fall of Rangoon, the Japanese reorganized and began a drive to the north; the 55th Division using the route to Toungoo and the 33rd Division pressing up the Irrawaddy Valley toward Prome. In early April the British and Indian forces in Prome were routed by the Japanese with strong assistance from the Burmese fifth columnists, members of the Burma Independence Army. The 200th Chinese Division in the Toungoo area gave a good account of itself, but it was running short on supplies and ammunition and withdrew a short distance to the north. Meanwhile the Japanese were busy reinforcing their troops by landing two additional divisions in Rangoon. The 18th Division reinforced the 55th Division in the area of Toungoo and the 56th Division supported the 33rd above Prome.

The Japanese Air Force also had been busy. It had lost heavily to the small RAF-AVG forces in Burma but concentrated in Thailand. In late March it conducted a heavy raid on Magwe Airfield and, for all practical purposes, put the RAF out of action.

The AVG was also put under severe pressure and was forced to move from Toungoo to Lashio and later all the way to China. Now the Japanese Air Force was supreme in Burma, and there remained no effective air support for the Allied ground forces.

In the Irrawaddy Valley the Japanese pushed rapidly beyond Prome toward the oil fields at Yenangyaung. On 14 April the oil fields were set to the torch by the retreating British and Indian forces to prevent their falling into enemy hands.

For a brief spell the Allied cause in Burma brightened at the word that the Chinese Sixth Army was starting its movement toward Burma. If its three divisions (49th, 55th and 93rd) had been in position in Burma, the Japanese tide might have been stemmed. However, the Japanese advance was so rapid that the forces of the Sixth Army had no opportunity to affect the outcome of the battle. It was not a matter of being too little; rather, too late. Two divisions of the Chinese 66th Army also were to figure in the Burma campaign. These were the 28th and 38th. Only the latter became engaged. In the aggregate of the eight Chinese divisions made available for Burma in 1942 (approximately 60,000 men) only three-plus divisions or about 20,000 troops were ever engaged with the Japanese.

After reaching Toungoo the eastern Japanese force divided itself into two columns, the 55th Division continuing northward in the direction of Mandalay and the 18th Division flanking to the east and north along the Mawchi-Loikaw-Lashio Road. The movement of the 18th Division was particularly effective. In mid-April they dislodged the Chinese from the area of Loikaw and in less than two weeks their motorized column had reached Lashio, over two hundred miles to the north.

With this action the entire left flank of the Allied Forces was completely uncovered. The remainder of the campaign in Burma was a rout. For the Allies the campaign from then on was simply a matter of trying to save the maximum number of troops and supplies from falling into the hands of the Japanese.

In the center the combined British, Indian and Chinese forces put up a stout defense, but were eventually forced to withdraw. Mandalay fell on 1 May 1942. The remnants of the British and Indian forces withdrew over the Kalewa-Imphal Road to India. The remaining Chinese forces moved northward with hopes of withdrawing to China by way of Bhamo. However, the rapid advance of the 18th Japanese Division to Bhamo and later to

Myitkyina severed this route and they were forced to withdraw through the inhospitable Hukawng Valley to Ledo in northeast India.

Generals Alexander and Stilwell met for the last time on Burmese soil near Mandalay in early May. By this time the rout was on. General Alexander withdrew with the forces through Kalewa while General Stilwell and his small staff walked out of Burma through Indaw and Imphal. Also in early May, the Governor of Burma, Sir Reginald Dorman Smith was flown out of Myitkyina.

General Stilwell summarized the Allied defeat in Burma when he said, "I claim we got a hell of a beating. We got run out of Burma and it is as humiliating as hell. I think we ought to find out what caused it, go back, and retake it."

A word must be said concerning the heroic efforts of the small group of American pilots working with the Chinese National Airways Corporation. With hundreds and thousands of refugees — men, women and children — crowded on the small, rough and rocky airfields at Myitkyina, they continued to fly them to India in spite of Japanese air raids on the field and kept on until the Japanese ground forces reached the very outskirts of the town itself. They also parachuted tons of food and medical supplies to the refugees walking out along the trails. Many of these pilots later joined the United States Air Corps and served the Air Transport Command with distinction in flights across the Hump to China.

One of the principal causes of confusion for the Allied forces during the Japanese campaign was the activities of the Burma Independence Army. The actual size of this force has been variously estimated at anywhere between five and twenty-five thousand. The Japanese had been clever in their propaganda for a greater southeast Asia — "Asia for the Asiatics" and "down with the white men." Japanese agents had been active and stirred up the people so that by the time their advanced military elements reached Moulmein and Rangoon, they had a well-organized fifth column. The Buddhist pongyies, "Yellow Robes," appeared to be the most active. Their activities against the Allies were so outrageous that in some places they were shot on sight. Not many of these Burmese insurgents were armed with guns but many carried knives and other weapons. Neither soldiers nor civilians could distinguish friend from foe and the result was confusion. To make matters worse, in the larger cities, large segments of the population joined in looting and pillaging. The civilian picture in Burma at that time was one of terror and panic.

The attitude of the Burmese toward the British and the Japanese is difficult to describe. It can only be considered in general terms, as there were so many exceptions to the rule. Taken as a whole the Burmese people were not anti-British. The British had done much for Burma: roads and railroads had been developed; mines and oil fields were in operation; the economy was sound; there was an effective educational system, and social and industrial achievements for which the Burmese were grateful. However, the winds of nationalism were fanned by the Japanese, and many Burmese mistakenly accepted Japanese assurances about their own self-determination and independence.

Dr. Ba Maw became the Japanese-supported premier of Burma; he ruled in name only, as can be expected of any puppet ruler. Major General Aung San was made Chief of the Burma Independence Army, later modified as the Burma Defense Army. These two leaders and the Burmese people were completely disillusioned by the Japanese. They had welcomed the Japanese with open arms, and received increasing contempt. In practice, the Japanese came as conquerors. Whatever the slogans said about co-prosperity for Asians under the Japanese, Burma had been absorbed, not liberated.

There was an undercurrent of strain and resentment in Burma against the Japanese; to our plans this gave beginning hope for success. British intelligence verified that a little flame of resistance flickered among the hill tribes. Soon we hoped to see it brandished as a torch.

V

The Light Begins to Burn

A GUERRILLA UNIT begins with a base camp. But where is the best place? Our own notions were unanimous on one point. It had to be as close to North Burma as possible. We could anticipate having to supply and communicate with our guerrillas in the field, so we knew quite well that the base camp would have to be near by. A difference of one hundred miles would mean the difference between success and failure.

In our search for the base camp we bore in mind General Stilwell's advice that we make a special effort to get along with the British. There was no end to their experience and their fighting in Burma, and they could do us much good, if we approached them with courtesy and with the idea that this was an Allied show. The British were understandably nervous about the impending Japanese thrust into India, nervous, too, that their lines and forces, on land and at sea, in southeast Asia, had received more than one shattering defeat from the Japanese.

American and British minds and talents combined to lead us in the direction of Assam in northeast India. I recall our arrival there — the alien landscape of precise tea fields, and, almost lost among them, airfields for the Air Transport Command flying to China. Hourly, one could hear the engines lifting the planes into the sky and, watching them, be aware of the vast distance, of the myriad mountains to recapture before there would be direct land communications between the ports of India and the Allied forces in China.

Our role, as we arrived in Assam, was envisaged in realistic terms. Already we knew that any attempt on the part of the Americans to get into Burma as agents was out of the question. This cast a shadow over many hopes.

The reasons stand out; a white American, even with the cleverest of make-up, would be sure to attract attention. We were all conspicuous by virtue of height and appearance. No one in that initial group of Americans had the lithe, the almost delicate frame of the peoples of Burma. The initial missions behind the lines would be doomed if Americans were to play the role of agent.

So, from the first day of our arrival in India, a continual search began for natives of Burma who would go back for us in a role that promised them more than one kind of trouble. In order to find these people, close contact was necessary with the British. Without their aid, their knowledge of individuals who could fit into our plans, we would have been in extreme difficulty. And it was British insight that took us to Nazira, Assam.

At first glance, it was clear that Nazira was the right place. Among the vast acres of tea fields, an approaching man or vehicle could be sighted easily. The English people working the plantations were pleased to see us; they had been cut down to a small group overseeing the battalions of native laborers. Sometimes there were long periods when they did not see a white man, so they looked at us with interest and anticipation. They were eager to do everything possible for us.

The English planters after all wanted to have a role in the war, and having an American unit, a secret one at that, in the midst of their tea plantations would be useful to the Allied effort and relieve a great deal of their boredom and routine.

The site we finally selected was ideal, a model for a base camp. It was far enough away from the main British and American Army installations in Assam so that we could minimize trouble, the probing of inquisitive eyes and embarrassing questions. It was close enough to jungles, rivers and mountains so that the last phases of training before actually parachuting, walking, or being flown in by plane to Burma could be done with a high degree of realism. There were large buildings which had once served the plantation as a tennis club, and overseer homes were available. And there was physical distance, enough stretching room so that agent groups could be kept separate from one another. This latter point was of great importance to us; if one group was to be aimed at one target, and a second at another, it was good to keep them separated and out of contact with each other. In that way, the complications of their knowing anything more than their own mission was avoided. We could not eliminate the chance that once in Burma these agents could be captured and tortured. Though they would not want to, they might hand over to the enemy valuable information concerning far more than their own group.

It was a gray monsoon day in October, 1942 when our reconnaissance party of Carl Eifler, John Coughlin, Bob Aitken and myself arrived at a plantation close to the Naga Hills in Upper Assam. We had tea with Allan Richardson, the general manager of the Assam Company, with whom we hit it off immediately. I knew at once that we had ended our search. Detachment 101 would put down its roots here amid the chatter of monkeys, the smell of elephant trails, the lazy rhythm of the passing Dikoo River.

When, after two days of talk and inspections and some convivial hours late at night over whisky-and-sodas, we had taken in the breadth of the company plantations, seen all its advantages of privacy, almost of innocence, and noted the proximity of the Naga Hills over which men might infiltrate into Burma, there was no question about it. Not only were Richardson and his company prepared to lease to us ample space for our needs, but they could build camps and roads to our specifications and could produce the domestic staff required for the dull routines of cooking and keeping the place shipshape.

"You should really not look so abject," said Richardson, after he had described the score or so of bearers we would inherit. There seemed legions of servants for each specific task. The man who swept floors could not wash down the shower room. The man who cooked did not serve. "This is a tea plantation, and without the proper bearers," he said, "the word would soon get out that there was something sticky about you all."

We were honestly amazed at the number of bearers needed. But there were no broken hearts among any of us that the dark horde of servants joining 101 would take our minds off the responsibility and drudgery of keeping the camp fed and maintaining neatness. And there was sense to it — for the days ahead we needed every man to put his mind and body to far more important tasks than housekeeping.

Established with this as our camp, we gave it a name: THE U.S. ARMY EXPERIMENTAL STATION. For months other military units wondered idly what it meant, and wrote it off as just another place where a bunch of goldbricks were serving out time pursuing a research project into some phase of malaria. If such were the illusion, we did nothing to spoil it.

We had brought along secret texts and training manuals, all based on espionage and guerrilla experiences in Europe; these were meant to serve as the basis for our teaching. The basic precept of the works was sound preparation before a team of agents was dropped behind enemy lines. In most cases, the techniques recommended to maintain communication with agents, to provide them with money and supplies, and finally to get them out safely, presupposed a more sophisticated situation than ours. Now, as we went over the text, we saw how radically different was our problem in Northern Burma. The terrain and the methods of the enemy involved were of a kind that allowed no conclusive preparation because we were so unfamiliar with what was going on in Japanese-occupied Burma. We saw at once that as much as we might render instruction to our first group — now known as "A" Group — they in the end must teach us as well. The range of their knowledge of Burma was needed by us before we could select what points in the text would be of value to their operation.

In "A" Group were educated men. All had gone to English schools. None were backward intellectually; three were college graduates. We counted on their mental aptitude and we revealed the problem: if they were to derive profit from our teaching, they in return must tell us all they knew about Burma, in response to detailed questions on the history and customs, dress and habits of specific towns, villages, even of specific individuals. Reason and memory were engaged in a vital learning process that was of value to both speakers and listeners.

Away from the classroom, quite informally, but no less intensely, it went on. What are the trinkets an itinerant peddler sells? How much daylight filters through a rain forest? What is the name of the headman's son in the village of Wadat Ga? Is the root of the jacaranda tree used as medicine?

We used to sit around bamboo tables, intensely collecting such particles of information so that one day in the near future this same group might sneak into Burma. And all the time there were practical exercises involving demolitions, weapons and the correct formulas for destroying bridges, locomotives, parked airplanes and motor vehicles.

There was much intensity, but no argument. We had all realized what was happening, and no moment was misspent. At bottom, every particle of knowledge was to put a foundation under 101 that would last for many missions beyond this first one; knowledge that would be shared time and time again. The faculty of 101 had no precedent. It was shaping its own material, its own ways, and it was shaping a form of espionage and guerrilla warfare that would tax all its resources to a scope no one of us dared dream of. But now only one thing was of interest: to train the first element in as careful and orderly a manner as seemed possible. We were going on what few facts we could gather; what actually was true on the other side of the Naga Hills was not known. It would not be known until we got "A" Group behind enemy lines; and we would not know how to grade the present procedure until they returned — if they returned. If they did not make it back, then all our procedure would have been wrong. The grades for this kind of teaching could be earned only by the operations themselves — this was an essential truth.

The base in Nazira was about four hundred miles away from the proposed area of operation: the vicinity of Myitkyina in Northern Burma. At that time no radio equipment was available which was small, light and powerful enough to operate successfully over that distance. We were seeking a radio which weighed no more than twenty-five pounds; we envisioned power by batteries or a hand generator weighing no more than twenty-five additional pounds. We deliberately wanted something one man could carry as a unit. The element of range was madly ambitious — 1,000 miles, to allow for operations as far south as Rangoon.

Since no such radio set was at hand, Captain Huston and his signal technicians in 101 set out to design and construct one. They were fortunate in one respect. In and about the Service of Supply (SOS) warehouses of Advance Section No. 2 there was a large number of V-100 radios waiting for air shipment to China under the Lend-Lease Program. A microscopic part in the V-100 set was valuable, available nowhere else in India. Twenty-five were obtained, and the critical segment was taken out. Then began, with much patience and diligence, a search beneath the surface irrelevancies of radio shops all over India. A slender wire here, a capable condenser there, finally produced enough of the structure and parts for an entirely new radio.

The technical capabilities of Sergeants Allen Richter and Donald Eng were given full rein by Captain Huston. By the first of December 1942 they had put together a working model. It weighed only twenty-three pounds, and the battery pack and carrying case weighed another thirty pounds, or a total of just three pounds over the original specifications. Sergeant Eng tested the range of the set by moving about by rail to the various cities in eastern India and communicating with the Nazira base radio station. As a final test he took it to Madras, about 1,200 miles south of Nazira along the east coast of India. At that range the set proved highly capable, receiving and transmitting in category 5, allowing us to hear it loud and clear. The radio seemed a good omen. Anything but impressive, and looking like a discarded cigar box, it was, however, just what we had wanted. Furthermore, it was proof of 101's affirmative answer to its own question — could we be self-dependent?

During this period Carl and John were away from the Nazira base camp a great deal of the time establishing contacts with the British authorities, recruiting agents from the refugee camps, developing a supply base in Calcutta and a variety of other things. They pretty well left it to my judgment to build the base, estab-

lish the instruction, and get the agents trained and ready for operations. All told, we took over nine tea planters' bungalows and were
building twenty agent training camps.

The Japanese Air Force began bombing raids, which for us had
one result: they hit our supply warehouse at the Chabua airfield
and destroyed the structure. The supplies and equipment we lost
through that raid were a blow. Some could be reordered from SOS
or purchased on the Indian market; but many were unobtainable
in the CBI Theater and had to be ordered from the States. That,
sadly, entailed a wait of twelve to eighteen months. The supply
lines were long, and our theater suffered the lowest priorities.

By now, the preliminaries with "A" Group were over. One thing
was left to conclude their training: they were divided into groups
to carry out an operational test in the Naga Hills. We had the
greatest regard for these hills, for they would reveal any weaknesses in "A" Group. The terrain was rough and the Nagas still
practiced head-hunting.

Two lines divide the Naga Hills; crossing over the "outer line"
one found pleasant, relatively safe villages, and might cross paths
with an occasional British or Indian Civil Affairs Officer. Should
one trek on twenty miles into the hills, he crossed the so-called "inner line." Here a party depended upon weapons for safety and was
on the watch for Nagas; alert, hardy warriors, these Nagas were
at times friendly, but could for one cause or another turn into
enemies.

In their foray, "A" Group got themselves into a kind of trouble that had not been anticipated. They were reconnoitering a
coal mine with an eye to sabotage, when the Nagas became suspicious and alerted the civil magistrate. The magistrate, with Indian troops and Nagas, surrounded "A" Group. They might have
escaped by shooting their way out, but they gave up. Later, one
of them said, "That would have been a foolhardy way to die; if I
must die, I would prefer doing it in operations." They were put in
jail, suspected of being Japanese spies. They did not reveal their
true allegiance until we appeared to release them from jail. All in
all, it had been a hardening process, and though they were a little
tired from lack of sleep and food, our men had experienced something of what they could expect in Burma. Now they were ready

to embark on a true mission, one where they would have to depend entirely on their own resources. To what extent they would succeed in staying out of prison and avoiding the firing squad reserved for spies would depend on how well we had all done our job of preparation.

"A" Group was to begin our penetration behind the Japanese lines. We were all agreed that they were to be flown to Fort Hertz (Putao), the last remaining town in Burma where it was possible for reconnaissance forces such as ours to make a landing. The town was defended by a British-commanded force of Kachin Levies who formed a defense line south of Sumprabum, the nominal capital of the Kachin Hills. The Japanese were not interested in Fort Hertz at the time. Their forces were pointed westward toward the heart of India. As a place, Fort Hertz had only one importance — it had an airfield, and from there it was possible to move south into North Burma.

Carl Eifler and John Coughlin accompanied the group to assist them in their initial passage through the Japanese lines. Once arrived in Fort Hertz in December of 1942, "A" Group worked with the Kachin Levies, learning from them where the Japanese fortifications were heaviest, where the Japanese line was thinnest. This required endless patrols, probing, not for a kill, but to locate the weak spot. Sometimes a fire fight ensued; they found getting through the Japanese lines a laborious assignment.

Here the suspicion began to grow that if indeed we expected "A" Group to operate deep behind the Japanese lines, where their presence would be totally unexpected, and where they could attack bridges and cut railway lines, we could not afford to gamble away the secrecy we wanted. The probing south of Fort Hertz was a risky and nerve-racking job. The Japanese were dug in with collective depth. The notion grew that trying to infiltrate the Japanese lines from north to south into Burma should be done by small groups of two or three men who could sneak through — but certainly not by the eight members of "A" Group plus the myriad of porters needed to carry their radio, explosives, food and other equipment, who traveled as secretly as a circus arriving in town.

The other thing that we found out was that every time a small hole was made in the Japanese lines through which our people

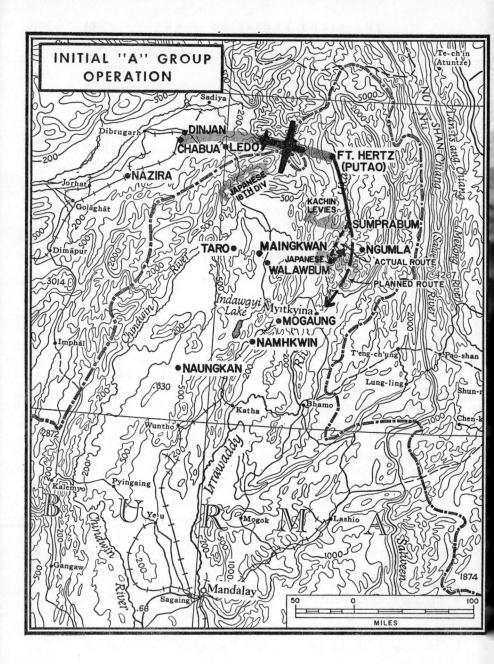

INITIAL "A" GROUP
OPERATION

could infiltrate for a short distance, the hole became a swarm of Japanese infantry; then our patrol was forced to withdraw. What headway it had made was obliterated by the increase in enemy troops, and by the setting up of new roadblocks. The condition of security we had envisaged for "A" Group was gone. The Japanese had more than caught on; they were clever at infiltration and they could read the signs in our first awkward attempt.

The group at Fort Hertz also began to realize that passage through the Japanese lines would only be the beginning. There remained over one hundred and fifty miles of mountainous jungle trail behind the lines just to reach the area where we hoped to carry out sabotage operations. There was also another feature. Carl and John were doing their best to carry out General Stilwell's desire to cooperate with the British. However, the British Commander of the Kachin Levies felt that he should command any Allied forces in the area. This was totally unacceptable and considerable friction developed. Fortunately for 101, this commander became ill shortly thereafter and was replaced by Brigadier Bowerman, a fine soldier who remained a great friend of 101 throughout the war.

The day came when we decided to give up Fort Hertz as a jumping-off place for significant guerrilla and espionage operations. The battalion of Kachin Levies were doing a good enough job maintaining the Allied presence in the no man's land of extreme Northern Burma. And right there and then the cardinal rule of our operations came into being. Guerrillas essentially require surprise. As they travel to their target area they should not be seen, known, heard or identified. Any identification, even the most fleeting, by the enemy, of a guerrilla potential poised against him severely limits the guerrilla's chances for realizing his full mission.

Our first attempt had not been a success. "A" Group had made the mistake of aligning itself with regular troops. This had frustrated its own identity and, further, had brought to an end any possibility we had for submerging into enemy territory unseen. For being guerrillas means just that: to submerge and wait through dozens of limited opportunities for the work you specifically want to do in an area before rising swiftly and submerging again to appear in a totally different area. The guerrilla gives no notice of his appearance. He commands the time of his attack. No matter what lures are placed in his way, the guerrilla helps himself only to those situations where the enemy is in a helpless position. The guerrilla resists temptations until he has studied them. When the enemy appears unexpectedly, the guerrilla is wary of a trap. He should know when and where the enemy hunts him, and he strikes back only after careful preparation and planning. Precarious as his existence can be, a guerrilla does not expose one inch of himself until the conditions are just what he wants them to be: all in his favor.

"A" Group was our first experiment, and it had been not so much a failure as a limited reconnaissance. Again a lesson in reality had been learned: operations such as ours would need reconnaissance, reconnaissance and reconnaissance before a proper operation could take place. The trek into the mountains of North Burma and the probing of the Japanese lines south of Fort Hertz had taught us that a first operation such as ours into an enemy-occupied country must be a *vertical* penetration — that is, that we must reach our target area by parachute. The discovery was an important one. Equal in importance was the knowledge we gained about the Kachins.

We had observed the Kachin Levies closely and had seen that the armed troops with the Levies were equal to the Japanese. There was a rugged staunchness to the Kachins. They did not like their land occupied by an invader. Their talk was simple, but convincing. The war was not yet over, and when the last battle had been fought, the Kachins would be found victorious. Their eyes, like their tongues, were full of enthusiasm for a fight. For Asiatics, they were rugged physical types of short stature. In their look was the fierce pride of mountain men, and years after the war, when I saw the first picture of Tenzing Norkay, the Sherpa of Mount Everest fame, I was to be reminded of a Kachin, for the high places of the Himalayas are their ancestral homeland. As guerrilla soldiers they were ideal. The difficulties of following invisible tracks through jungle or crossing towering peaks they looked upon as a natural contest. Weapons they understood as a fact of life; demolitions were not beyond their powers. Four Kachins from the Levies, all sons of headmen, were recruited and added to "A" Group to serve as its eyes and ears.

The Fort Hertz reconnaissance had also given us a firsthand understanding of money and opium as other tools of guerrilla operations. Early as it was then in the Japanese occupation, we found that the paper money which the enemy had distributed was received with indifference; forthwith we gave highest priority to gathering together large sums of British silver coins. It also was necessary to enter the opium business. We had all read that once the habit is formed, it takes extraordinary will power to break it. There were no clinics in North Burma for mastering the fastening bite of opium. Our decision to use opium was based on the fact that it would give our troops a certain amount of freedom, of buying power; we did not question it as just or unjust. The fact remained that opium, along with its multitude of sins, was also a palliative for the thousands of older people, who suffered from a complex of maladies for which there were no cures. Even so, it should be noted that opium was not used to recruit guerrilla troops. We went out of our way to make this clear. Simply stated, paper currency and even silver were often useless, as there was nothing to buy with money; opium, however, was the form of payment which everybody used. Not to use it as a means of barter would spell an end to our operations. Opium was available to agents who used it for any number of reasons, ranging from obtaining information to buying their own escape. Any indignation felt was removed by the difficulty of the effort ahead. If opium could be useful in achieving victory, the pattern was clear. We would use opium.

Now that we were back at Nazira, with the year 1943 just beginning, we sat down in earnest to figure out what should be done. We could see that parachuting "A" Group into Burma was the next step. But to get the parachutes and the planes for the job was not easy. The subject of planes at that time was painful; for the character of the theater was such that every aircraft was part of the most critical link with China, with America, with England, with Australia. We knew that there were not nearly enough to go around, and the importance of aircraft was not unknown to the

Japanese. They had taken immense steps to shoot them down as they flew over the Hump, and they had not failed. As we sat huddled over our maps, we noted that the concentration point of these Japanese attacks came as the planes reached altitude on the Burma side. This meant that the planes shot down crashed into the mountains of the Kachin people. Rescue attempts had so far not been contemplated. We were in effect surrendering the crews of these planes to the forest or to the Japanese, because we saw no way of getting them out of a huge, primitive, multi-dangered area full of tigers, snakes, mountains and Japanese. Even on the map the area was forbidding, with contour lines so thick that the mountain peaks seemed to jut out of the flat heavy chart paper. Suddenly light struck us; the Air Transport Command surely would give us planes if we would make an effort to bring back their men!

At Air Transport Command Headquarters we sought an interview with General Alexander. When we talked about the lost crews, his voice became bitter:

"I'd give anything," he said, "to guarantee my people that they had a chance."

"That's why we are here."

"But what can you do?"

"We can promise that if your crews crash in North Burma, we will go in and lead them out."

"That's the sort of thing they show in movies."

"No, sir. Those hills, those mountains are Kachin country. They are on our side and if we could get in and show them that we mean to stay, we should be able to get your men out."

"It would help morale a great deal," the General said, "just to say to my flight crews, 'Look here, men, don't expect a miracle, but there are guerrillas down there in the mountains. They are on our side. We can contact them by radio and if you are shot down, or you crash, why there's a good chance they will come in and help you get back here.' "

And that was the way we left it: we would work closely with Air Transport Command; we would make it our job to help their men get out of North Burma. Our operation would act as an underground railroad for American and British aircrews. In exchange,

Air Transport Command would provide planes and parachutes to us.

Our parachute instruction was started by Master Sergeant Wayne (Pop) Milligan, transferred to us by General Alexander from the ATC at Chabua. He moved in and immediately accommodated himself to our needs. He was a short, stocky Oklahoman who had done a little bit of most everything — ranch hand, rodeo roper, oilwell wildcatter — and he had also made sixty-two parachute jumps barnstorming about the United States. Parachute training had to be near an airfield — and we found another tea planter's bungalow near Dibrugarh, only a few miles away from the Chabua airfield.

Pop stepped into his new role, working all twelve men from five in the morning until well after sunset when "A" Group would head for their bunks, exhausted. Competition was strong to get Pop's approval. Whenever he told one of the men that he was doing fine — the highest praise he allowed — that man's day was made.

Looking over the intelligence reports of the Japanese air strength in Northern Burma, we decided that the aircraft for the jump should be armed. A C-87 was chosen to see our men on the way. The C-87's were B-24's converted to flying cargo over the Hump. They carried heavy firepower with guns of .50 caliber in the turret, nose, waist and tail; should Japanese Zeros spill out of the skies over the drop area, the C-87 could put up a fight. Its maneuverability was slow, making larger circles to drop men than was customary. But we were after protection, and what inadequacies the C-87 offered were hardly large enough to offset its striking power. The exit door was quite small with a little step alongside it which added complications. Also, the door was so located that it looked to the jumper as though he would be cut in two by the tail.

Since the C-87 was not designed for parachute drops, it had no hook-up cables to fasten static lines. Pop arranged to have rings installed in the aircraft to serve as tie-downs for the static lines. Within a few days he was giving the group dry run training while the plane was undergoing maintenance after each of its trips over the Hump.

Tension was at its peak, so close now was the second attempt to lodge "A" Group behind the lines. As the drop day drew near, all their supplies, from demolitions to food and medicines, were packed, with every man a witness. Each man could see what each numbered container bore and in fact, memorized the look and contents of every container. The age-old question of the quantity of supply to give a soldier, whether conventional or unconventional, was answered arbitrarily by how much we could air-drop as they jumped.

The simple, inexpensive containers of woven bamboo measured about eighteen inches on each side. They were forty inches deep and covered with burlap. Rice husks swelled out the sides of the container, acting as a resilient buffer. The supply parachutes were broadcloth and quite inexpensive.

A dozen or more aerial reconnaissance flights had provided good photos of our drop area — the Koukkwee Valley, approximately one hundred miles south of Myitkyina. "A" Group was to establish a base camp there and initiate operations against the railroad line about forty miles to the west. Our operational plan for getting the men in was cautiously planned in two steps. I mention this because in every way we wished to proceed with the strictest discipline and security. "A" Group would not have been much good to themselves or 101 if they were dead upon hitting the ground.

The parachute drop was to be done in two parts on separate days. On the first day the group leader, Captain Jack Barnard, and the radio operator, Saw Egbert Timothy (known as Saw Judson), were to be parachuted in and that night establish radio contact. If they did, that would be reason enough to send the main group in on the following day.

In the meantime we were absorbed in searching the aerial photos for evidence of Japanese anywhere near the drop zone, an area that was isolated, entirely removed from villages and paddy fields. Then we made a discovery that was bewildering.

The photos clearly showed large logs spaced somewhat evenly over parts of the area. The logs spoke like a language. They appeared to say that the enemy had gotten busy putting the logs there as a practical measure to prevent what we planned: parachute operations. We showed the photos to "A" Group to see what they would say, and much to our surprise, they were quick to say there was nothing to worry about. The logs must have been carried there by elephants working for a teak extraction company before the war. This again opened our eyes to the wisdom of having in "A" Group British and Burmese who knew the area as we never would. They had lived and worked in Burma, they shared this in common. Having understood the meaning of the logs, we set the hour of departure for the first flight.

Carl Eifler and John Coughlin were to supervise the jump of Captain Barnard and Saw Judson on the first day. They had briefed them in detail and everything was set. It was 26 January 1943.

The C-87 stood ready, engines throbbing, the fighters were also ready. I said a few noisy words of luck to Captain Barnard and Saw. The engines beat louder, and Saw was shouting in my ear, "I've lost my watch."

"Watch?" I said, and he nodded his head up and down unhappily. There was no time to procure one anywhere, but correct time was essential in his business. The entire operation of the radio involved making contact with Nazira on exact time. I held out my watch to him. I had had it for years. It was made of fine gold, acquired in college as security against a small loan made to a fraternity brother. The original owner had never reclaimed it, and I had become fond of its accuracy.

As he entered the plane, I asked Saw to take good care of the watch and return it to me when he came back. Then I watched the take-off, stood there on the airstrip well after the C-87 had disappeared in clouds, and hoped for the sake of all, that we had not overlooked some important detail . . .

Later, we heard about the flight, how Jack and Saw sat inside the plane, tight in their parachute harness. In the clouds, all was cold, rough turbulence, and they turned and climbed in every direction; the pilot, Captain Jake Sartz, could not get out of the mounting, swirling clouds elbowing fast against his aircraft. The four planes of the fighter escort tried to stay with the C-87 but the difference in the flying speed of the aircraft (about 175 m.p.h. for the C-87 as compared to 350 m.p.h. for the fighters) and the dirty weather separated them from one another. Presently, the fighters returned to base, dangerously short of gasoline. The C-87 was left to contend with Japanese Zeros — if they appeared — on its own.

Upon reaching the area the pilot, Captain Jake Sartz, made a couple of anxious passes over the drop zone. Beneath him, on the ground, the land looked peaceful. He brought the plane lower. Captain Barnard and Saw Judson jumped on the third pass. There was no doubt, their chutes opened. They were seen to land, two figures pulling off their parachute harnesses. On the next pass the two supply containers were dropped. One chute opened perfectly, but the other was a streamer and did not open fully until just before the container hit the ground. The moment of parting, of breaking visual contact with the two men was signaled by the C-87, almost as if shouting goodbye, diving down in a final pass over the drop zone. As it did, the two men waved and then were lost in the unknown of the jungle — they were on the ground. From then on, Captain Sartz flew the C-87 at treetop level, choosing the low altitude to avoid detection on the way home.

All the room in the radio shack at Nazira, a few hours later, was taken up. Hardly a man present did not find himself tense. They had left jobs and sleeping quarters — for now at 10 P.M. we were to hear the first message from the advance party of "A" Group. The air was oppressive and hot. Danger washed over us as the base operator listened — listened and heard nothing. The bamboo floor crackled with the impatience of men's feet, with private movements, sometimes with a tap like the tick of seconds sliding by. An hour passed, and still no signal from Saw Judson. The silence was as firm as the night outside the lighted shack.

Ambush was our first thought. It was written on our faces. But no one cared to say it. The next schedule for Saw was at 2 A.M. I thought of the gold watch. We sat up waiting for 2 A.M., counting on hearing Saw's signal then. And that hour came and stood empty, smelling of no signal, of no good, and infesting our thoughts with a sense of tragedy. Two of our men were missing. Later, we were to discover that the container with the chute which had been delayed in opening held the radio, and it had been hopelessly smashed.

We had guessed as much that night, but we had no proof. These facts we knew. Two of our group were in Burma; but in what circumstances? Threatened? Dead? We could not tell. Now we were surrounded by questions: if the remainder of the group were dropped on the next day, would they be jumping into a trap? Then there was the possibility of another photo-reconnaissance flight — but wouldn't that pinpoint our intentions, and act as a betrayal of the two men if they were alive? And if captured, how long would Captain Barnard and Saw Judson be able to sit tight-mouthed through torture?

Until daylight we talked, and everyone agreed that even if Jack Barnard and Saw were captured, the Japanese would not have had time to interrogate them, nor have enough information to arrange for Zeros to intercept our aircraft. And we told each other the main party of "A" Group would parachute in, as originally planned, with John Coughlin and myself operating the drop.

We ran over the procedures. Captain Patrick (Red) Maddox, leader of the second part of "A" Group, conducted the briefing session with calm. It was Red's decision as to whether the operation would go or not. All he had to say was he did not think it wise and nobody would have thought the less of him. However, Red, who during the initial Japanese operation had twice gone behind enemy lines to blow up tin mines, never wavered, nor did he display a single emotion. Without saying so, he gave the impression that he had confidence in the operation and that, if this is what we thought best, he was for it. In his certainty, there was more than courage: regardless of what happened, he felt that "A" Group's assignment was to get in and find out.

Parachutes and weapons were issued, the C-87 alerted, and we took off on the second part of the "A" Group mission. Looking them over, I saw all ten men calm in appearance. Going with them were eight supply containers, including two with radios, and about a dozen bags of rice. The rice was to be free dropped: that is, without parachutes. To do this, each sack was filled about half full of rice, then sewn so the rice was loose inside, and finally encased in two additional sacks, also sewn loosely. Although we had never seen it attempted, Pop believed in the experiment — and it was worth the try.

We had six P-40 fighters for an escort. They stayed with us until we passed over Hopin in the railway corridor, whence they had to return to base while they still had gasoline. Our plan was to arrive over the drop zone at about 4 P.M. and allow about thirty minutes of daylight and early dusk to complete the drop. The plane would return to base under cover of darkness.

When we arrived in the drop area, Jake flew directly over the drop site of the previous day. There stood Captain Barnard and Saw Judson. They had ground panels displayed: they were well. No sign could have made us feel as buoyant as the sight of two minute human figures appearing miraculously amid the logs and the strips of parachute cloth. We had found them alive, and we had found our faith justified.

In this revived atmosphere, the members of "A" Group sprang to the door, Pop Milligan telling them a jump was a moment of beauty. They were laughing now. All of Burma was there in the English faces, the Kachin faces, the Burmese coloring of the Anglo-Burmans, the professions of the past, whether student or foreman or mining engineer, making way for what they were now to do. They were going back home to fight.

The drop was crude and primitive. In the first place, the men used seat chutes of the kind used by pilots and aircrew members in crash emergencies. We would have been better off with the United States paratrooper chute, but they were not then available. We had to be sure that the iron release handle on the chest strap would be pulled so as to eject the pilot chute and pull out the main chute. To do this we made static lines of one-half-inch Manila rope, about twenty feet long, which were fastened to the tie-down rings in the airplane. Then, to insure that the iron handle, which weighed about half a pound, did not hit the jumpers under their chins and injure them, John and I stationed ourselves on either side of the door to assist the jumpers out. As each man left the door of the plane, he was given a twist so that he actually jumped backwards out into space, allowing the handle to be pulled free in front of him.

It was a busy time getting them out, and it was rewarding to see them descend without mishap.

They jumped from an elevation of six hundred feet and they landed perfectly. It was truly remarkable to see the calmness of the entire group. They knew of the difficulties ahead, as well as the inherent dangers. Not one man showed the slightest bit of trepidation or hesitancy.

A few moments after the men were on the ground, we dropped six containers of supplies and, on the following pass, two additional containers, each packed with a radio. On the final pass we free-dropped the twelve bags of rice. They were not dropped in the same drop zone but in another area about two hundred yards away, because if one of the rice bags, moving along at two hundred or more miles per hour, were to hit a man, it would kill him outright.

The drop appeared to go off with professional skill. The entire aircrew were so elated they could hardly contain themselves, but the operation was not over until we had made the run home.

Again, Jake Sartz put the plane down to treetop level and flew low enough to count branches. We crossed the Mogaung River and, proceeding to the north, Mogaung Town could be seen on the left and Myitkyina and its airfield on the right. There had been so much talk about Myitkyina that it was quite a thrill to see the Japanese airstrip, and alarming too, since we were in a cargo aircraft over a field full of Japanese fighters and bombers. It was just turning dark, which gave an element of protection. After crossing the railroad, Jake headed eastward into the valley of the Irrawaddy, which he followed northward to Fort Hertz. He then took a heading for the Chabua airfield and landed at about 8 P.M. that evening. John and I immediately jumped into a jeep at the Chabua airfield and drove back to the base camp at Nazira. It took a couple of hours. As we arrived, "A" Group's radio had just come on the air. They were safely in operation, they said, and signed off. It had been a long, hard day for all. This night we could sleep without apprehension. We had done it. Our first group was in Burma alive.

PART THREE

The Guerrilla Potential

Uneasy Moments

THE "A" GROUP spent a couple of days getting themselves ori-
ented and establishing their camp. Their plan of operation was
to leave Captain Oscar Milton, Saw Judson, the radio operator,
and the four Kachins behind to guard the camp. The remainder
of the group, six in number, were to proceed to the west, across
the Hopin Hill Tract and into the railway corridor to carry out
operations against the rail line.

The straight line distance from their camp to the rail corridor
was only about fifty miles. However, the trail led through dense
jungles and over some extremely rugged hills so that, taking into
account the ups and downs and going around obstacles, the actual
distance approximated one hundred miles. All members of the
group were in excellent physical condition and were accustomed
to the area and its climate. It was well they were in good shape
because each of them carried a full load of explosives and Captain
Barnard set a grueling pace. By the evening of the second day they
had reached the last ridge overlooking the corridor. To avoid
detection they did not build a fire that night but ate an uncooked
supper. After another cold meal in the morning they again started
on their way, and by late afternoon were within a few hundred
yards of the rail line.

In the early hours of the night, parties were sent out to reconnoiter the rail line to the north and south. Aside from a couple

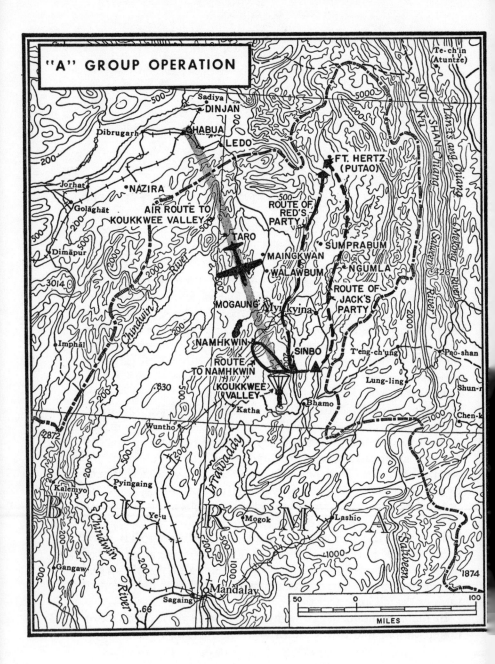

of walking patrols they reported all clear. Alternating between sleeping and guarding, each of them got several hours' rest. Shortly after midnight and under a bright moon they started on the first phase of their operation, which was to lay explosives rigged with delayed fuses along the track. The explosive to be used was composition C, which was much more powerful than dynamite or TNT and was highly stable, meaning that it could stand rough treatment and wide variations in temperature without its being set off. A quarter-pound charge of composition C well placed and packed against a rail will easily blow it in two.

The delayed fuses were what were known as chemical delays. They resembled small pencils. Through the center of each of them ran a taut wire under spring pressure. Also enclosed was a small glass vial of acid. To activate the delay mechanism, after it had been attached to the fuse and the explosive, the operator simply broke the vial of acid. The acid worked on the wire until it ate through it; this in turn released the spring which ignited the fuse and set off the explosive charge. These delays were made to go off in as little as one hour and as long as twenty-four days depending upon the thickness of the wire and the concentration of the acid.

That night the group, working in three teams of two men each, planted a total of twenty-seven charges up and down a five-mile stretch of railway. Most of the delays were set for two to five days, although some longer ones were used. After placing each of the charges it was carefully covered over with rock, gravel and cinder to avoid detection by the Japanese. The group finished its task at about 4 A.M. and all of them returned safely to the rendezvous point. The remainder of the day was spent in sleeping and resting for the next night's activities.

Their plan of action for this night was to divide the group into three working parties of two men each. The northernmost party, consisting of Captain Red Maddox and Lieutenant Dennis Francis, was to use explosives to drop one or two spans of a large railway bridge just north of the town of Namhkwin. A short distance away Lieutenants Quinn and Aganoor were to destroy a smaller railroad bridge. The other group, consisting of Captain Jack Barnard and Lieutenant John Beamish, was to destroy a one-span bridge about three miles or so to the south across the Dagwin Chaung (river).

All went well for them until Red had just about completed laying the demolition charges on the large bridge. At that time, Lieutenants Quinn and Aganoor were surprised by a Japanese patrol and came under heavy rifle fire. When he heard this activity, Red set off his explosive charges, which tore one span from its abutment and dropped it into the river. Red and Dennis then disappeared in the jungle. A Jap patrol, augmented by the local Burmese militia and police, gave chase to Lieutenants Quinn and Aganoor. Lieutenant Aganoor was cut off while trying to serve as a rear guard and was killed by the Japanese. Lieutenant Quinn was very fortunate to get away with his life.

When Captain Barnard's party heard the rifle fire and explosions to the north, they suspected that something had gone amiss. They abandoned their demolition efforts and returned to the rendezvous point. The Japanese continued to pursue Lieutenant Quinn and caused him to take a circuitous route to the rendezvous point, delaying him for a couple of days. Red and Dennis were also forced into the jungle and delayed in getting to the assembly point. Before any of the others had reached the rendezvous point, Captain Barnard and his party had given them up for lost. They buried the remaining demolitions and, taking the last of the food with them, proceeded across the Hill Tract to their base camp in the Koukkwee Valley. As they climbed up and over the Hopin Range they could hear the explosive charges which had been set with the chemical delays going off up and down the line. They at least had the satisfaction of knowing their work was doing damage to the Japanese war effort in Northern Burma.

When Red and Dennis arrived at the rendezvous point, they were in an absolute dilemma. There was no sign of the other members of the group; no word had been left for them; they had no food; and, worst of all, there were numerous indications that the Japanese were making an intensive search. It was not a very comforting situation. They spent the rest of the day hiding out and observing the rendezvous point. That night they hit the trail to return to their base camp.

While the operational part of the "A" Group had been mining the railway corridor, Captain Oscar Milton with Saw Judson, the radio operator, had maintained radio contact with the base camp in India. Oscar had no information to pass on and only came on the air long enough to exchange recognition signals so that we knew the group was still there. When Captain Barnard returned to the base he sent in a message which provided a fairly comprehensive picture of the operation, as he knew it. He expressed the opinion that the members of the other parties had been killed or apprehended. He also advised that the Kachins in the villages they had passed through had informed them of a most unusual amount of Japanese activity during the last four or five days.

Captain Barnard and the other members of the group remained in the base camp area for a couple of days, resting and hoping for the arrival of Red's group. Jack was very concerned about all of the reports of Japanese activity and surmised that they were trying to locate this group and their base camp. He took into account the possibility that the other party may have been captured, which, in time, would provide the Japanese with a great deal of information concerning "A" Group's activities. He prepared a detailed message in which he outlined the entire situation and proposed a plan to break camp immediately, to cross the Irrawaddy River, and to establish a new camp somewhere near the road between Bhamo and Myitkyina, along which "A" Group would gather information of Japanese movements and also carry out raids and ambushes. When the message reached India, Carl and John and those of us concerned with operations studied it at length. We concluded that Captain Barnard was on the ground and certainly knew the situation better than any of us over three hundred miles away in India. Accordingly, we gave approval to his plan and requested that he advise us when and where he wanted their next airdrop. At the same time, however, none of us were convinced that the personnel of the other parties had been killed or apprehended. In the short time they had been with us in training these men had made a most favorable impression. It was obvious that they were without peers in the jungle and their courage and spirit were such that they would be killed before they were captured. Considering the spirit, faith and enthusiasm they had shown, it behooved us to maintain our faith in them.

Captain Barnard and the other members of the group broke

camp the following morning and hit the trail to the northeast in hope of finding a place where they might cross the Irrawaddy. Between Myitkyina and Bhamo the river varies in width from a few hundred to a thousand or more feet. It traverses a low range of mountains and flows through an area known as the Gorges, where it is narrow, swift and extremely treacherous. The first places to the north where the group could possibly cross would be in the area of Sinbo and it was there that they were headed. The Japanese, however, had picked up their trail and were in hot pursuit. It was fortunate that the four Kachins were with the group. Even though they were youngsters, their knowledge of junglecraft paid off handsomely. They were able to use old abandoned trails and employ various ruses and feints that completely misled the Japs. Also, in the hills the population, meager as it was, was almost entirely composed of Kachins and they provided all possible assistance.

From the local Kachins the group learned that the Japanese were trying to locate elements of a British combat force and thought that the "A" Group was a part of it. This information was relayed to us by radio and it was the first inkling we had that a British-Indian force had entered Burma. In accordance with General Stilwell's directive we had advised the British authorities on the Imphal Front of our planned operation with the "A" Group. For some reason they had not considered it necessary to advise us of their own plans. When we checked with them and confronted them with the information coming from within Burma, they revealed that it was Major General Orde Wingate's Chindit Force, composed of about 10,000 British, Indian and Burmese troops. They had crossed the Chindwin River near Imphal and, by land routes, had reached the railway in the area of Wuntho. They had conducted several successful raids and ambushes against the enemy and their unorthodox tactics initially stunned the Japanese. The Japs, however, recovered quickly and in a short while were effecting coordinated attacks against the various Chindit columns. The Chindits were eventually forced to withdraw from the railway. Moreover, the Japanese pressure on the columns which had crossed the Irrawaddy River became so intense that it was necessary for the Chindits to break up into small groups to try to work their way back to India. The Japs pursued these groups night and day. In some respects, the actions of the "A" Group were quite similar to those of the Chindit bands and the Japs thought them one and the same.

By the end of the fourth day Captain Barnard and his group had progressed only about thirty-five miles, although in their evasive action, backtracking, circling and so on, they had covered well over one hundred miles. They were tense and tired from their pursuit but were in good health and eager to move on. That night as they made camp they were on the crest of the hills overlooking the Irrawaddy River Valley. They were in the village of friendly Kachins whom they knew they could depend upon for protection while they caught a few hours' sleep. They also sent us a radio message in which they requested an airdrop two days hence in a cleared rice paddy area about eight miles northwest of the town of Sinbo.

Bright and early the following morning John and I drove to Chabua to see if we could again arrange for the C-87 to carry out the drop. To our chagrin we found that it had carried a load across the Hump to China and had developed engine trouble. It would be at least three or four days before the plane could possibly become available. This, of course, was too late for our purposes and would place the "A" Group in a most serious predicament. With this in mind we contacted General Egan of the 5307th Air Group. He was most sympathetic and called in Colonel Sanders who commanded the 56th Fighter Group which also had a few light bombers, B-25's, attached to it. Colonel Sanders agreed to use a B-25 for the drop and we drove to the Dinjan airstrip to check the bomb bay to see how many containers it would hold, and to meet the crew. The pilot was Captain Thompson. He and his crew were ready for anything. We looked the plane over closely and estimated that we could suspend only six drop containers from the racks in the bomb bays. We also checked the strength of the bomb bay doors and estimated that they would hold six thirty-five-pound bags of rice, which would be free-dropped with the instantaneous opening of the doors.

Since the drop would take us fairly close to the old base camp of the "A" Group it seemed wise to conduct an air search for the other members of the party at the same time in hope that they were still alive. If by chance we were fortunate enough to locate them, we should be prepared to give them an emergency drop to provide them food and supplies until we could return a few days later with another more complete drop including a radio and radio operator. There was no conceivable way of getting additional containers out of the bomb bay so we finally decided to try to use the rear escape hatch, which was just large enough for a small container to be pushed through.

Captain Thompson said he wanted to get started as early as possible the next day so that we would not be arriving in the area the same time as the previous flights and have the Jap Zeros waiting for us. It was getting late and we had a long drive ahead of us to return to the base camp, pack the containers and get them to Dinjan and loaded in the plane. With this in mind, we set the departure time for the plane at noon the following day and told Captain Thompson we would be loaded and ready to go.

Several of us worked through the night assembling the supplies and getting them packed into containers and the chutes attached. There was not much time to catch an hour's sleep and get a bite to eat before we had to depart again to load the plane at Dinjan. However, at 11:30 A.M. the bomb bays were loaded and we were ready to go. Sergeant Milligan was to handle the emergency drop through the escape hatch and I was to fly in the nose with the navigator-bombardier to identify the panels and to effect the drop. We took off exactly as scheduled without any fighter escort and headed directly toward the old base camp to see if we could first locate Red and the rest of the group. In about an hour we were over Lake Indawgyi, a magnificent lake completely surrounded by tropical forests. From there we flew over the railway corridor and could plainly see where one span of the bridge over the Namyin outside of Namhkwin had been dropped in the river and another section had been severed. All of the work of the "A" Group had not been in vain — the traffic to Myitkyina would be cut off until the Japs could repair the bridge.

About ten minutes later we were approaching the site of the original parachute drop. We had not given up hopes for Red and the others, and were greatly concerned about them, especially in light of Captain Barnard's latest message concerning the Japanese activities. One can well imagine the pleasant surprise when we made the first pass over the drop zone. There in the middle waving their arms were Red Maddox and Lieutenants Pat Quinn and Dennis Francis. They also had emergency panels displayed to indicate that they needed supplies and that it was safe to drop. We made another pass and Sergeant Milligan dropped a message on a streamer telling them to sit tight and that we would return in a few minutes to give them an emergency drop of food.

Seeing Red, Dennis and Pat together was most surprising. It wasn't until sometime later that we were able to piece together what had happened. Red and Dennis had reached the base camp and found nothing to eat. They heard a suspicious noise and hid out in the jungle to watch. To their amazement Pat Quinn emerged and they were reunited. After Lieutenant Aganoor had been killed, Pat was chased by the Japs for three days. He eventually reached the rendezvous point, which had been cleaned out. Then it was another couple of days before he reached a friendly village to get some food. After that he proceeded to the base camp, where he joined Red and Dennis. They were no better off than before, but it buoyed their morale to be together again.

After dropping the note to Red's party we flew northeast to the Irrawaddy and, from the village of Sinbo, took a heading for Captain Barnard's drop site. We flew directly over it and identified the panels. As we were approaching it for the drop run at a speed of 140 M.P.H. and at an elevation of about three hundred feet, the navigator gave me the signal and I pushed the handle forward to open the bomb bay doors to free-drop the rice bags about one hundred and fifty yards from the drop zone. The handle stuck and as I jammed it forward again we felt the plane lift in the air from the sudden loss of its load. As we were making the turn I looked back and the drop zone appeared snow-white. I had a sinking feeling, because all I could think of was the bags breaking and spreading the rice all over hell's half acre. We lined up for our next pass to release the parachute containers from the bomb bay. As we approached the drop zone it became clear that what I had thought was rice, was, in fact, the entire load, parachutes and all. When I had pushed the handle forward my first touch had opened the bomb bays and released the rice. The next push had released the containers, so that they followed directly after the free-falling bags of rice. The rice bags were carried forward by the momentum of flight so that they landed almost at the same spot and simultaneously with the parachute containers. Everything was together in an area about fifty feet square. It could not have been more perfect. It was an act of pure providence, but I am sure that Jack's group on the ground thought it had been planned just that way.

Captain Thompson headed back toward the Koukkwee Valley and Red's group. Captain Thompson and I talked over arrangements for the signals for dropping the two emergency containers; about two hundred yards before the drop zone he was to give us a horn so that Pop and I could get the containers out as quickly as possible. I then crawled over the top of the bomb bay and joined Pop. We prepared a hasty message to Red telling him that we would be back in two days to drop a radio and operator to them. The message was placed in an envelope and put in the top of one of the containers. In about ten minutes Captain Thompson gave us a preliminary signal that we were nearing the target. A minute or so later, he gave us the drop signal and the containers were dropped through the emergency hatch with hardly a second between them. We stuck our heads out the hatch and watched the containers and their parachutes float to the ground almost at Red's feet.

We had now been in Jap territory for over three hours and it was high time for us to get back to base. All in all, it had been a successful day. Pop and I were elated upon our return, despite the fact we had had only a couple of hours' sleep during the past two days.

Two days later we returned to Red's drop area in a C-87 with a radio and an operator who was to jump in. We flew over the drop zone several times but there were no signs of either personnel or panels. We stayed in the area about half an hour with still no signs of our people; we were greatly disheartened when we returned to the air base in India. Two days later the search was repeated but still there were no signs of them.

We tried to analyze what had happened, but the only logical

conclusion we could arrive at was that the Japs had closed in on the area and driven them out or possibly captured them.

To make certain we arranged with General Egan of the Air Group to have a photo-reconnaissance mission flown over the drop zone a couple of times during the next week to see if they could locate any display of ground panels. The photos were beautifully done, but there were no panels. We had done all possible and reluctantly decided to abandon the search.

In the meantime, Jack Barnard's group was faced with an immediate problem. The Japanese were on their trail. To their front was the beautiful but broad and treacherous Irrawaddy River. Their only salvation lay in their ability to get across the river and into the almost impenetrable jungle on the far side.

There was no time to get rubber boats to them, so in the drop we had included eight rubber air mattresses which they were willing to use as floats rather than be captured by the Japanese. However, from some of the nearby Kachins they learned of a spot on the river where the local Shan fishermen tied up their boats. They laid their plans, got a bit of sleep, and, at about 3 A.M., under a clear half moon, went to the spot where the boats were tied. They commandeered two boats and set off poling and paddling across the river. All went well until they reached the far bank. There, as luck would have it, they rowed directly into the center of a huge herd of wild elephants taking a bath. Fortunately, the elephants were frightened off by the boats. Splashing, thundering and trumpeting, the herd fled from the river and into the forest. After Jack and his party landed they pushed the two boats out into the current of the river and set off on foot due east through the jungle.

They were headed toward the area of Man Pang. Nearby there was a single extinct volcanic peak, Lampha Bum, rising about eight hundred feet above the nearby hills. This mountain was a sacred area to the Buddhists and it was reported to be infested with snakes. Since nearly all of the snakes in Burma are cobras, it was an area that people avoided. The group reached Man Pang's safety at the end of the third day and set up their new camp in a nearby abandoned rice paddy area called a *tongyaw*.

Tongyaws are numerous throughout the jungles of Northern

Burma. The Kachins burn off a small area of jungle and plant their rice to obtain the rich vitamins in the fresh topsoil. Their rice is highly nutritious and has a fine, rich flavor. After two or three years the field is abandoned to return to the jungle. The nomadic Kachins move on to a new area to burn it off and repeat the cycle.

After Jack and his group reached their new base camp site, the four Kachins in the party immediately started erecting a bamboo hut, called a *basha*. The Kachins are experts in such construction and can put up a three- or four-room house elevated three to four feet off the ground in a matter of a few days.

Their radio contact with the base continued in nearly perfect order. Soon after their arrival they asked for another supply drop but, at the time, every possible aircraft was needed on an emergency Hump run to China.

It was two weeks before we could get a drop aircraft, and the situation for Jack and his group was becoming desperate. They had consumed all their food and were living entirely off what they could forage in the jungle: wild game, bamboo shoots, berries and a few grains of wild rice. Several times in his radio messages Jack, a devout Christian, cited Biblical quotations about food and its scarcity.

When we were at last able to obtain a drop aircraft we were lucky enough to get the C-87 with Jake Sartz and his crew. It was a difficult drop. After each pass the plane had to bank sharply and turn away from the side of a sheer cliff. Because of the pitch inside the plane, stacking supplies and fastening static lines was difficult. The winds, however, were perfect for the drop, and we delivered Jack the food he so desperately needed. Jack now set up observation posts along the road from Bhamo to Myitkyina manned mostly by young Kachins he had recruited in the field. He reconnoitered and made plans for the demolition of numerous small bridges along the route.

Jack's group stayed in place gathering information until the first week in May, at which time he sent in a message requesting permission to withdraw by land trails from Burma before the coming monsoon. The group's route would lead them north into the Triangle area and thence to Fort Hertz from where they could be flown to India. He also asked for another supply drop to provide provisions essential for the trip. We approved of Jack's plan and arrangements were made to give him a final airdrop.

It was made under the worst possible conditions. There had been an unseasonal rain and the clouds were right down to treetop level. A strong wind was blowing diagonally across the drop zone. The pilot had to fly the plane at an angle across the drop zone and then put it into a violent banking maneuver to avoid flying into the side of the mountain. Captain Sartz was fatigued, so Captain Grube was piloting that day. Flying the C-87 on a drop mission requires two people at the controls, and Grube's co-pilot was inexperienced in dropping. The sensation at the drop door was like a roller coaster running amuk.

We managed to get only 50 per cent of the supplies in the cleared drop zone area. The remainder fell in the jungle and got hung up on trees. In the end, Jack and his group lost about one-fourth of that drop.

Two days after the drop they were ready to move. They crossed the Bhamo-Myitkyina road and then turned north along the mountain range between Burma and China. This region is fairly well populated with Kachin villages located about five to ten miles apart. These Kachins belonged to the Gauhri and Maru tribes. The Gauhries are noted for their colorful dress and a distinct culture of family life. The Marus, on the other hand, were nomadic, primitive, but had an unparalleled knowledge of the jungle. They assisted the movement of Jack and his group by providing guides and porters. In about two weeks the group had reached the Nmai Hka (river) and were ready to cross over into the Triangle.

Japanese intelligence was not to be caught napping. They were able to keep track of the movements of the group through spies from the Shan and Burmese villages, along with a few from the Kachin villages. Up to the Nmai Hka, Jack and his group were in radio contact with the base camp on a schedule of alternate nights. When they crossed the Nmai, into the Triangle, radio contact was lost and, as days passed into weeks, we became greatly concerned for their safety. The next word we had of them was from a new group we had sent in under Captain Wilkinson, then located in the Triangle at a place named Ngumla. He advised us that some of his agents had contacted Jack's group and they were on the way to his base fifty miles behind Japanese lines.

When he finally reached base camp at Nazira, Jack filled us in: they had progressed about a day's march beyond the Nmai Hka when the Japs closed in on them. They had to abandon the trail and strike off directly through the jungle. To reduce their loads to a bare minimum they destroyed the radio, food, ammunition, everything, so that each man was left with only his clothes, weapons and a few rounds of ammunition. Day after day, the Japs stayed on their trail and at the end of ten days had them cut off. The situation seemed hopeless. Out of nowhere there appeared an old Kachin headman who was a close relative of one of the Kachins in the group. He knew every inch of the ground and that night led Jack and his party through the Japanese encirclement so that by dawn they were twenty miles away. Five days later, they were at Captain Wilkinson's camp at Ngumla.

They stayed at Ngumla for about a week resting and regaining their strength. Then, with guides and porters provided by Captain Wilkinson, they passed around the Jap lines in the area of Sumprabum and walked on to Fort Hertz, where Captain Aitken had them flown to India.

We were in for still another surprise. Two days after Jack and his group had left Fort Hertz, Captain Aitken received a message from Kachin Levies Headquarters that Captain Maddox and Lieutenants Quinn and Francis had reported in to them. They had been intercepted by Subedar Zhing Htaw Naw who fed them and directed them to Captain DeSilva of the Kachin Levies. He gave them money, salt, rice and other necessities and had them guided to Levies Headquarters.

After all this time, we had given them up for lost. In the three months since we had last contacted them with an emergency drop, they had covered a thousand miles by foot, circling and crisscrossing areas of jungle and mountain where there are no marked trails. They took the Kachins into their confidence and, of necessity, lived entirely off the land. They became so independent, so sure, that they stole into Jap camps to steal rice and other foodstuffs, yet were never seen.

They even pretended to be natives. Captain Maddox was light-haired, yet he was able to hide this fact with a turban such as the Kachins wore. He darkened his face and, with an assurance that struck no false note, seemed nothing more than a native. They were never once detected by the Japanese even though their route passed within a mile of Myitkyina. They came out of the operation with rags on their backs and not a single complaint — they had exercised a guerrilla's talent to stay alive. Pop Milligan and I picked them up at the airfield. They trotted out of the airplane hollering, "Here we are!"

Red's next remark was, "You Yanks certainly make good shoes. We have been wearing these shoes since we dropped in almost five months ago and they are still in good shape."

I could see that he was right, and though they had all lost weight their eyes were clear, their handshakes strong, and I knew they had come through hardened. They had found the enemy's weakness. They knew that they had done something good.

On the plane ride back to India, Red told us of his encounter with a leech. These bloodsucking creatures were the bane of our men in the jungle. Varying in size from about an inch (common leech) to three inches (buffalo leech) and up to five inches (elephant leech), they attach themselves without being felt and swell to balloon-like proportions on the blood of their prey. In the jungle they seemed ever-present; personnel of 101 made a practice of stopping once each hour to look over all parts of their bodies and remove any leeches before they could do much harm.

One night while he was sleeping one of these leeches had gotten into the tube of Red's penis. When he awakened it was swollen to the point where he could not urinate. It was becoming extremely painful and there seemed nothing they could do to remove the leech. When the pain became most excruciating, he was actually thinking of gouging it out with a knife. Lieutenant Quinn finally suggested making a forceps-shaped tool out of bamboo. It worked fine and they were able to get hold of the leech and pull it out.

Detachment 101 was now moving forward. New missions were coming up. We would, in part, be better for the mistakes and the success of "A" Group. Once we had these men together at base, we went over their operation in detail, fitting together what we had learned.

The first and most glaring shortcoming was our inadequate parachute capability. We had been extremely lucky; the next time, however, we might not be so fortunate. Twelve men had been jumped under the crudest of conditions. We had parachuted and free-dropped approximately fourteen tons of supplies with comparatively little loss. But we could not gamble that our luck would hold. This time we recognized the need of men to serve as jump instructors and dropmasters. It was almost a year before the first qualified parachutist would arrive from the States. Back-pack-type personnel chutes were also requested. These were provided immediately, some by air freight via the ATC Red Ball Express direct from the States to Chabua, and the remainder by ship to Calcutta. All of the subsequent drops were made with this equipment and it greatly eased the problem. We also asked for United States Army-type cargo parachute containers with chutes. This request was purposefully kept low because the bamboo, burlap-covered container with the broadcloth chute had worked so well and was so inexpensive that we decided to use this as our primary cargo container. We made the containers ourselves and the chutes were purchased on Lend-Lease from the British and Indian governments.

It also became apparent that a twelve-man group was too large, too unwieldy, too likely to attract attention, and seriously limited in its mobility. We all owned up to the necessity of smaller teams held together by a stronger link among themselves. The operational results of several small groups, as it worked out, were considerably greater than those of a single large group. From that point on, the size of our operational teams was kept to a maximum of six men, preferably three or four.

We had not foreseen sufficiently how we would respond to "A" Group's silence. We had been at a loss, and feared disaster the moment contact ceased. Not only must we now prepare more detailed plans required for keeping track of our field stations, but more specific alternate plans in case something went wrong. This had been particularly evident when the groups became separated. We were able to locate Red purely by chance, for we had not developed a procedure to maintain the contact. We could well have lost all of Red's group. Such contact procedures were now incorporated into the training and monitored by the operational staff. This had a tremendous effect upon the quality of 101's future operations.

Another weakness in "A" Group's operation was the failure to utilize rally points. If things had been handled properly, the three groups should have been able to contact one another after the effort to blow the bridges in the Namhkwin area. It is true that both groups were under tremendous strain and pressure. But, had their training been more perceptive, they would have automatically done those things which must be done to re-establish contact. Instead of running from danger near a rally point, it is necessary for the sake of the group that a few men remain behind. The only hope of retaining contact is the formula of risking a fight to carry out contact. This insight was incorporated into our training — and it worked. Never again were our men in the field unable to establish contact at a designated rally point.

It also became evident that the power for our field radios was inadequate and would have to be increased. The radio itself worked beautifully. Even over vast distances, across jungle and mountainous terrain, it was never seriously lacking a strong signal; what we now sought was still greater range and a lighter load. In order to keep the set going in field operation, it was necessary to drop hundreds of pounds of dry cell battery packs. At the maximum, the batteries had a life-span of only thirty hours and, on occasion, as little as ten hours. The jungle dampness took life from the batteries, and with the rain and dampness of the approaching monsoon, we expected an even more dramatic sapping of energy. It was obvious that we would have to provide a form of power generator to future groups.

To provide for the field station with a moderate-size traffic load, Captain Huston experimented with hand generators. Every type of generator tested set up a whine which could be heard one hundred to four hundred yards away. This, it was thought, would be a dead giveaway, so they were encased in boxes with insulating material to lower the noise level. This increased the size somewhat, but it was effective in reducing the sound. Shortly thereafter, the insulating material was discarded because in the Burma jungle there is almost always a continual buzzing noise going on, from crickets, cicadas and similar creatures. These are so loud that they drowned out the noise of the hand generator, so that it could not be distinguished at a distance of over twenty-five feet. For the larger field stations, small portable gasoline generators were ordered from the States.

All but two of the original twelve members of "A" Group insisted upon future roles in operations. Their wishes were granted and through the ensuing months and years they were to go forth again and again behind the lines.

When the debriefing for "A" Group came to its conclusion I asked Saw Judson about my gold watch. He said it had worked fine and in a burst of praise cited its help in making radio contact exactly on time. He looked at his empty hands and even then I knew: he pointed to the place on the map where the old Kachin headman had led them out of the Japanese encirclement. The watch was there, I could sense it. Saw told me that when they had ended up safely he could not leave the old man without a reward.

"He showed us the way," Saw said.

"So he got the watch," I said.

"He liked it," Saw said. "He said it was bright as the sun."

"It's much better with him," I said. "He does need something to show around that we were there."

Saw agreed. The headman was a fine old man and he would be considered important owning an American watch. Besides, part of our business was to make friends.

V I I

The Enemy Answers

OUR RECRUITING for new teams had flourished, largely because of the retreat from Burma. The people who had fled their homes were in refugee camps in India, and it was there we found men willing to undertake the dangerous activities we had in mind. We narrowed the initial list down to fifty people; some of these had been engaged in smuggling and illegal trading, work which seemed to fit naturally into what we expected them to do in war; others were college professors, merchants of various commodities, or managers of teak forests who had had their holdings taken over by the Japanese. For some, the reason was the money we were prepared to pay; for others it was what they felt about the war. We moved them from the refugee camps to Detachment 101's training base in the Nazira area. They learned quickly, and our concern now was to get them into new operations.

Some of us wanted to concentrate in North Burma. Others suggested that we expand our activities to Southern Burma, to the Arakan coastline, and even as far south as the fabled city of Rangoon. We were a group that did not relish an internal argument over purpose, and in the end we settled on a compromise. The operations in Northern Burma would continue as the primary objective, but at the same time, we would also begin operations further south on a minimal basis. Then, following up that decision, we requested from OSS in Washington a PT boat and skipper to aid us in sea operations along the southern coast of Burma.

Carl Eifler was more excited by the southern operations than either John Coughlin or myself. He shook his fists over the maps, snorting contemptuously at any suggestion that we were moving too fast. If there is one thing that a unit such as ours needed it was a dreamer, a dreamer strong enough by the force of his will and personality to penetrate beyond dream into reality. Carl gave us this stimulus.

It seemed to me we were moving perhaps a trifle too fast. In this business a man's life depended upon not making a single mistake. I felt quite strongly that it was best for us to do a little and do it well rather than try to do many things and not do any one of them with the perfection that was necessary. I didn't know why, but I felt apprehensive. We were getting into something we were not yet prepared to do.

Our new target area was the Lawksawk Valley in Central Burma about seventy-five miles southeast of Mandalay. This area was approximately two hundred miles further south than the "A" Group operational area; it would be a long flight by C-87, well beyond the range of fighter support from bases in India. Hence, in order to parachute the group into operations it would be necessary to have it done from the China side.

Accordingly, in March 1943, arrangements were made with ATC to use one of their long-range C-87's piloted by the old hands, Captains Jake Sartz and Grube. The agents to be dropped were eager to get into operation. We completed their parachute ground training and packed all of their equipment in parachute containers. Then the group, accompanied by Coughlin, now Lieutenant Colonel, Captain Frazee, Pop Milligan and myself, flew to Kunming, China, the Headquarters of General Chennault's 14th Air Force.

Some preliminary arrangements had been made for the drop with the 14th Air Force but, at the time of our arrival, they were not overly enthusiastic. The fighter escort was essential because we knew we would be flying directly into the central base area of the Japanese Air Force in Burma with bases in Namsang, Laihka, Heho and Meiktila. John and I finally ended up talking to General "Butch" Morgan, the A-3, and, subsequently, with the Chief of Staff, General Casey Vincent. Basically, they were not against the flight, provided we could convince them that the benefits to be derived from the operation were greater than the risks involved. John used every point of logic trying to convince them of the intelligence values of the operation, and I put in a word or two concerning the capability of rescuing downed aircrews. Evidently, the dialectic must have been somewhat convincing, or perhaps we wore them down; after two days Casey advised us he had talked it over with General Chennault and that the flight was approved. Then he added "except that," and here came the hooker, "we must bomb Lashio on the return flight." The 14th Air Force did not have any B-24's at the time and their fighters and medium bombers could not carry the bombs and enough fuel to make the round trip. Our C-87, although it was a converted B-24, did not have a bomb bay. In order to get the bombs out of the aircraft, somebody was going to have to pull the arming pins on the bombs and throw them out of the door. John and I thought this over for quite a while, but we knew that if we were going to get the group into operation we would have to agree to their terms.

Take-off time for the flight was set for 11 o'clock the following morning. They agreed to provide an escort of four P-40 fighter aircraft with Lieutenant Colonel Johnnie Alison leading the flight. Colonel Coughlin and I spent the greater part of that night going over the details of the flight with Jake Sartz.

The flight from Kunming to the target area was without incident except that Johnnie Alison put on quite an exhibition of precision flying for our benefit. He flew his fighter directly into position between the wing and the tail of our aircraft. He stayed there for quite a while; so close that it seemed we could reach out and touch him. His fighter escort remained with us to a point about one hundred miles beyond Lashio, where it broke off to return to home base. When we arrived in the target area, Colonel Coughlin and I scanned the land below, and saw villages no more than two to five miles distant from the proposed drop zone. Wasn't that too close? I said, and John agreed. We talked it over with the group leader, who said there was no reason to be concerned. He knew the area and suggested we go ahead.

The drop was completed in three passes, one for the men and two for equipment containers. We dropped from a low altitude of four hundred feet in order to screen the drop behind low hills and trees.

As we made our last pass, we could see a discomforting sight: villagers streaming out from every direction, heading toward the drop zone. I had an aching feeling that their lines looked hostile. I couldn't get it out of my head that they were out to kill. And because of this, I felt this had been a bad decision. As I sat in the plane, I felt miserable about the whole affair and wondered why I had ever got mixed up in this sort of business.

I have yet to see an operation that was not without a sense of good or evil omen. The dismal sense of warning, of disaster, is stronger with some than others. It may get you nowhere to listen too carefully, but when it pounds, then another place, another day is wise.

Our mistake was in not calling the operation off when we became alarmed. In such a situation, an agent going into operation becomes so physically and emotionally keyed up that he cannot exercise prudent judgment. Then somebody with an objective viewpoint should make the decision. I know that I learned a tremendous lesson: when so much depends on secrecy, it is pitiably certain that observation also means treachery. Thereafter, I relied upon my own judgment, because we were dealing with men's lives; if I made a mistake, it would be my fault and there could be nobody else to blame.

I can still see those lines of villagers. With so many people around, our group had no chance. They went no further. The mission was scuttled the moment we let them jump.

John and I looked at each other and shook our heads. It was distasteful to say anything. Then we saw the bombs — the whole thing suddenly was important as it had never been when we wanted the plane to drop our men. It suddenly seemed generous to have twenty thirty-pound bombs. Our hands moved, touching them, waiting.

Over the highway between Hsipaw and Mandalay, Jake Sartz and Grube spotted a Japanese convoy of about thirty trucks. Were we interested?

A truck convoy doesn't show up every day.

They dropped the C-87 down to treetop level and flew the length of the convoy spraying it with all available .50 caliber machine guns. It was like seeing a crazy dance, Jap trucks going off the road, afire, careening wildly.

We could have cheered, but we didn't. Our turn was next.

Then Jake climbed back up to 6,000 feet to put us 3,000 feet above ground elevation. John and I were going to drop the bombs by sitting sideways in the doorway, pulling the pins and chucking them out. Neither of us had any idea where they would fall, so we test-dropped a couple to get the feel of it. The first one was way off, but the second one came within a few feet of one of the buildings of the Namtu mines.

Shortly thereafter Jake gave us the green light: Lashio. We saw the airport, the town. We started, scarcely aware of unloading bombs on the target, aware only of death. Brilliance as our bombs flashed, and the innocent puffs of ack-ack fire close to the wing-tips . . . we might not have been there, so strange was the sense of detachment . . . and listening, as cannons and machine guns became a hellish nightmare somewhere else . . . and, mouth wide open, like an Indian in a movie battle, shouting at us, one of the aircrew, his eyes ice, saying it as if he did not believe it — "I'm hit, I'm dying."

John and I disposed of the remainder of the bombs in a hurry. About this time the nose of the plane went down and it seemed that we would certainly crash. The pilot, trying to get out of the ground fire, was skimming over the crest of a mountain, using it as a shield.

Jake kept the plane low in the valley until we came to the gorge area of the Salween River, a hundred or so miles north of Lashio. Meanwhile we checked the airman. He had a small flesh wound in the leg but no bones were broken; he was more scared than hurt. Jake asked whether we should return to India as planned or go on to Kunming. India was four to five hours away and Kunming only one and a half or two. We were all tired and it was starting to get dark, so we decided to go to Kunming for the night. This was one of the luckiest decisions we were ever to make. When the plane landed, its motors stopped for lack of gasoline.

The gauge showed plenty of fuel, but later it was found that some of the Japanese ack-ack had knocked out the gas transfer system so that the gas in the reserve tanks was not being transferred to the main tanks. After they had towed the plane off the runway we got a good look at it. It looked like a sieve. There were over two hundred and fifty holes in it, varying in size from a pinhead to two or three inches.

Later I found out from General Stilwell that he had opposed the drop from the beginning, even assuming the operation was successful. It was too far away to have any direct effect on operations in Northern Burma and he felt this talent could have been used more profitably further north. He did not, however, want to countermand Carl's orders, so he let it go.

It required another day to patch up the airplane, and the following day we returned to India. We proceeded to our base camp that night to see if there had been any radio contact. I don't think either John or I really expected any then — or ever. We monitored their radio frequency and not one signal came through; our prearranged efforts to locate them or their panels by photo-reconnaissance flights made no difference. We knew that the group was lost. For days upon days we hoped, and then the Japanese radio boasted — we got your men. The announcement was brief: the men were dead.

VIII

The Prisoner

ᒧᒥᒧᒥᒧᒥᒧᒥᒧᒥᒧᒥᒧᒥᒧᒥᒧᒥᒧᒥᒧᒥᒧᒥᒧᒥᒧᒥᒧᒥᒧᒥ

ALTHOUGH THE LOSS of our second group was a blow, in no way did this defeat — and it was that — bring about doubts. We were dazed momentarily, but we were also preparing additional groups.

By the spring of 1943, our training of volunteers had begun to take effect, and the members of our unit were, in their variety of backgrounds, in their human types and characteristics, almost a microcosm of all the nations fighting for the Allied cause.

Among those on our roster were two priests: Father MacAllindon and Father Stuart. One was a Scotsman and the other Irish, both of the Dominican Order with its home office in Omaha. Although they were offered a good deal of money for their services, their real objective was to return to the people they considered their own; both converted every cent of pay into clothing, school materials and the like for the Kachins.

These two had a thorny answer to Japanese occupation forces. The Japs were going to arrest them as Englishmen, but they were adamant that they were Irish and that Ireland was neutral. The Japs released them north of Myitkyina, but they knew they were being followed. The same night they turned in for sleep in a Kachin house where there was a box of hand grenades and a couple of shotguns. When the Japanese started looking through the village for the padres, the two threw grenades out of the windows and fired shotguns through the roof. It sounded impressive long enough for them to escape into the jungle. They reached an

Allied outpost minutes ahead of the enemy. We found out about them, and naturally sought out their invaluable help. They were only too anxious to aid our cause and when one of our men in the field, Captain Wilkinson, asked for an interpreter, Father MacAllindon volunteered to go. Father Stuart later joined Lieutenant Curl of KNOTHEAD.

Usually, once our men were in the field, we had no way of reaching them save through radio or airdrop. There was an urgent need for a third way — landing an aircraft — for the loss of personal control of units in the field could be solved once and for all with light planes.

We directed both FORWARD and KNOTHEAD to build airstrips. They managed it by putting hundreds of natives to work, and, leaving nothing to chance, they built numerous dummy bamboo houses which they set on the strips. From the air, the strips looked like native villages. When a light plane came, it was a matter of minutes to remove the houses and quickly make the strip ready for landing. Now we had to deliver. The strips were there but we had no light aircraft.

The problem was given to Captain John Raiss, a Wall Street broker in civilian life, and he launched into the project as though he alone could corner the market in A.T. & T. stock. The United States Air Corps had no light aircraft in India at the time, so the obvious answer was either private Indian sources or the RAF. After a bit of preliminary checking Raiss decided the best approach was to go directly to the RAF. Somehow, he arranged a meeting with Air Marshal Peirse, head of the RAF in India. He took along as a modest token two cartons of Camel cigarettes: these, along with John's cosmopolitan charm, must have worn down resistance, if there was any: within a couple of days the RAF delivered a Gypsy Moth to Detachment 101. We were jubilant. She was a two-seat biplane of 1925 vintage, in excellent condition; she flew and handled well. There was no mistaking the fact that 101 was in the flying business.

And in a matter of days we were glad to have the plane.

In the radio shack, there was a shout, "A Jap! We've got a Jap."
A new operation, a few miles north of Myitkyina, had just radioed

in an urgent message: a Jap fighter plane had crashed and they had moved in and captured the pilot. He was uninjured. This was an intelligence opportunity that opened up enormous possibilities for unthought-of information. Understand that since the initial Burma campaign not a single Japanese had been taken prisoner in all of southeast Asia. None of what we knew of the enemy came from firsthand interrogation. The details the pilot could provide! The implications shook us all, not so much with surprise as with the challenge of getting the prisoner out of Burma. He was a prize worth a lot of trouble.

The Air Corps, for instance, was in foul temper because Burma seemed to have swallowed up every Japanese aircraft. Many aerial photos had been taken, often at great danger to pilots, and still the secret of where and how the Japanese were hiding their aircraft had not been revealed. They were there, we knew, because they attacked the transports flying the Hump in strikingly large numbers. The Air Corps had sent us word that they would appreciate anything our men in the field could find out about the location of the phantom Japanese air bases. The same mystery greeted our men. They could not find a trace of aircraft on the ground. Now the closely guarded secret of the Japanese air bases in Burma could perhaps be solved. We were consumed with the necessity of bringing the pilot out of Burma.

But how? The ordinary way would have been to walk him out, something that involved time and physical strain; and there was always the chance that the patrol escorting him would be ambushed. The recovery of the pilot was as important to us as it had been to the enemy to see that he did not fall in our hands.

Then the answer opened up. The Gypsy Moth, of course. Why had we gotten it in the first place but to make speedy contact with field units? The point was raised, and correctly, that this first mission involved far more daring, far more distance than we had envisioned. The prisoner had been captured over three hundred miles away, beyond the range of the Gypsy Moth, and in the thick jungles and mountains it would take weeks or months to build an airfield. Our problem then was to move the prisoner to an airfield within the range of the airplane. The answer was KNOT-HEAD, but this involved a move of over a hundred miles behind the lines and through Jap-infested territory. But the risk had to be taken and instructions were sent to effect the move to KNOTHEAD with the most reliable men and for KNOTHEAD to notify us immediately upon his arrival.

Carl, who embodied so much energy, and the courage that does not falsify danger at hand, made the decision. He himself would pilot the Gypsy Moth — along with his many talents, he could fly a light plane, a skill he had acquired on the Mexican border when he was a Treasury Department agent hunting down smugglers. Now we set about planning the flight in detail.

The Gypsy Moth's fuel tanks at capacity would just get the aircraft to KNOTHEAD at Nawbum. That is: if Carl were lucky and did not have to deviate his flight, which was all over jungle, most of which was uncharted. This meant that for the flight back Carl would need fuel; therefore, a sufficient amount was parachuted into KNOTHEAD where they had just completed construction of a strip long enough to take the Gypsy Moth.

When Lieutenant Vince Curl at KNOTHEAD signaled the arrival of the prisoner we learned that he was behaving in the style of a samurai. The prisoner had let it be known that he understood why so much effort was going into the leveling out of a paddy field; obviously an aircraft was coming in to take him out. Vince was certain the Japanese had an escape attempt in mind. His look was restless, as if something were going to happen. He knew airplanes and we guessed that in some way he hoped to take over the controls, destroy the plane and Carl and himself. We absolutely had to figure on his making trouble after the plane was in the air. The suicidal tendencies of the Japanese, especially a samurai disgraced by capture, we recognized with respect, if not awe.

Our solution was simple; the Japanese would be given a strong enough injection to knock him out for the length of the trip. As an additional measure of safety, once he was asleep he was to be bound to his seat, so that even if he returned to consciousness early, he would find his arms, hands and legs properly secured. In addition, we rigged up a device with a slipknot around the prisoner's neck so that if he started breaking loose, Carl could pull it tight and strangle him. This was not necessary, however, as the plan worked so well that afterward, when Carl returned to base, the prisoner was still under the slumbering power of the drug.

When he did come to, he looked us over coolly. You could see that the man was no coward. Under the interrogation, he betrayed no sign of giving in; no amount of threat or cajoling did any good. The prisoner remained silent. After two days of interrogation, the whole thing had gotten nowhere; we were exhausted and the prisoner stared at us with the same impassive contempt. And still, we sensed that he knew many things about those bases.

We studied his diary and it revealed him as the kind of man who only writes down what should go into a diary — a personal kind of monologue that is expressed in terms that are obscure to all but the author. There was also a photograph, showing him standing by his aircraft. The picture was clear, and then somebody pointed out that the grass in the rear of the plane was irregular and appeared to have holes in it. We used a magnifying glass and Sergeant Moree, the photo technician, enlarged the picture to bring out the details — the answer to what the Japs were doing to hide their planes was no longer a mystery. Instead of building revetments around their airplanes they had dug holes and covered them with sod. The runways leading into these dugouts were also sodded so that in an air photo it all looked like a pasture, except for a few small shadows.

We still did not know where the Japanese air base was located so we went back to work on the pilot. Finally, he talked: he was based at the Meiktila air base a few miles south of Mandalay. With this information we went to the A-2 of the 10th Air Force, Captain Burman, and he produced the air photos of Meiktila. Sure enough, the odd-looking shadows were there, appearing around the edge of the airfield and in nearby cleared areas. All told there were about thirty of them. This was all the information that was needed. A few days later a large flight of B-25's from Lower Assam bombed and strafed Meiktila. It did not take all of the pressure off the Hump because the Japs had many other fields: but our flyers were subsequently conscious of less pressure, fewer attacks.

Shortly thereafter, operation FORWARD also captured a Japanese and Carl flew him out by way of Fort Hertz. The prisoner was a private first class who did not have much information of imme-

diate military value, but did provide a lot of data concerning desig-
nations of units in Burma and background data on Japan.

During this period, the addition of new personnel did not keep
pace with the expansion of operations. During one of his trips to
the Headquarters of the New Chinese Army in India (Chih Hui
Pu) Carl had met Captain David Hunter. They had much in
common: Dave put in for a transfer to 101 and, much to his surprise, it was approved. Shortly thereafter Lieutenants Tilly, Larsen
and Peterson and Sergeant Schreiner, a cryptographer, joined 101
from OSS in the States and they were greatly needed. Sergeant
Hemming, our demolition expert, had been hurt when a jeep rolled
over on him. Lieutenant Peterson was an engineer and wasted no
time in taking over. Lieutenants Tilly and Larsen spent a short time
as instructors in the training base and were then sent to the field;
Tilly to KNOTHEAD and Larsen to FORWARD with Wilkinson, now a
Major.

We also received a shipment of seven NCO's from the New
York National Guard. Most of them were supply and administration specialists and were sorely needed. They arrived at Calcutta,
and Carl happened to be in the area at the time. Captain Little,
who was in charge of our Calcutta base, had them lined up so
Carl could get acquainted with them. He went down the line from
one to another asking, "What is your name, soldier?" etc., and got
such answers as "Sergeant Banker, sir"; "Sergeant Richardson, sir";
etc. Finally he came to one sergeant and asked — "What is your
name, soldier?"

His reply was "ssss-ssss-ssss-sergeant ssss-ssss-ssss," and then he
nudged the fellow next to him and said, "you tell him." This was
Sergeant Straub, who proved to be one of the hardest-working and
best-liked persons in the unit, and, above and beyond that, his
occupation as a chef in one of the larger hotels in New York made
him a welcome addition as our mess sergeant.

During the course of an airdrop from the Dinjan airfield, John
and Carl became acquainted with Major Bill Cummings. Bill
belonged to the Seagrave Hospital Unit but at the time was as-
sisting in a supply drop to the V Force (a combined British-
American unit formed by General Stilwell to recruit and train
native personnel to be used on reconnaissance patrols, flank pa-

trols and scouts for the combat forces). Bill did not agree with some of Colonel Seagrave's policies in handling members of the native staff of the hospital unit and felt it best if he were transferred elsewhere. He asked for a transfer to 101 and it was approved immediately by General Stilwell's Headquarters. Bill had been born and raised in Burma, educated in the States, and was a graduate of Purdue. He was the kind of Burma expert we could use.

Through the courtesy of Lieutenant General Stratemeyer, the United States commander of the newly formed Eastern Air Command, we were suddenly blessed with another light plane, an L-5. A few days after it arrived, Carl flew it to Fort Hertz where he stayed overnight, gassed up, then headed for the strip which Major Wilkinson had built at Ngumla. On his approach for the landing, he overshot the strip. He gave it the throttle to make another pass but, in the high altitude, he lost flying speed and suddenly crashed into a bamboo jungle about half a mile beyond the field. He was shaken up, but not hurt, and after a couple of days he hit the trail and walked back to Fort Hertz. It took ten days, but it seemed longer because of the loss of the plane.

For the Fourth of July, we put on a party for the benefit of our friends, the local British tea planters. They had devoted a great deal of time and effort in our behalf, always in the best of moods, building camps and roads, supplying food and labor, and responding with answers to any number of problems.

Together we spent that evening toasting the President, the King and each other's good fortune in working and fighting side by side.

A Voyage by Submarine

By THE WINTER of 1943-1944 the Japs in the Hukawng Valley were becoming increasingly active with their patrols into the Naga Hills. Headquarters of the Northern Combat Area Command (NCAC) asked us to organize several forward outposts to report on their strength and locations. Three teams of five men each were organized from the group of Anglo-Burmese trained at Nazira.

L Group under Skittles, a Chinese from Rangoon, was established in the area of Tagap. The group escorted Major General Raymond Wheeler, Chief of Service and Supply in the CBI Theater, on his initial reconnaissance of the forward trail of the Ledo Road, but they encountered a strong Japanese patrol and were subsequently withdrawn. Robby's M Group was to go into the area of Taro but their Naga porters, fearful of losing their heads or their lives to other Nagas, wanted to return home, so this group was also withdrawn.

Further to the north in the valley of the Tarung Hka (river) there was an unprotected route into the Brahmaputra River Valley in India. Into this gap was sent J Group, named after its Anglo-Burmese leader, Jocko. The group advanced about seventy-five miles into the Tarung Valley and located a base. They set up outposts that stood off small enemy probes, and within a short time the Japanese pulled back, believing that they were confronted by a much larger force.

J Group had an odd radio hookup. Their forward outpost was located at Miao about a hundred miles from Ledo, where they wanted the reports delivered. However, the communications systems of the 101 field units and the Army system were entirely different. Our Nazira base camp was about a hundred and fifty miles south of Ledo. So J Group communicated with the Nazira radio station, from whence the information was immediately relayed to Ledo. We did not realize it at the time, but this procedure had the primary benefit of security for 101 communications and, equally as important, it gave 101 complete control of all of its field operations.

J Group led a lonesome existence. There were only a handful of natives in the entire valley. After about three months its usefulness was over and it was withdrawn to base camp.

The results attained by these three groups were insignificant; however the lessons learned from them were highly important. Our mission was to raise and organize guerrilla forces. These operations dramatically pointed out that this could not be done along the periphery or front lines. It could only be accomplished well behind the enemy lines and thereafter all of our effort was exerted in that direction.

Captain Oscar Milton from the initial "A" Group was also put back into operation. Oscar was English through and through, an adventurous spirit ready for anything. He selected two of the four young Kachins who had accompanied him on the A operation and we provided him a radio operator. After being flown into Fort Hertz, his party proceeded due east and set up a field station. We had always wondered why the Japs did not put on a drive to take over Fort Hertz and its airfield, which they could have done with a little extra effort. Since we believed that they would do this sooner or later, Oscar was directed to set up a station, a redoubt near the headwaters of the Nmai Hka, in order that other field units could fall back to it in the event the Japs did take over Fort Hertz. He set up the field base, but after a while it became dubious that the Japs would try to take over Fort Hertz. Consequently, he was directed to cache the spare radio set and other camp equipment and proceed south along the Nmai Hka and continue south through the hill tract toward Bhamo.

Oscar had the ability to live with the natives and like it. With no Caucasian companionship, he stayed in the jungle for a solitary period of almost nine months and we heard no complaints from him. There were not many Japs in this remote region. Oscar's agents fanned out to the south and there still were no Japs to be reported. Even this negative intelligence was valuable.

In the same way, we sent numerous teams into areas where we could take nothing for granted until reports from Detachment 101 agents in the field confirmed or denied the presence of Japanese activity in a specific area.

To augment our now far-flung operations, a boat finally arrived for use along the southern coasts. Though not a PT, it was almost as good, sleek-looking, about forty feet in length and powered by a 250-horsepower engine. She carried out her first mission in November 1943. What happened can perhaps best be described by the commendation sent to 101 by General Howard C. Davidson of the 10th Air Force:

APO 465
8th December, 1943

SUBJECT: Commendation.
TO   :   Commanding General, Rear Echelon, U. S. Army Forces, CBI, APO 885.

1. The Tenth Air Force wishes to express its appreciation for the action performed by Col. Carl F. Eifler and the members of his command in the rescue of a B-24 crew shot down in the Bay of Bengal west of Rangoon.

2. This B-24 was badly shot up and the aileron controls completely shot away. Two motors on one side were out, and when the pilot used sufficient power to keep the airplane in level flight, torque of the engines would push down the wing on their side to such an extent that the airplane could not continue on its course. It crash landed on the water, and the crew took to their rubber life rafts. An unsuccessful search was made by a USAF Catalina the next morning at daybreak. On the same day, an RAF Wellington, carrying an extra life raft, food and water to be dropped to the stranded crew, was successful in its mission, and a further report was made back to this Headquarters.

3. Col. Eifler was in this Headquarters in connection with an attempted rescue mission being carried out for a fighter pilot forced down on a previous mission. Upon learning details of the stranded B-24 crew, he immediately started making plans to launch his rescue boat which was still in a cradle and organize a search and rescue mission. After overcoming many obstacles, Col. Eifler and crew departed on the following morning at daybreak on a 450-mile trip deep into enemy waters and within sight of enemy shore line to attempt to rescue this crew. The USAF Catalina was dispatched the following night to search again for this crew, and after a short period, sighted Col. Eifler's boat and the dinghy at about the same time members of the rescue launch sighted the airplane and the dinghy.

4. The B-24 crew was immediately taken aboard the rescue launch, and medical aid was given to members of this crew on the return journey. The crew was successfully brought into Chittagong and later flown to Calcutta and hospitalized. They were in fairly good condition except for one man who had some fingers shot off by the attack of the Japanese fighters.

5. I wish to commend Col. Eifler and the members of his command for this splendid action and the efficiency and speed at which it was carried out, resulting in the rescue of this crew and raising the morale of all combat units under this command.

> HOWARD C. DAVIDSON
> Brig. Gen., U.S.A.,
> Commanding

The operation supported those who advocated expanding our work to Southern Burma. Carl conferred with Lieutenant General Irwin, the British Commander of the Eastern Army. The supply route to the Japanese force on the Akyab front was over a single road from Prome, through Taungup pass. The blocking of this road would restrict the Jap resupply to sea routes.

General Irwin asked 101 to establish an operation in the area to gather information and cut the road. Carl sent word to get a group organized to land by boat on Ramree Island. Ramree is about sixty miles long and about twenty-five miles wide and sparsely habitated by Burmese and Arakanese. The team, which was termed W Group, was selected from the Anglo-Burmese group at Nazira. All were familiar with the island and approached the mission like a returning army. They could swim, and they were graduates of our training program.

A Royal Navy submarine was to get them to the island, and so urgent was the mission that only after they were aboard ship was there time to show them how to maneuver the rubber landing boats that would carry them from ship to beach. The cramped quarters aboard the submarine made a bedlam of the instruction period in how to handle the landing boats.

When they arrived close to the island, it was night and foggy. Two rubber boats composed the landing armada — boats to be buried as soon as they landed. The submarine resurfaced, the captain was reluctant to move in close to the shore for fear of the fog, and the scene as the men got into the rubber boats was unfortunately comic. Carl was sure the boats could not be buried. There was a solution: bring them back. He decided to take one boat carrying two agents and equipment; after that Carl was to return the two boats through the surf to the submarine. The sea had turned rough as they cast off. They somehow landed the second boat without incident, but Carl's craft hit a trough in the labyrinth of fog, then poised on breakers. They were pounded through the surf. Carl's boat took a lethal pitch, he was thrown out, hitting his head against a submerged rock. Each man somehow in this desperate moment held on, Carl was pulled back in, groggy from the blow, and in some obscure and miraculous way they waded to shore, saving a good part of the equipment. Their faces revealed the weariness of the moment, their clothes were drenched, their hands cut and bleeding. They were nevertheless confident. Carl took the two rubber boats back through the surf to the submarine six hundred yards out. The fog grew thicker, but he made it. In a clear voice, as he got on the submarine, he said, "Ruddy good boys we put on that island."

For the boys, danger stretched out across the beach and on into the jungle, suffused with an unearthly light. They made it through, reaching a sanctuary of dense undergrowth where they spent the night.

They did not look back. They should have. On the beach, a wave washed in and deposited a lone hand battery cell on the beach. It lay there, glistening — as it was found by a fisherman walking the beach early the following morning. Inevitably he was suspicious and turned it over to the Japanese. The forgetfulness sprang a manhunt, the boys were followed, routes blocked, until there was no way out. They never came on the air. Later, we learned they were shot standing close together, faces covered with mud. Even then, they were extraordinarily together and shouting defiance to the enemy.

Carl's head injury did not clear up. He complained of headaches. He would hold his head and admit agony. He emptied bottles of aspirin and sipped tumblers of bourbon, but the prescriptions failed. He finally conceded that he should check into the hospital, where he was able to get at least temporary relief.

The tragic silence of the radio from the island left us face to face with another loss, with the biting fact that we had made mistakes. Now we made another survey to direct us in correct ways.

We led ourselves, step by step, through what we would have to do — find men and equipment for safer, surer landings by sea.

When he got out of the hospital, Carl still remained hopeful of getting operations established in Southern Burma. He and John planned another operation with its target the tin mines along the Tenasserim strip of the Malay Peninsula, about two hundred miles south along the coast from Rangoon and about halfway between Tavoy and Moulmein. Still another team was selected out of the Anglo-Burmese group. It consisted of five men with a highly competent individual as its leader.

They were outfitted in the base camp at Nazira and Pop Milligan gave them a short but intensive period of training on parachute operations. Meanwhile, John Coughlin had made arrangements with the Air Corps to have the drop made by B-24's stationed at Ranigungh about one hundred miles north of Calcutta. When all was set, the team with its equipment was moved from the base camp to Ranigungh and turned over to John.

The operation had been planned for the first full moon in September. A section of beach over two hundred yards wide and nearly a mile long was selected as the drop site. It appeared to be ideal. The drop went off on schedule and John indicated that it was executed exactly as planned and he had every reason to hope for success. However, that was not to be. We had every one of the base radio stations, plus an extra we had set up in Chittagong, listening for them to come on the air with the radio, but they never did.

We had arranged emergency panels and smoke signals with them in the event their radio did not function, so John asked me to see if I could locate them at the alternate control point. John must have known that I was about worn out. Those of us back at the base camp had been working day and night for almost a year, building camps, receiving groups, revising the training program, organizing, equipping, supplying teams in the field, and, after every mistake, going over every action that could have been done better and could have saved lives.

I knew very little about the lay of the land in the Tenasserim area so I asked Captain Red Maddox who had been raised in the area and had been with the initial "A" Group to accompany me. We would be operating in and out of the American air base at Ranigungh, so Red donned the uniform of an American enlisted man to avoid attracting attention. The flight from the air base to the alternate point was a long one, about twelve hundred miles each way, and over the waters of the Bay of Bengal. We tried it four times on alternate days and each day we ran into huge fronts of monsoon clouds. On all four occasions we were within fifty to sixty miles of shore when we encountered a wall of clouds. The pilots did not want to fly into this on instruments for fear of flying into the mountain range which paralleled the shoreline. Each time we had to turn back. On each of these trips we took off from the air base at about four or five o'clock in the morning and returned after dark, so it was anything but a joy ride.

The second day I felt miserable. I started going through alternate spells of chills and fever, one minute under ten blankets and the next in the bomb bay to cool off. I had malaria. Red was an old hand at this sort of thing and kept giving me large quantities of quinine. I survived and we made three more search operations. We found no sign of our men. Now I found myself sick in a different, dark, lonely way.

After four failures, the air base commander told me that he needed the airplane for other missions. He finally consented to run one more mission using three airplanes and combining the

Close to the battle lines in Northern Burma, General Stilwell, left, and Colonel Peers discuss how 101 will support the Allied drive on Myitkyina.

The first commander of OSS Detachment 101, Colonel Eifler, holds in his hand one of the thousands of fire-hardened, lethal *pungyis*. These handmade primitive booby traps caused many enemy casualties.

After Stilwell's departure from the CBI Theater, these four men drew up the plan for the final defeat of the Japanese forces in Burma. Seated from left to right are Lieutenant General Sultan; Lord Mountbatten; Major General Donovan; and, standing, Major General Wedemeyer.

"A" Group posed for this picture just before boarding the plane to parachute into Japanese-occupied Burma. Captain Barnard, the group leader, is fourth from the left; Captain Red Maddox, the deputy, is holding a cigarette; Captain Oscar Milton is at the extreme left. The Burma Army lieutenant standing to Captain Maddox's left was an Armenian and was killed on this mission.

The main building at the base camp of Nazira, Assam, where 101 began its education in guerrilla operations.

Future agents, mostly Burmese and Kachins, learn how to set up intelligence nets in the field.

Agent Saw Judson at the head of the desk instructs future agents in the processes of cryptography. Agents were taught that, at all costs, the cryptographic books were to be destroyed before falling into enemy hands.

Here an American field commander inspects Kachin recruits, who in many cases traveled several days from their homes to join the guerrillas. The two uniformed men to the right of the American are Kachins who now possess the equipment and experience of many months as guerrillas of 101.

PHOTO BY U.S. ARMY SIGNAL CORPS

A Kachin muleteer with one of the guerrilla companies. He carries both the rifle issued to him by the Americans and the *dah*, or sword, he has worn on his person for years.

Bearded Captain Curl and Kachin headman Zhing Htaw Naw at a rendezvous

The problem of supplying the
guerrillas was entirely in the
hands of airdrop crews. Of
necessity, guerrilla encamp-
ments were in wild, remote areas
where the only practical way of
reaching them was through air
supply.

The initial guerrilla movement
began with the parachuting of
small teams behind enemy lines.
Here three Americans land in a
Kachin area.

Elephants were often the foundation of a guerrilla battalion's
transport logistics. They ate off
the land, and always traveled a
day or two behind the main
column.

A hundred miles away from any friendly forces, this small detachment of guerrillas moves toward a Kachin village where they will find friends. The stealth, the silence and loneliness of this scene are typical of what operations were like in the early days of 101 when units moved quickly, lightly, and their dress was left to their own imagination.

During the later stages of the campaign, the guerrillas achieved a solidity of formation and movement. Here they have built their own version of a Bailey Bridge. They have now gained the ability of sustained offensive action and move like a seasoned combat force.

This successfully sabotaged bridge in Japanese-occupied Northern Burma was the work of a 101 guerrilla force.

One of the missions of the 101 guerrillas was to rescue American Air Force crews, like these four men, shot down behind Japanese lines.

A victory for the guerrillas was the capture of Japanese prisoners like the three wounded men in the wagon below. They are being interrogated by a 101 Nisei. Leaning against the wagon without hat is agent Betty.

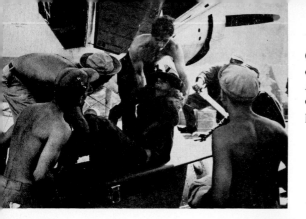

Guerrilla troops were not without casualties. Here a wounded American operations leader is evacuated from the field by light plane.

As the campaign moved south from the Kachin Hills, recruits came to the guerrillas from a variety of tribes. Here Chins are issued rifles by a Kachin noncommissioned officer.

After the Japanese defeat in Burma, the guerrillas were discharged with ceremony and honor. The rifles and swords seen here were awarded to those who endured the cruelest tests of battle.

search with a bombing raid on the Kanbauk tin mines. On this one everything went off perfectly. We broke out of the clouds about fifty miles from the shoreline and proceeded inland to the designated point. It was easy to locate, and all three aircraft stayed in the area almost an hour, but we were never able to pick up any form of emergency signals. In all the interrogations of later periods we hoped anxiously that someone would reveal what had happened to the group. We never learned a thing, even to this day.

After the search the flight set a course on the Kanbauk tin mines, which were located on an inlet at the base of a steep mountain. The bombing was done at low level by coming in through a pass and almost immediately dropping the load. As the bombs from the lead plane hit, a most unusual sight was created. Huge geysers of water 200 to 400 feet high started spurting into the air, some of them quite near the second and third planes. What had happened was that bombs had hit the aqueduct bringing water off the mountain to the electric power plant near the mine. The bombs had cracked the line and the water pressure was forcing fountains of water straight into the air. The other bombers had to dodge around these fountains but managed to make perfect hits on the main buildings. This part of the mission was successful.

After the bombing run the flight leader took his heading across the Bay of Bengal toward home base. The course led across the southern tip of Burma, and as we passed the delta area of the Irrawaddy, in the distance we could see the sun slanting off the Shwe Dagon, Rangoon's fantastic gilt-covered pagoda. I felt a silent confidence that one day we would get there, that in the summing up of 101 the forlorn facts of missions destroyed would be more than compensated for by the accomplished missions that did not die away.

The next day Red and I started driving toward Calcutta, a distance of 85 or 90 miles, which we had expected to make in three to four hours. It turned out to be one of the most horrible experiences that either of us had ever gone through. The area of Ranigungh-Assinsol has a high incidence of elephantiasis, a disease carried by a species of mosquitoes. For some reason it seems most prevalent among men. This day, however, it was beyond belief. Nearly every male we passed had a thick trunklike arm or leg and some of them had testicles swollen like pumpkins. Seeing this ravaged humanity was, in itself, almost enough to make one sick.

This however, was mild in comparison to the effects of the famine which we soon encountered, concentrated with such deadliness that it was like seeing skeletons striding the earth. It became increasingly worse as we neared Calcutta.

India, and especially the provinces of Bengal and Behar, did not raise enough rice to meet the needs of the huge population. In peacetime this shortage of rice was alleviated by imports from Burma, but with the war this source was cut off and Indian stocks had been depleted. The monsoon rains of 1943 had been inordinately heavy; crops were flooded out and villages were isolated. The peasants were starving. And as we went on, we saw a cruel paradox. In some places there was food, kept sealed by calculation.

Many of the shopkeepers capitalized on the famine and the plight of the people. In some cases we saw whole warehouses full of rice, but the merchants had raised their prices from a normal rate of about twenty rupees for a mound (eighty-four pounds) bag of rice to eighty and one hundred rupees, which few, if any, of these starving people could afford.

We went on into the prolonged lane of death, roads often lined with corpses like a thicket of disaster on both sides. Red and I must have seen nearly twenty thousand bodies on our trip, and when our auto lumbered into Calcutta, the wind reeked with the evil smell.

Conservative estimates showed that two to three million people died in this famine; other estimates ranged from four to six million; while one estimate put it at ten to twelve million. Nobody will ever know which figures were the most valid, but even the lowest was bad enough. A landscape such as that, steeped in death, a land desiccated by war and its effects, comes back to me now and again these days, a choking reminder of what might happen in the aftermath of an all-out atomic war.

X

"The Yellow Rose of Burma"

⎍⎍⎍⎍⎍⎍⎍⎍⎍⎍⎍⎍⎍⎍⎍⎍⎍⎍⎍⎍⎍⎍⎍⎍⎍⎍

THE YEAR 1943 was drawing to a close and we had reason to be grateful. In Northern Burma nearly every operation was successful and was developing according to plan. All told, we had four operations in existence and two more on the drawing board ready to be put into effect. However, the situation in Central and Southern Burma was not so bright. We had tried four group operations and had failed in all four.

At the same time, the Air Transport Command was undergoing its severest test in the CBI Theater. As a result of Madame Chiang Kai-shek's appearance before the assembled United States Senate and House of Representatives, every effort was made to increase the volume of war materials being provided for the Chinese. The principal result was that the new C-46 was being pressed into service across the Hump before it had been thoroughly flight-tested. Unfortunately, the aircraft had numerous bugs: lack of defrosters on the carburetors, gas transfer system failures, and undependable engines.

One could hardly blame the crews for being on edge. Some openly revolted at flying the Hump. In their flights, if an engine missed once, they bailed out immediately. It was better to parachute into hostile Burma than to take a chance on riding the plane into the jungle. During this period, units of Detachment 101 rescued over one hundred and twenty-five crew members. They were heartily glad to find our agents in the remote regions of North Burma. So many were being picked up that our station at Fort Hertz was crowded with rescued aircrews, and we jokingly accused Major Aitken of running a hotel there. As the rescues became more frequent, we sent in a lieutenant and some medical personnel to help him out. The lieutenant, Ted Barnes, was a marvelous addition. He personally had a hand in the rescue of about twenty-five airmen.

Here, it should be added that once the bugs were worked out of the C-46 it became a highly reliable airplane and did yeoman service on the Hump. Because of its ruggedness, most pilots preferred it to the other planes.

Of these who bailed out, Detachment 101 rescued perhaps 25 to 35 per cent. Some were killed in landing, others were captured by the Japs, and an unhappily large percentage roamed about, became lost and died of starvation. The following brief of one of the rescue operations is somewhat representative.

When C-46 #634 enroute from Kunming to Chabua rapidly lost altitude and failed to respond to emergency measures the pilot ordered the crew to bail out. Lieutenant Starling and Corporal Wyatt bailed out seconds before the transport plane crashed into a mountain side and exploded with the other two members still on board the aircraft. Corporal Wyatt was badly burned when the plane exploded against the mountain just after he bailed out. Though both men encountered different natives, in each case the natives were very friendly. They understood the word American. Kachins hid Wyatt in a cave and treated his wounds with native poultices. The enemy was in the immediate vicinity. At one time Corporal Wyatt looked out of the cave and watched a party of five Japanese soldiers search the home of his benefactor, which was located barely fifty feet away. At this time the natives with knives drawn stood by to protect him should the Japanese discover the cave. Runners carried his messages to the nearest Allied outpost and returned with medical supplies and an air mattress. Risking their own lives the natives smuggled Wyatt out of the cave and carried him to the nearest Allied outpost, Ngumla, where he remained for three weeks recuperating. Lieutenant Starling, who landed on a mountain north of Nanchang Hka (river), about ten miles northwest of Hpimaw, was also fed and given shelter by the natives and taken to Ngumla.

One fate that befell some of these crew members was unbelievably gruesome. As they parachuted into the tall trees, often 100 to 150 feet high and with huge trunks, their bodies traveled beyond the upper foliage, but the parachute was stopped in its descent, caught upon the branches. A man caught in this position, and hurt as most were, would stay suspended in jump harness more than one hundred feet off the ground, like a puppet. The man could neither drop down nor climb up. The result was a slow, agonizing death. In several cases, by the time 101 people located the hopelessly hung-up pilot, ants had eaten away so much flesh that all they found was a skeleton hanging in a tree.

Suddenly, to add to disaster, the weather began playing havoc in late 1943. To increase the amount of supplies delivered to China, night flights had begun; but just after this ground fogs began to make their appearance on some of the Assam air bases. These fogs, sometimes stationary, sometimes shifting, fifteen feet in depth, spread over the ground with amazing speed. From the air, they looked like the flow of an ocean tide. The danger was great. Numerous airplanes crashed in the process of landing; and this, of course, did not enhance morale.

One night the Chabua airport was encircled by thirty airplanes trying to land. Their roar was ominous, their signals for clearance desperate. Captain Hugh Wild, one of the old-time pilots, took over as operations control officer and from the tower started talking them in. Under the circumstances he did very well; eighteen were brought in safely, seven crashed on landing with varying degrees of damage and five of them ran out of gas and the crews bailed out. A few days later Hugh flew a load of supplies into Fort Hertz for us and took off, gaily waving goodbye. He had to make a routine flight around a mountain and through a pass. The winds were always fierce and, with the mystery of such things, that day blew him to doom, a downdraft forcing him into the side of a mountain. He had been close to 101 and having him killed was another sort of failure. It hit us deep in the stomach.

We performed two other services for the ATC, in order to take some of the pressure off the aircrews. The first thing was a course in jungle survival training. The crew members had little knowledge, strange as it may seem, of woods. Many of them could not read a hand compass, though familiar of course with the compass in their aircraft. They lived a military life removed from jungle warfare, and they had to be taught from the start. For example, one of the first rules for a person who is lost is to follow a stream downhill. In Northern Burma, however, going downhill meant entering the lowlands occupied by Shans and Burmans who, in most instances, would turn them over to the Japs. So they had to be taught to do the reverse, that is, walk upstream into the hills, the habitat of the Kachins, where they were most likely to get assistance. We set up several such courses. They lived in the jungle for a period of two weeks with nothing but rations, survival tools and a blanket. This gave them a tremendous amount of confidence and undoubtedly saved hundreds of lives. We trained the leaders first and they in turn set up their own survival courses within their units, so that in a relatively short time this training was extended to aircrews flying the Hump.

Another service we extended to the Air Corps was a by-product of 101 radio communications. Some of our radio operators were old hands at the business and in their spare time monitored the traffic between the air bases and the aircraft. The ATC had lost several planes setting down through the weather and crashing into mountains for no explainable reason. As a result of monitoring, our operators were able to pinpoint two stations which were operating on the right frequency but seemed to be located in the wrong places. They were giving the signals for DF or homing stations, and the pilots, combating all kinds of weather, were glad to pick up their homing signal to guide them into their base. A thorough check proved that these stations were very cleverly operated Japanese deception stations and were so located that when the planes homed on them they crashed into the nearby mountains. Captain Huston and his radio operators were able to warn the ATC of the presence of these two stations so that they could instruct their crews and change frequencies. Shortly thereafter the Jap stations went off the air and the crashes ceased.

The fellow who gave the survival course for 101 was an Anglo-Burmese of better than average size, six feet one and about a hundred and eighty pounds, whom we called Rocky. His ability with

guns, rifle or shotgun, was uncanny. I have considered myself a reasonably good shot, particularly with the shotgun, but I always
enjoyed hunting with Rocky just to see him shoot. I was with him
on several jungle drives for green pigeons, jungle fowl, pheasants
and wild boar and I don't recall ever seeing him miss a shot.

Rocky was well known throughout Burma for his knowledge of
the jungle and his use of firearms. All of his life had been spent in
the jungle, and he looked upon it as home. He had killed so many
tigers, leopards and other wild game that his ability was legendary.
On one unfortunate occasion, however, when he was out shooting
with an old, dear friend, for no apparent reason Rocky's mind
went blank. He looked at the friend and saw some horrible, frightening apparition — a sort of werewolf — Rocky opened up with his
gun and shot his friend between the eyes. He was arrested, and it
seemed best that he be committed to a mental institution in Rangoon. During the Second World War, he was still in the institution at the time extensive rioting and pillaging spread in Rangoon, prior to Japanese entry into the city. It was easy for the
inmates to break down the doors of the institution. Rocky went
with them. He headed north and joined the retreating, panic-
stricken population. He mingled with the British units and eventually, when he reached Myitkyina and the Triangle area, he posed
as a Burma Army captain and did a commendable job of organizing parts of the Kachin Levies.

When the Indian Army Headquarters in New Delhi and the
governor of Burma made available to 101 the military personnel
for the initial "A" Group they also sent us Rocky. However, before he reached us the British had discovered who he was and
withdrew his commission. But since he was already at Nazira and
seemed a decent sort of chap, we decided to keep him for what he
was worth. Captain Maddox had known him before the war and
told us his entire story, including his good points as well as his
weaknesses. For obvious reasons, they did not want him on the
"A" Group operation, but suggested that if we ever wanted to
teach people about the jungle, Rocky was without a peer. At the
time he had only one weakness, and that was his fear of the Japs.
He must have picked this up during his flight from them in Burma,
because it was a form of manic phobia. At the slightest mention of

Japs he would become nervous and almost frantic. I tried every-thing I knew to reassure him and at times he seemed to lose his fears. He did an outstanding job of organizing and running our survival course, perhaps a better job than anyone else could have done, and he was the subject of numerous letters of appreciation and commendation. He was an expert on the tiger and could spot its spoor with uncanny sense. My own hope was some day to bag a tiger, so I listened avidly to all of Rocky's tales. Such luck I was never granted.

But there wasn't too much time for thoughts of tigers, espe-cially the day three prominent people were to be gotten out of the Naga Hills. They were Eric Sevareid, then a war correspond-ent, Jack Service of the State Department and Duncan Lee of OSS. The engine of the airplane returning to India from China, started to cut out, and the pilot ordered the passengers to bail out. They landed in the jungle and, with the aid of some of the local Nagas, were able to assemble. The pilot meanwhile was able to get the engine smoothed out. He flew on to his base. An air search followed and the three men were located by their panel display. The ATC borrowed Sergeant Milligan from 101, and he dropped supplies to them along with maps and directions to trails leading out to base camp. Two days later the colonel who headed the ATC Air Medical Evacuation Section parachuted into the group to give them any medical attention needed and, so pre-pared, they trekked out to Mokachung where they were picked up by jeep and brought to our camp, arriving in good physical condi-tion, not too much the worse for wear. The ATC did a fine job on this rescue operation.

About 50 per cent of all of the agent personnel lost by 101 dur-ing the entire Burma campaign were Anglo-Burmese. Some knew insecurity and lacked self-confidence because of their mixed par-entage; other shortcomings may have been in the training, and possibly some errors were made in operational planning. Yet, de-spite all this, none of these fellows once refused to take a mission. On the contrary, every one of them went into operations at least once and some of them went behind the lines three, four and five times. In the aggregate they served their country and the Allied cause in a most admirable manner, and we are indebted to them.

Sometimes in the evenings and on Sunday a few of us would drive over to their camp to have a meal with them and pass the time of day. They loved to sit around a campfire in the evening singing songs, putting on little skits and other acts. They all seemed to have a natural flair for entertainment. One of the songs they sang as a group was "The Yellow Rose of Burma" with the following words:

YELLOW ROSE OF BURMA

I'm a fellow that was born in Burma and I'll sing to you a song
Of a Burmese girl in Mandalay on good old Burma ground.
She's a young and charming little maid, her age is ten and eight
And she smiles at everyone that passes through her little gate.

Chorus: She's my Yellow Rose of Burma that the Burmese never knew
Her eyes they shine like diamonds that sparkle in the dew.
You can talk to me of Calcutta girls or the girls from Bangalore,
But the Yellow Rose of Burma beats the whole darn lot and more.

Very soon I'm going back to Burma on a bright and sunny day,
Without any leave and any pay I'll get there any way.
And the Calcutta girl can go to hell for I have a story to tell
To my Yellow Rose of Burma and to Burma I belong.

None of us had ever heard the tune so we assumed it was original. It was not until "The Yellow Rose of Texas" was revived in the 1950's that we realized it had not been their own composition. In any event the music, and the lyrics fitted well with 101 and everybody in the outfit knew it and sang it.

Before 1943 ended, we proceeded with plans to expand 101 operations in Northern Burma. These plans included four things: first, to establish a new field base camp in the Pidaung Forest Preserve located at the apex of a triangle with Myitkyina and Mogaung as a base; second, to start another group in the Chindwin River Valley between the Hukawng Valley and the Imphal Front; third, to get an operation started in the Lashio-Mandalay area; and fourth, to strengthen the other groups already in the field.

For the Pidaung operation two Anglo-Burmese, Lieutenants

Patrick Quinn and Dennis Francis, from the initial "A" Group, were selected as leaders. These two officers had been raised together in a small village on the Irrawaddy River named Shwegu gale' about midway between Bhamo and Katha. They were an unusual pair. In many respects they differed greatly, for one was quiet and reserved while the other was gregarious and aggressive, but they were the closest of friends and almost inseparable. Pat was the older by a few months and militarily was the senior, so we considered him the group leader, although they both looked upon it as a form of dual command. At the time the operation started in November 1943, Dennis was in Calcutta on a recruiting job for us so the initial job fell upon Pat. He selected one of the native radio operators who had been trained in the base camp and two other Kachins to accompany him.

Pat and his three companions were flown into Fort Hertz, where Captain Aitken and Lieutenant Barnes arranged porters for them. Then they slipped through the Japanese lines and after a ten-day march arrived in the Pidaung Forest Preserve. Pat made a hasty survey of the area and decided to establish their field base in a small village by the name of Arang. In this location he was surrounded by Japanese bases. It was about thirty miles from Myitkyina and Mogaung, which had relatively large Japanese garrisons, about twenty miles west of Nsopzup, a large supply base and hospital area, and about twenty miles south of Ritpong where the Japs had an outpost of 300 to 500 men. We assigned the operation the code name PAT, obviously after the name of its nominal leader. Lieutenant Francis arrived back at Nazira at about Christmastime. A few days later he was on his way to join PAT.

It was necessary to delay setting up the second new base, in the Chindwin River Valley area, because we lacked a competent leader. Captain Red Maddox, a veteran of the "A" Group who had also participated in the search flights to the Malay Peninsula, was finally selected to head the operation. The personnel chosen by Red to form his group consisted of one Anglo-Burmese, a Burmese radio operator and three Kachins. We allowed him six weeks to complete the field training of the group. The land route to the proposed operational area was one hundred and fifty miles long;

the answer was to infiltrate them by parachute. This operation was known as TRAMP.

A group of five Anglo-Burmese had been recruited and trained as a unit to set up a base in the Lashio-Mandalay area. They were known as the HATE GROUP. It was decided that the best way to infiltrate them was to use a land route from the China side. We flew them to Kunming and started them down the Salween River Valley. Communications with them were excellent even though they were seven hundred miles away. But it was neither the Japanese nor natural barriers that sabotaged this group. We soon discovered that bands of Chinese war lords were placing every possible barrier in the way of the HATE GROUP. In the final analysis they wanted to be paid to guarantee safe passage through their territory. Control by the Nationalist Government over the local leaders was nominal at best, and the war lords practiced war or bribery as they pleased. The first demands on HATE were small, but the shakedowns became increasingly large and the situation became unbearable. The Chinese Headquarters could do nothing to stop it, so, after about three weeks, the group was ordered out of the field. They returned to Nazira for additional training and possible infiltration by air at a later date.

The final action, that of building up the groups already in the field, was carried on continuously as resources would permit. However, our resources were quite limited. We were halfway around the world from our basic source of supplies, the OSS home office in Washington. They were responsive to our requests, but the delay from the time we requested an item until its receipt was anywhere from three to six months. The SOS Advance Section at Chabua assisted us in every way possible, and we supplemented this through purchases by our own supply office which had recently been established in Calcutta. Even so, the supply situation in those early days was such that we had to scrounge and live off the land. The majority of our meals were native dishes, curries and the like.

Our personnel situation was making slow progress. We had started off with twenty American personnel arriving in India in July 1942. A year and a half later, in late 1943, our gains had been offset by losses, and our personnel strength stood at only twenty-five Americans. Considering the extent and scope of our operations, we were stretched to the absolute limit and simply could not expand operations until we received some trained, qualified personnel. Our policy, however, was to give the maximum to the field in terms of personnel, supplies, etc., which meant that those remaining in the base camp would have to work just that much harder.

In this period, however, much was done to improve operations in the field. The flow of intelligence became so heavy that it severely overloaded the radio circuits and priorities had to be established to insure the transmission of important information.

By October 1943, we had in the field a total of thirty-five men, American, English, Anglo-Burmese, and others. Twenty of these people had parachuted into operations. Captain Sherman (Pete) Joost joined 101 in October and he and Pop Milligan made successful supply drops to the units in the field.

In November we were helped by the arrival of several new volunteers from the States: Lieutenant Gorin and Sergeant Pendergast took over 101 Finance; Lieutenant Mykland USN set up a 101 Finance Office in Calcutta; Ensign Shepard established a 101 Maritime Base in Chittagong, and Pharmacist's Mate Cloyd was sent to Fort Hertz to provide medical aid to the ever-increasing number of Air Corps personnel being rescued. Cloyd's arrival permitted the release of Captain Aitken to return to Nazira to take over direction of intelligence operations, and Lieutenant Barnes took over our station in Fort Hertz. Commander Luce (a Navy medical officer), Lieutenant Damen (a signal officer), and sixteen Anglo-Burmese were dispatched by land routes to join Major Wilkinson at FORWARD.

In early November, 1943, we were advised that General Donovan would visit the theater during the latter part of the month and would spend a few days at 101. He arrived at Nazira on schedule and spent the first day or so looking over the base camp and observing some of the agent and operational training. He stated he was impressed with how much was being done with so little. He had seen the critical messages which had been addressed directly to him requesting men, equipment and funds, but he had not seen all of the messages; thus it was not until he saw 101 firsthand that he realized the true situation. He responded in two ways: first, he sent off a few blistering cables to Washington which left no doubt that 101 needed some assistance; and, second, he arranged for some of the Stateside chiefs of section to visit Nazira and gain personal knowledge.

The afternoon of the second day of his visit Colonel Eifler suggested that he fly General Donovan into KNOTHEAD to visit Lieutenant Curl and his field group. General Donovan could hardly say no, and so it was arranged. Curl's camp was located about one hundred and fifty miles behind the Japanese lines and about two hundred and seventy-five miles from our base, well beyond the round-trip capabilities of 101's only airplane, the Gypsy Moth. We would have to parachute a supply of aviation gasoline into KNOTHEAD to refuel. We arranged a flight with the ATC and dropped the gasoline into them, along with other needed food, supplies and ammunition.

Carl and General Donovan took off the following day from the improvised strip at our base camp; we saw the Gypsy Moth out of sight across the Naga Hills. A series of radio signals had been arranged with KNOTHEAD, and about three hours later we received the flash that they had arrived safely. The flight was a highly skilled job of navigation. The route was across an endless tract of jungle with few recognizable landmarks, and even though Carl had been into the strip twice before, the approach was from a different direction. After landing, General Donovan spent the remainder of the day talking to Lieutenant Curl and other members of the operation. Father Stuart was interpreter, and General Donovan conferred at great length with Zhing Htaw Naw and some of the Kachin headmen. What doubts General Donovan might have had about the Kachins were swept away that day.

Fortunately, the return flight was without incident and they returned safely to Nazira the following day. I shudder to think what would have happened to the Allied cause if General Donovan with his knowledge of world-wide military operations had fallen into the

Japanese hands. General Donovan stayed with us a day or so longer and then departed for a short trip to China with a promise to return.

During this period Carl Eifler's health and mental attitude were deteriorating noticeably. He couldn't sleep, was nervous as a cat, would not submit to medication as recommended by the 20th General Hospital at Ledo, and completely disregarded all advice. As a result, when General Donovan returned to 101 in mid-December, Carl was in a terribly run-down condition. OSS and General Donovan had much at stake in the success of 101 and in the development of strategic operations in the CBI Theater. Carl had done a magnificent job, but simply could do no more. General Donovan had to face the issue and make a decision, which he did by relieving Carl for physical and medical reasons. Colonel Coughlin was placed in charge of all strategic operations in the CBI Theater, with instructions to pay particular attention to China. Colonel Coughlin asked me to take over 101, so on 17 December 1943, I assumed command of the unit. John Coughlin was a most unselfish, unassuming person. He could have insisted that I report through him to Washington and CBI Headquarters, but he did not do so. He gave me absolute free rein but told me to let him know if we needed assistance.

The departure of Carl Eifler was like the end of an era. His peculiar quality was imagination. He seemed to call forward the condition necessary to guerrillas — restlessness to fight the enemy. The stress of getting 101 on its feet had taken its toll, nevertheless. He went home with the pain in his head relentlessly sapping his funds of almost superhuman energy and endurance.

Now I found myself in command of 101. I had seen the impossible happen under Carl, seen America represented in the Burma campaign with a whole new set of rules, with a combination of Allied talents, black men, yellow men, white men, brown men, a little army that had an organizational structure of its own. The command came easily because there were so many faithful, brave men ready to serve. I was not there to betray them.

PART FOUR

The Road to China

The Guerrilla Influence

Now, in February, 1944, General Stilwell gave Detachment 101 a new, more ambitious mission. On that rainy day in his tent which I have described in Chapter I, he demanded a major breakthrough before June — the liberation of North Burma.

He had enough confidence and belief in 101 to have taken the pains to outline his plans; and he had asked my opinion on whether we could do the job. It would have been unfaithful to all of the men, to Carl now back in Washington, to have considered Stilwell's plan aimed at recapturing Myitkyina and control of North Burma in any light but that of a challenge. Our mission would be to make Stilwell's belief a reality. There had indeed already been moments during my command of 101 that I had sought the counsel of Stilwell. I had found him always gracious, always ready to put aside enough time to answer my problems. Now he wanted to produce an Allied victory. However determined and bold was his plan, it would not work without the sustaining intensity of 101 guerrillas behind it.

Our brothers in arms, the conventional warfare warriors, with all the support they would get from the Air Corps, from the supply forces, would still, in the end, depend upon guerrillas; with our help, they might stay together, withstand heat and humidity, march where they knew there was no enemy, and come upon the enemy out of the tangle of jungle. War can be distorted into disaster more quickly in the jungle than anywhere else. The jungle on your side can spread this disaster to the enemy; with the jungle against you, death explodes in your face.

What would follow now could be managed possibly without guerrillas; but we were there, ready to serve as guides, as a screen and to immobilize as best we could the rear echelons of the Japanese Army in North Burma. How well we did this might mean the difference between advantage or disadvantage for Stilwell. 101 had been saying they owned the jungle; now 101 must prove it.

After we had a little time to digest fully the implications of General Stilwell's new directive, it was apparent that changes were necessary in 101's operational procedures.

The most likely change was in the system of command and control of operations. There were six major bases in the field. Radiating out from them were about a dozen other radio-equipped agent operations. The radios of the field base stations were small sets, powered by batteries or hand generators, which were incapable of carrying on radio communications with their agent stations. For this reason, all of these agent operations, as well as the field base stations, worked directly into the base radio station at Nazira. This imposed a tremendous load on the small group at the base radio station, and much of it was relaying messages back and forth between agent stations and the field bases. This centralized system of control could have continued, provided the operations did not expand beyond the existing load. However, Stilwell's new directive called for an increase in the size, scope and area of operations as well as a stepping up of the tempo.

We found the solution to our expansion in what we called "Area Control." Northern Burma was divided into four operational areas. In each area one man was to be designated that area's commander. He was to be responsible for all operations in his area, from guerrilla operations, espionage and sabotage through psychological warfare and escape and evasion.

The four areas of Northern Burma were Area I — east of the Irrawaddy River, commanded by Commander Luce; Area II — between the Irrawaddy River and the Kumon Range, commanded by Lieutenant Pat Quinn of the Burma Army; Area III — between the Kumon Range and the Hukawng Valley

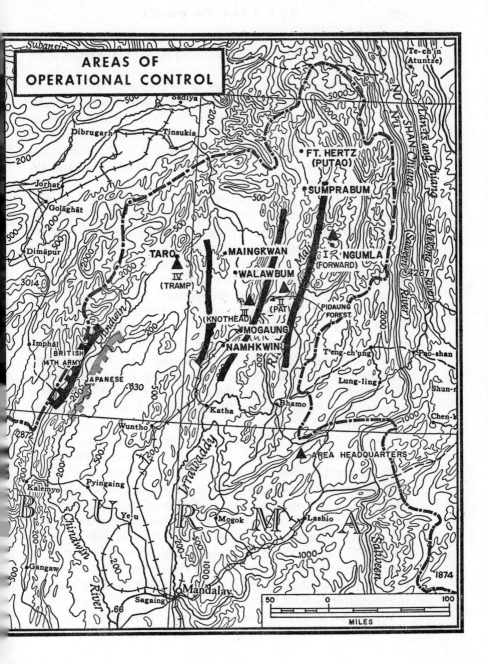

AREAS OF
OPERATIONAL CONTROL

Road, commanded by Lieutenant Curl; and Area IV — to the
west of the Hukawng Road, commanded by Captain Red Maddox
of the Burma Army.

Since the area commanders would be communicating directly
with their agent stations, the means had to be found for setting
up a more elaborate network of radios. We promptly sent to
Washington a request for more powerful radio sets, capable of
twenty-four-hour operations, and powered by a small gasoline generator. These arrived by air, were assembled, checked out and air-
dropped to the four field bases.

The theory of placing operational control with the four area
commanders was perhaps the biggest single step taken by 101 toward the improvement and expansion of operations during the entire Burma campaign. It meant that I, as 101's commander, no
longer had to deal directly with eighteen or more field stations; I
now directed the activities of the four area commanders and they
in turn were my means of communication with the rest of the
men in the field. The rewards were initiative and flexibility such
as we had never known. Moreover, our enlarged radio net provided far more rapid and efficient radio schedules, at the same time
greatly reducing the excessive load on the Nazira base station.
Nazira continued to handle the traffic of long-range agents as well
as the traffic to Washington, the logistics net and the vital communications with a large number of military headquarters in the
CBI Theater.

How good our new system would be was dependent, too, on our
airdrop capability. The detachment average of one to two planeloads of supplies each day would, with our expanded activities,
have to increase to a daily average of nine to ten planeloads. This
would mean packing twenty-five tons of supplies for airdrop each
day; and we would require a further increase if we were to push
our guerrilla numbers up to 10,000 men. Luck was with us in getting at this time qualified paratroopers with a spirited tradition of
getting difficult jobs done fast. Under their control the airdrop expansion went ahead and achieved in little time the bold and precise standards required.

We started to increase our guerrilla force from about nine hundred to three thousand, as directed by General Stilwell, by charging the four areas with orders as follows:

FORWARD (Area I) — expand to a force of approximately 1,500 guerrillas; harass the Japanese along the watershed of the Irrawaddy; extend guerrilla operations to the south in order to oppose Japanese reinforcement of Myitkyina, and expand espionage operations southward into the Bhamo area.

PAT (Area II) — raise a force of about 400 guerrillas; harass the Japs along the road and railroad from Myitkyina to Mogaung; and expand intelligence activities south in the Koukkwee Valley.

KNOTHEAD (Area III) — raise a force of 1,000 guerrillas to operate behind the Jap lines in the Hukawng Valley; and extend espionage operations into the railway corridor and into the Lonkin Jade Mines area.

TRAMP (Area IV) — move the base camp out of the Naga Hills into the Chindwin River Valley; raise a force of about 300 guerrillas; and extend intelligence operations southeastward toward the rail corridor and southward in the rear of the Japanese forces on the Imphal front.

Orders by radio are one thing for the men behind the lines; execution may not be as easy. My intent was to give the commanders maximum latitude, and not handicap them with a hopeless listing of minutiae. They were seasoned and experienced. Nevertheless, to supplement the words they received by radio, I felt it necessary to go in by light plane and talk to each man; thus allowing time for questions and to learn firsthand what needs they had.

Again the ancient Gypsy Moth was rolled out of her hangar. She seemed to gaze around, looking for Carl; but after her new pilot, borrowed from ATC, reached for her controls, she settled down and we were off.

We stopped first at KNOTHEAD. The guerrillas seemed poised, even though their most recent contact with the enemy had almost led to the death of two top agents, Skittles and Hefty, when Japanese unexpectedly came to their village. The two agents escaped by flinging themselves through an open door into the jungle; the Japanese were no wiser.

This first conference convinced me that there was reason to be hopeful that 101 would match Stilwell's expectations. On my day of departure, I went to the Gypsy Moth happy that all was running smoothly. In the plane, the pilot signaled take-off, we gained speed down the rough runway, the plane bucked like some charging animal, careening wildly as if she did not wish to leave the ground. Then with a twist, less resistant, she swayed up into the air, hung there momentarily, and came back down. The crash exploded us into a thatched hut. I was well strapped in; I gave frantic thanks that I could see, feel; I was unhurt. In the sunshine, I saw the wings of the Gypsy Moth unexpectedly shorn of dignity, spread about in bits and pieces. I thought of Carl and what he would say to see her body so naked. Now a cluster of guerrillas helped us out, the pilot looked numb. "My head," he said, leaning on a guerrilla, "my head hurts."

To which I could only add my own sense of bewilderment. I was two hundred miles behind the enemy lines, a twenty-day march from base. Before the day was over, I found, as if I needed it, more reason than ever for light planes to be part of 101. The use of such aircraft is lifeblood to guerrillas: with all their weapons and men, with all their courage, guerrillas still cannot live their dangerous life without the flexibility, the freedom that a light plane — or in this day, a helicopter — permits. The next morning two L-4's from NCAC came in and took out the pilot and myself. During the night, the guerrillas had dismantled what remained of the Gypsy Moth. She might easily have led the Japanese there had she not been removed.

The Eastern Air Command, under Lieutenant General Stratemeyer, grateful for the airmen we had rescued, gave us a light plane to replace the Gypsy Moth. She was an L-1, large for a light aircraft, weighing about 5,000 pounds, with a 285-horsepower radial engine, and equipped with both slots and flaps on the wings. Her cruising speed was only 65 M.P.H., but she could land and take off at about 30 M.P.H. and could carry over 1,000 pounds payload. She could operate from short, rough and muddy runways. She might be thought obsolete, but we did not argue the point. For us, then, she was an angel. With her, I continued my tour of the areas.

A week or so following our meeting General Stilwell suggested that the American personnel in the V Force be transferred to 101. The V Force was a combined United States and British organization charged with screening to the immediate front of the combat forces. The five officers and thirty enlisted men would be of considerable assistance to 101 and I told General Stilwell we could certainly use them. I then arranged a meeting at Taro to introduce myself and 101 to the new Americans. Captain Red Maddox (in charge of Area IV) was there too. I explained the organization aims of 101 and assigned two of the new officers, Captains Dow Grones and Pete Lutkin, to organize small teams of American and native guerrillas. They would infiltrate into Japanese territory and establish field bases to attack the Myitkyina railway line and the rear of the Japs on the Imphal Front. I liked the coolness with which they responded; getting to their target area would demand an unusually difficult trek through an area that was unexplored; indeed, the land was so wild, with so many stretches of swamp and dangerous river crossings, that the Kachins themselves described it with awe. Red Maddox helped to train and brief them for the rugged days ahead.

In early February, 1944, Merrill's Marauders arrived by train in Ledo from their jungle training base in Central India.

I talked with General Merrill and his second-in-command, Colonel Hunter, shortly after their discussion with General Stilwell and, in broad terms, they told me what they were to do. Their job was to act as an envelopment force; first to swing around the Japanese flank, then to set up roadblocks in the enemy rear and force the Japs to fight their way past them while the Chinese maintained pressure on the front. Their first job was to get the unit assembled at or near Shingbwiyang. General Merrill said that in order to condition the troops, shake them down, he was going to move the unit from Ledo to Shingbwiyang by foot over the Naga Hills portion of the Ledo road which was then under construction. I advised him against it and suggested he fly or truck them over. An individual has only so much stamina in the jungle and after periods of exertion must rest to recoup his strength. We had run into it many times in our behind-the-lines operations, not only with Americans but with natives as well. Consequently, we believed in going full out when we had to, but our people were taught to conserve their strength, rest, and eat whenever they could. I pointed out all this to General Merrill, but he was convinced that his troops and animals needed the march of approximately one hundred and twenty-five miles prior to engaging the enemy in combat. In my position I could hardly argue with General Merrill's decision. I remain convinced that this act had much to do with the later tragic events that overtook Merrill's Marauders.

The first operation of the Marauders was a military classic. The two Chinese Divisions, the 22nd and the 38th, abreast of one another, were applying heavy pressure on the Japs along the road northwest of Maingkwan. With the Japs so engaged, General Stilwell ordered the Marauders and a composite American-Chinese Tank Group around the north flank. The Marauders were to continue around the flank, pressing on the Japs' rear and setting up a roadblock in the area of Walawbum. They set up the block in perfect style and thought they had the Japs cut off. However, unknown to them, there was a trail which permitted the Japs to avoid the block and hit the road several miles below it. The Japs worked feverishly repairing and widening the trail so their motor transport could be moved over it. In order for the Japs to protect this trail they had to engage the Marauders' roadblock. They attacked, crossing a small stream, and were exposed to the murderous Marauder fire. In this fantastic and stupid attempt, the Japanese were defeated. The final count of the comparatively brief action of Walabum was eight hundred and fifty Japanese dead to seven Americans wounded.

Meanwhile the two Chinese Divisions had been throwing everything they had at the Japs. The Japanese began withdrawing their troops and transport over back trails, the Chinese lashed in, overran the enemy rear guards, swept through Maingkwan and linked up with the Marauders. In the battle for Maingkwan the Chinese and Japanese probably each suffered 2,000 to 3,000 killed. At the same time, the 101 guerrilla units were attending to small Japanese columns of no more than company strength which were trying to make their way to the battle. Largely because our men were capa-

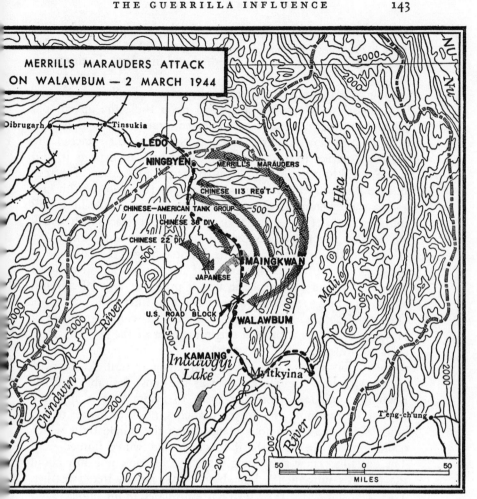

MERRILLS MARAUDERS ATTACK
ON WALAWBUM — 2 MARCH 1944

ble of using jungle trails unknown to the enemy, they repeatedly managed to catch the Japanese attempts at re-enforcement by complete surprise. Agents were close at hand to Japanese motor pools and supply dumps. They observed sudden movements of troops early enough so that the guerrillas could prepare ambushes.

An excellent illustration of what can be done in such a situation is the experience of Lieutenant Tilly about thirty miles behind the Japanese lines in the area of Walawbum. He was part of KNOTHEAD and had been sent into the area to ambush, raid dumps and attack weak defenses from the rear. In four days of operation, he and his fifty guerrillas killed over one hundred and fifty Japs. Their casualties: one guerrilla wounded.

All guerrilla tactics, whether the operation be in Burma, Algeria, Laos, Russia or elsewhere, are based upon the same operational principles. Guerrillas are not organized, trained or equipped to fight as orthodox military forces. Accordingly, their tactics are harassing tactics, to hit the enemy where he least expects it, and where it will hurt the most. This involves the application of secrecy and stealth to effect maximum surprise upon the enemy; to hit him with a short period of violent shock action; and, while he is still confused and before he can take effective counteraction, to break off the engagement and disappear into the surrounding terrain.

Thus, as the Marauders and the Chinese fought the Japanese in conventional warfare, the guerrillas of 101 applied unconventional tactics upon the enemy: basic was a primitive type of ambush which was used successfully against the Japs time and time again. On several occasions, this ambush resulted in score upon score of Japanese casualties without a single member of the guerrilla force even so much as getting scratched. The first requisite was a proper ambush site along a well-used Japanese trail. A site overgrown with heavy jungle foliage was the most desirable and the Kachins would take particular pains to insure that it appeared natural; no footprints, no broken branches, no disturbances of any kind. There were numerous plants along the jungle trails which could forecast the ambush: if touched, they wilted immediately. The guerrillas knew everything there was to know not only about the enemy's movements, but about rocks, plants, trees, weather. Their efficiency was based on their knowledge of all things. They undertook an ambush with the same preoccupation one finds in an architect planning a building.

When the site was selected the Kachins took strips of bamboo about two feet in length and cut them into knife-like spears about three-fourths of an inch wide. These they hardened over a fire until they were as strong as steel, sharp as daggers. They called them *pungyis*. The *pungyis* were then set in the ground in the undergrowth alongside the trail with the heads pointing in toward the trail. In effect, this was an ingenious kind of natural trap, deadly as a land mine. Then automatic weapons — British Bren guns approached the ideal automatic weapon for jungle warfare — were sited to fire up and down along the long axis of the ambush area. This done, the ambush was complete and ready to go.

Through their own intelligence nets our guerrillas learned when a Japanese column was moving and about when to expect it. When the Japanese column came into the ambush area, the scouts and advance guards were allowed to pass through. As the main enemy body reached the ambush area, the guerrillas with automatic weapons opened fire on the column. This, in itself, generally took quite a heavy toll, but the principal reaction it caused was for the enemy to run and dive for cover into the underbrush. Rather than cover, they found the planted *pungyis:* men flinging themselves down were impaled before they hit the ground. No clothing was protection. The *pungyis* passed through leather easily. The low *pungyis* tripped a man over, so the longer ones caught him full in the chest. Rarely could a human being survive the physical and psychological shock. The bamboo caused a ragged wound that festered readily, was painful and slow in healing. It was a cruel death, and would have been more so if some of the guerrillas could have had their way. They proposed treating the *pungyis* with poison. This was in violation of the rules of land warfare and, remembering General Stilwell's strong views, I said no. To the best of my knowledge, poison *pungyis* were not used. Even so, the ambush was charged with death.

Another type of ambush that came nearer to modern techniques but still employed the elements of surprise, shock action and disengagement, was the grenade ambush. Twenty-five to fifty grenades were planted one by one at intervals of about five yards along a trail. These were then connected with electric wire so they could be set off simultaneously by an electrical device. The ambush area was covered by automatic weapons. The timing with respect to the Jap column was similar to the *pungyi* ambush. Here, however, when the main body of the Japanese column was in the ambush area, the grenades were set off. They always took a heavy toll, and inevitably those uninjured were caught by the automatic weapons and the whole column suffered heavy casualties. During the ensuing pandemonium the Kachins melted away into the nearby jungle, receiving few, if any, casualties.

There were other variations, but all were based on the crushing element of surprise. The Kachins had experienced guerrilla fighting for several centuries. They saw no cowardice in breaking off an engagement with an enemy once you had scored an ambush. Their philosophy was that it was far better to run; that way, a guerrilla lives to fight another day, eventually to kill enough of the enemy so that he can stand and fight a full-scale battle, on terms and grounds of the guerrilla's choosing.

The main problem was the trouble caused by the American personnel. They, at first, preferred to stay and fight. They thought it shameful to run, but after they had been left behind a couple of times by the Kachins it did not take them long to learn that a guerrilla's business is to inflict maximum casualties upon the enemy while receiving minimum casualties in your own force.

Indeed, the fact that a relatively small total population of about 300,000 Kachins could oppose groups totaling several million attested to the tenacity and security of guerrilla tactics. No one had yet conquered the Kachins. We learned the principles of ambushes from them. The casualty ratio worked out at about one Kachin Ranger killed for every twenty-five Japanese.

Our guerrillas took full advantage of civilian sources of information. Friendly villages were an underground intelligence network for revealing enemy locations. Every one of these reports was confirmed by our own guerrilla patrols. Wherever our people camped, they set up guerrilla outposts for local security and, in addition, made extensive use of trip wires and various other alarms to warn of enemy approach. Nor did they neglect setting an assortment of both primitive and modern booby traps. Very, very rarely did the Japanese or the Burmese quislings ever catch our men off guard. If they did, the Kachin's superior knowledge of the jungle usually permitted escape. Only once during the entire Burma campaign were the Japs able to penetrate to the inner portions of a 101 guerrilla encampment, and even then, during the bloody engagement that followed, the Japanese casualties were over three times as great as those of the Kachins.

The guerrillas of 101 turned the Japanese rear areas into chaos.

The Japanese had to maintain continuous guards; they could never relax; could only move troops in combat formation. It became a war of nerves. The threat of guerrilla ambush made the Japanese taut and tense, slow, cautious and finally paranoic. Several Japanese prisoners volunteered the opinion that in the jungle the Jap forces so feared the guerrillas that they rated one Kachin equal to ten Japanese.

It was not only the ambushes that were effective in supporting the conventional forces. Frequently the guerrillas made quick raids upon Japanese camps and depots. They would infiltrate such an installation at night, shoot it up, set demolition and incendiary charges, and get away before the Japanese could react. The raids followed the guerrilla principle of ambush: surprise, shock action, rapid withdrawal and as rapid breaking off of engagement.

In all of these operations, however, there were two critical elements: intelligence and planning. The guerrilla had his own intelligence and this was supplemented by information made available from other 101 sources. Plans were carefully prepared to the finest detail. The operation was then reviewed and rehearsed several times to insure that every man knew his job. In unconventional warfare a single error of judgment can spoil an entire operation.

The Japanese were not without cunning. We could not count on the same tactics working every time. To give us variety, OSS in Washington provided a diabolic anti-personnel device — a hollow spike, about six inches long, with a .30 caliber cartridge in the top. Our guerrillas planted them on trails used by the enemy; when stepped on, the cartridge was fired through the foot, possibly up into the body. We always stationed a few guerrillas near these deadly places to keep away innocent people and prevent their being uselessly injured. The device was successful, and caused untold apprehension among the Japanese. Even when we dropped the use of the device because the enemy was too alert for it, the threat of finding the mine slowed down the enemy's advance.

During the initial weeks of the campaign to retake Myitkyina, the quantity and the quality of our intelligence operations came up against new challenges.

About ten miles northwest of Myitkyina there was a lone mountain peak which overlooked the town and its airfield. The Air

Corps was anxious to know what activity existed on the airfield. To get them the information they needed, we selected a highly intelligent Burmese, named Maung, who had gone through agent training with flying colors and was also a qualified radio operator. He was a loner, the breed ideal for such a job. He was given additional training in the use of a long-range telescope and binoculars, was briefed on the operation of an airport and drilled in the details of his job. He was then parachuted into Area II at Arang along with his specialized equipment. Lieutenant Pat Quinn had already selected a spot on the side of the mountain where the activities of the Myitkyina airfield could be kept under continuous surveillance. He took Maung to the selected site to help get him established, and also arranged a weekly courier to supply him with the necessary food, water and other materials.

This operation paid off immediately: at once we could maintain a minute-to-minute log and count of the air traffic of the field. However, between Maung, Area II, our base camp and Headquarters 10th Air Force, we were having communication difficulties. Area II was so busy with their other radio traffic that they were unable to provide a continuous monitor on Maung's channel. This was seriously delaying the relay of vital information, so we cut them out of the system and allowed Maung to pass his operational traffic directly to the base station. By this means, the elapsed time from the moment Maung saw a Jap airplane land or take off until his message was flashed to the 10th Air Force was reduced to a matter of a few minutes. This intelligence greatly assisted the security of the Hump route. In addition, Maung was able to locate a secondary field which partially explained the occasional heavy Japanese air traffic in the area even though there might be only a small amount of activity on the Myitkyina airfield.

Skittles, who had joined Captain Curl with KNOTHEAD, was put on his highest mettle in ferreting out intelligence that would aid the attack. His activity reached into the lower reaches of the Hukawng Valley, and there he developed some simple but ingenious ways to pinpoint and report Japanese supply installations concealed by dense jungle foliage. One method was to select a landmark such as a trail junction, bridge or prominent tree which could be identified readily on an air photo and by the pilots of the fighter bomber aircraft. From the landmark the location of the target was given by polar coordinates (distance along a given azimuth). Another method was to lead the pilot from such a landmark, to another landmark, and another, and so on, to the target.

Numerous Japanese installations located by these means were bombed or strafed without the pilot's being able to see his target; huge explosions or fires erupting through the trees would signal a successful attack. The Japanese knew that something was amiss. Since the targets were completely hidden from the air, they deduced the repeated attacks were being directed from the ground and correctly surmised a 101 agent. They went out to get Skittles, and he was kept on the run, yet he was not caught. He traveled light, with a minimum of equipment, and he was able to find and report new targets. There were apprehensive times when his radio was silent for days upon days; then he would come on, crackling out a location of a new enemy target for our bombers.

The guerrilla units now sensed the battle near. Small parties of British commandos who had been sent in on reconnaissance missions made their way to the safety of 101 camps. Sometimes they were badly wounded. The guerrillas provided a hot cup of tea, food and friendship, and were able to evacuate them by light plane. The talks around campfires were of the grim fight ahead. We at the base thought of the fight, too, and how it must produce giants — a doctor, or a rifleman, or a pilot. Everything seemed to point toward our kind of giant, General Joseph Stilwell. His was not the happiest of positions.

X I I

Uncle Joe

ⅬⅬⅬⅬⅬⅬⅬⅬⅬⅬⅬⅬⅬⅬⅬⅬⅬⅬⅬⅬⅬⅬⅬⅬⅬⅬⅬⅬⅬⅬⅬⅬ

THERE WERE THOUSANDS of stories about General Stilwell, but two in particular stand out in my mind, and they are directly related to one another.

At one time in the spring of 1944 it looked as though a Japanese drive from Central Burma into India might succeed. If it had, it would have severed the road and railroad between Calcutta, northeast India, and the Chinese forces in Northern Burma. For all practical purposes the Chinese forces would be isolated, except by air. Under these circumstances General Stilwell saw nothing to be gained by inactivity; he wanted to maintain the forward momentum of his attack. The Chinese, however, would not budge, they just sat. No amount of threatening, cajoling or humoring could move them.

It was obvious that they were under orders from somewhere. Some said it was from the Generalissimo; others, the Chief of Staff, Ho Ying Ching; but the fact remained that they would not move.

After going to the division commanders Sun and Liao, General Stilwell went to the regimental commanders, but still no results. Then he went to the battalion commanders, down to the company commanders, the platoon leaders, the squad leaders and finally, he, then a three-star lieutenant general, was out in front of the combat forces motioning them forward. The Chinese could not lose face to this extent. Soon one soldier, then a squad, a platoon, a company, joined in the attack until eventually both divisions were again on the offensive. Few people have the determination and sheer guts to do a thing like this.

The other story is one Stilwell liked to tell on himself. He was returning through the jungle after visiting one of these Chinese units. He stopped to rest, sitting alone on a log by the side of the road. He had barely paused, when a typical monsoon downpour erupted from the skies. He went on sitting there, his old campaign hat drenched, his cigarette glowing angrily in its holder. He had no insignia showing. A sergeant from one of the colored engineer battalions came over and sat down next to him. After they had talked for a while the sergeant said: "Soldier, you look too old for this sort of thing. Why don't you ask them to send you on home?"

During Stilwell's period of command he had many troubles, and I don't believe his position was ever fully understood and appreciated, especially in Washington. Most generals have one job; General Stilwell had several. He was the commanding general of CBI, and also of the NCAC. He commanded the Chinese Army in India. He was deputy commander to Lord Louis Mountbatten in SEAC. He was in charge of all Lend-Lease. He had two principal difficulties, with the British and with the Chinese. The British caused him many anxieties, and, to be sure, there were innumerable misunderstandings. Upon occasion, Stilwell had been at fault in ignoring tact and favoring sarcasm. His worst side emerged when he thought of the defensive holding tactics being employed on the Imphal and Arakan fronts. An army, he felt, thrives on attack and withers on the defense, especially when there had been so many Allied defensive actions that degenerated into defeat. Success for the Burma campaign, Stilwell felt, required aggressive commanders. In August, 1943, when General Slim took command of the British Fourteenth Army, Stilwell was relieved at the birth of an offensive spirit. He recognized General Slim as one of the great commanders in the Allied camp. Under Slim's leadership, he correctly anticipated a campaign that would destroy Japanese forces in Burma.

Stilwell's more immediate problem was the Chinese. This situation was much more complex than the British because American interests were directly involved. To make it even more difficult, Stilwell was at odds with both General Chennault and Generalissimo Chiang Kai-shek. To state his position simply, General Chennault felt that China's salvation rested on air power. Stilwell believed that without the foot soldier Chennault's air bases would be lost, and that to achieve final victory, the vast areas under Japanese domination in China and southeast Asia would have to be won back on the ground. Air support and air bombardment, Stilwell recognized, were not sufficient by themselves to defeat the enemy in Burma or in China.

Chennault disagreed. He asked that the bulk of equipment and supplies coming into China over the Hump go to the 14th Air Force and the Chinese Air Force (CAF). There were bitter exchanges over this issue. Stilwell's troops in Burma were fighting to protect the air bases in Assam. They were fighting to build a new land route into China. Stilwell wanted twenty-six Chinese combat divisions for operations in China and the arms and equipment to go with them. Every time there was a high-level meeting to discuss the allocation of the Hump tonnage, the argument between Stilwell and Chennault broke out afresh. Neither general would give in.

Although Stilwell was Generalissimo Chiang Kai-shek's chief of staff, Chennault had been with the Nationalist Government much longer, since 1934, and he had the ear of both the Generalissimo and Madame Chiang. The Generalissimo liked to think of China as a first-rate military power; the development of air power fitted nicely into this scheme of thinking.

In this session of the eternal debate between air power and ground forces, air power won out. The thin trickle of supplies reaching China could not support both Stilwell and Chennault; and in deciding for Chennault, Generalissimo Chiang Kai-shek felt he was doing the right thing for China. His decision aborted Stilwell's hope of creating a great Chinese Army.

I myself firmly believe that had Stilwell's plan for equipping, organizing and training the Chinese ground forces been carried through to completion, Japanese infantry would not have been able to overrun the air bases in Southern China in late 1944; they would never have been able to mount an offensive in early 1945;

nor would the Chinese Communist ground troops have achieved their ends after the war against the Japanese was over.

These were by no means all of Stilwell's difficulties. Some of his worst problems stemmed from the smallest incidents; to illustrate: the Chinese forces in Burma were at one time having a very difficult time trying to penetrate Japanese defenses in the huge clumps of bamboo. A group of newspaper reporters came into Northern Burma without authority and, as luck would have it, one of them visited a Chinese unit trying to crack these bamboo defenses. The reporter suggested a flame thrower for the job.

It did not take long for the word to get around, and the Chinese sat and waited for flame throwers. The difficulty, however, was that, at the time, there simply *were* no flame throwers in Burma, India or in the entire CBI Theater of Operations. General Stilwell returned from China and found the Chinese demanding flame throwers; he hit the ceiling, and ordered the whole planeload of reporters back to India. After a week of painstaking negotiations with the Chinese commanders, Stilwell got them to move again.

One day I was with the General and his son-in-law, Colonel Easterbrook, in the General's tent when a telephone call came through from an American liaison officer in the front lines with one of the Chinese units. He, too, had been trying to get the Chinese to move, without too much success. The American, as he spoke, got more incensed, described the Chinese in the most vivid of barracks-room epithets. The only tactful solution was to get the man away from the Chinese, and Stilwell said: "I agree, and I want you to come back here and give me a full report." To return to Stilwell's headquarters, the officer had to walk for four days — enough time to think it over and quiet down.

One day, I described a guerrilla success in the Lake Indawgyi area; General Stilwell said he would like to see the American running the show and also one of the Kachin leaders. Little did I realize what I was letting 101 in for. A liaison plane was sent behind the lines to pick up the two men and bring them to the airstrip outside General Stilwell's headquarters. They reported to the General and made a favorable impression, especially the Kachin.

Stilwell then asked them how many Japs they had killed in a particular engagement. This was always a difficult problem, because, after all, when you are two hundred miles behind enemy lines you don't spend much time standing around counting enemy dead and wounded.

They replied, and General Stilwell asked, "Well, but how can you know so exactly? How can you be sure?" With this, the Kachin unhooked a bamboo tube tied to his belt and dumped its contents on the table. The contents looked like dried prunes and the General said, "What are these?" The subedar major replied, "Japanese ears. Divide by two and you will know how many Japs were killed."

This left no question in the General's mind, but later, after they had returned to the field, Stilwell called me in to ask if I had heard of this means of counting the enemy dead. I confessed that I had heard of it but had never seen the actual ears. He then quoted chapter and verse of a pertinent paragraph from the *Rules of Land Warfare* and directed that I take action to stop ear-collecting immediately. This was easier said than done. Among Kachins, it was a mark of a warrior's courage to show the ears he had taken in combat. They were not easily discouraged, and it took six months of constant lecturing before the Kachins were converted to simply counting the dead.

During the winter and spring of 1944, with the rigors of the tropical jungle sapping his strength, Stilwell kept himself going by sheer will power. He was a sick man. Whenever he felt well he was out with the troops, both day and night. However, there were times when all the color left his face; it turned an ashen gray and he stayed pretty well within the confines of his tent. As soon as his strength and color returned he was out again with the troops. A couple of years after the war, he died from intestinal cancer and, as I look back upon it, there is little doubt in my mind that he was going through indescribable pain at the very time he was leading the most important military campaign of his career — the attack on Myitkyina, which, when it fell, would at long last allow us to open a new land route to China.

The Attack Mounts

FOLLOWING THE Maingkwan-Walabum operation, the First Battalion of the American Marauders moved south through the jungle and hills east of the Kamaing Road, then changed direction to the southwest to hit the road in the area of Shadazup northwest of Myitkyina. They were to be followed by the 113th Chinese Regiment. The Marauder troops, despite continual Japanese patrols, gained ground. Far more resistant than the enemy was the jungle; often they had to hack their way through, and they were several days late in attacking their objective near Shadazup.

It would have taken more time and men had not Lieutenant Tilly's guerrilla unit been situated in the area. Preparing to meet and oppose the Marauders, the Japanese had no knowledge of the guerrillas to their rear and paid no heed to the possibility of attack from that direction.

Lieutenant Tilly and his Kachins had a field day. They ambushed the Japanese in the area of Jaiwa Ga and Makay Bum, inflicting significant casualties upon the enemy. They broke up his counterattack patterns and repeatedly permitted the Marauder column to exercise fuller freedom in its advance. Moreover, the presence of guerrillas aiding the conventional troops gave the Marauders confidence that the jungle was on their side. Tilly and his group remained with the first Marauder battalion, sometimes delivering information on enemy numbers and locations, sometimes ambushing the enemy in his own backyard.

Colonel Osborne of the 1st Battalion of Marauders directed one platoon to make a feint toward Shadazup. He planned to use the remainder of his battalion to ford the Mogaung River and put a block on the road leading toward Kamaing and Myitkyina. The 113th Chinese Regiment was to be kept in reserve.

The attack went off as planned, achieving complete surprise. The Marauders enveloped the Japanese camp and pursued their advantage to set up a perimeter defense around the roadblock. The Japanese counterattacked fiercely but could not force the Marauders, now strengthened by the arrival of the 113th Chinese Regiment, to yield. The Chinese 22nd Division carried forward a steady pressure and, on 28 and 29 March, it broke through the Japanese defenses in the Jamba Bum area and established contact with the Marauder roadblock. The Japanese withdrew. The road to Myitkyina was now open all the way up to Shadazup; the Allies had moved, as planned, a considerable distance back into Burma.

To the east, the bulk of the Marauder force, the 2nd and 3rd Battalions, had as its object a wider envelopment, following the headwaters of the Chindwin River (Tanai Hka) to the area of Warong and thence west to hit the road at Inkangahtawng. They too were aided by 101's guerrillas. At Nawbum, the headquarters of Area III, they established contact with Captain Curl. He assigned a force of nearly two hundred Kachin guerrillas as reconnaissance patrols to screen the front and flanks of the 2nd and 3rd Marauder Battalions.

The plan was for Colonel Hunter with the 2nd Battalion and one combat team of the 3rd Battalion to establish a roadblock in the vicinity of Inkangahtawng, with the rest of the 3rd Battalion to remain behind to block any possible Japanese movement through the headwaters of the Tanai Hka. As the force neared Inkangahtawng, the Kachin guerrillas encountered strong Japanese patrols; so the Marauders were warned that the Japanese were holding the area in considerable force.

The 2nd Battalion crossed the Mogaung River and probed Inkangahtawng; they ran into gathering resistance. Colonel McGee's orders had been to hold the block for a day but not to stay

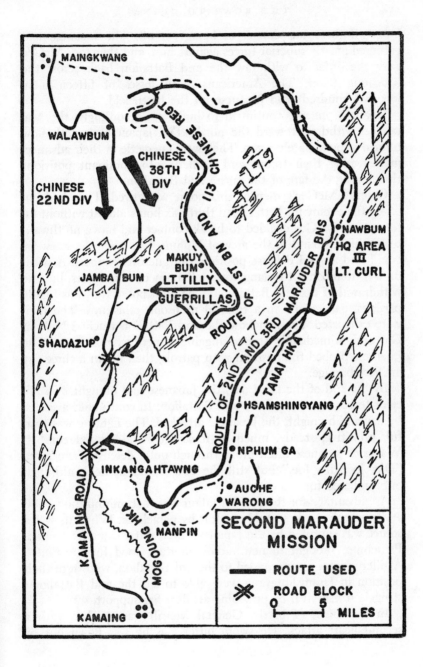

MAINGKWANG

WALAWBUM

CHINESE 38TH DIV

CHINESE 22ND DIV

113 CHINESE REGT

NAWBUM HQ AREA
III
LT. CURL

MAKUY BUM
LT. TILLY
GUERRILLAS

JAMBA BUM

ROUTE OF 1ST BN AND

ROUTE OF 2ND AND 3RD MARAUDER BNS

SHADAZUP

TANAI HKA

HSAMSHINGYANG

NPHUM GA

INKANGAHTAWNG

AUCHE
WARONG

KAMAING ROAD

MOGOUNG HKA

MANPIN

SECOND MARAUDER
MISSION

KAMAING

——— ROUTE USED
✳ ROAD BLOCK
0   5
MILES

longer if there was danger of being cut off. The Japanese had gathered greatly superior forces against him, and therefore McGee gave the order to withdraw the 2nd Battalion back across the Mogaung River. The Americans, with losses of fifteen men, left two hundred dead Japanese on the battlefield.

Japanese pressure continued to build up; accordingly, the Marauders withdrew toward the north. The Japanese strength now totaled approximately 2,500. They were energetic in their advance, maneuvering their troops and artillery into dominant positions threatening the fate of the entire 2nd Battalion.

Colonel McGee's men at this point were tired. They had engaged the enemy for better than thirty-six hours almost without interruption. McGee decided to break contact and move northward to the high ground in the area of Nphum Ga, where he knew he could find a good defense position and guerrilla support. A withdrawal from contact is dangerous under any circumstances, but the withdrawal of the 2nd Battalion along an exposed trail was highly perilous, particularly in a tropical monsoon rainstorm. The men were exhausted, but somehow the 2nd Battalion reached Nphum Ga, and immediately started digging a perimeter defense. The Japanese probed the position with patrols, then began a three-day artillery barrage.

By the end of the third day, the Japanese had brought up sufficient forces to surround the 2nd Battalion. In continuous assaults, by day and by night, the Japanese attacked. The fighting was fearful, primitive, steady, much of it savage hand-to-hand combat. Waves of Japanese often broke through outer defenses, screaming "Die, Joe; die, Joe," but still the 2nd Battalion held, although outnumbered four to one.

An advantage for the 2nd Battalion was that ammunition, food and medical supplies could reach it by parachute. When its water source was captured by the Japanese, even water came by airdrop. Parachutes brought in new radios, mortars, food for the mules. Artillery pieces were dropped to the 3rd Battalion, who from their position in Hsamshingyang were able to aid the 2nd Battalion's struggle for survival by providing artillery fire support.

In the midst of battle, General Merrill was stricken with a second heart attack. He swore bitterly as he was flown out by liaison aircraft to the 20th General Hospital in Ledo. Colonel Hunter assumed command of the Marauders.

The Japanese lacked an airdrop capacity. Nor could they call, with assurance, for air support, or count on the aid of the native population. They pressed the attack with courage, but when their ammunition ran low, they had to wait days for resupply to reach them overland. The guerrillas of 101 were given the job of ambushing their supply columns, cutting telephone lines, seizing radio stations and damaging the morale and fighting capacity of Japanese front-line troops. The Japanese troops waited for food and ammunition that would not arrive.

It was a battle for survival — a battle between two properly trained, highly disciplined, and capable opponents, neither side willing to give an inch. The 2nd Battalion was now compressed within a perimeter of a few hundred yards; nearly all of their mules were dead, a bloated grim spectacle within the defenses; and very near, their unburied comrades.

On the seventh day of the encirclement the 1st Battalion came to join the battle. With the 3rd Battalion, they began a double envelopment of the Japanese positions. Before the Marauders could perfect the counterattacking movement the Japanese, recognizing danger, broke contact and withdrew along the trail toward Kamaing.

When the pressure on the 2nd Battalion eased, General Stilwell ordered the entire Marauder unit into bivouac for a brief rest period. The 1st and 3rd Battalions were withdrawn to Nawbum, the headquarters of Captain Curl and Area III. The 2nd Battalion of the Marauders was bivouacked about twenty-five miles to the south in the area of Senjo Ga to guard against any possible Japanese movement into the upper Tanai Hka. It was during this period that dissension between the Marauders and General Stilwell began. From their association with Wingate's Chindit Division, the Marauders felt they had been promised that after ninety days in combat, they would be relieved. And shortly, the ninety days would be over. The troops were soon to find out that Stilwell had other ideas. Myitkyina was the key to the conquest of Northern Burma. Enemy control of North Burma had to be broken. Stilwell was going to do it whether it took ninety days or one hundred and ninety days. In this determined decision, he was to deprive himself of that which was nearly a necessity to him, a bond with the man who stood out in his mind in the front rank of soldiers anywhere — the infantryman of a rifle company.

The Drive Toward Myitkyina

THE NEXT STEP was Myitkyina.

General Stilwell's plan was concise. At Nawbum he assembled two battalions of the Marauders, one regiment of the Chinese 30th Division recently arrived from the Ramgarh Training Camp and a patrolling assignment in India during the Japanese Imphal offensive, and one regiment of the Chinese 50th Division just recently flown in from China. The 3rd Battalion of the Marauders and the 88th Regiment of the 30th Division were to form K Force under the command of Colonel Kinnison, and the 1st Battalion of the Marauders and the 150th Regiment of the 50th Chinese Division were to comprise H Force under Colonel Hunter. The plan further included M Force under Colonel McGee, to consist of the 2nd Battalion of the Marauders augmented by a small force of guerrillas from 101. The entire task force was to use the code name *Galahad* and would be commanded by General Merrill, who had made good progress in his recovery from his heart attack.

To take the pressure off Myitkyina, General Stilwell ordered the Chinese 22nd and 38th Divisions to capture Kamaing and clear the Hukawng Valley of Japanese. The 3rd Indian Division, the Chindits now under British General Lentaigne, were to throw a block on the railway corridor and prevent any major Japanese movement toward Myitkyina. The British-Kachin Levies were to capture Sumprabum and to continue their movement southward toward Myitkyina. Detachment 101 was to provide the maximum possible support to the operations of the combat forces, particularly to *Galahad*.

By mid-April, I presented the disposition and plans of 101 to General Stilwell.

AREA III. This area was to provide the principal support to *Galahad*. Of their roughly 1,000 Kachin Rangers, two companies, (350 to 400 men) were to support H and K Forces by patrolling and screening their front and flanks. Another 200 to 250 men were to join M Force, and the remaining four hundred or so were to stand by for the protection of the Nawbum area and to assist the Chinese 38th Division where possible. Espionage activities were to be pushed to the south along the railway corridor toward Katha and west toward the Lonkin Jade Mines.

AREA II. They were to provide guides and a small force of Kachin Rangers to *Galahad* when it passed through Arang. They were also to make their airstrip available for medical evacuation and airdrop. Until the passage of the *Galahad* force they were to arrest any Japanese movements from Nsopzup and the Irrawaddy River toward Arang and to keep the trails clear to the south. Subsequently, Area II was to operate along the road from Sumprabum toward Myitkyina to restrict any Japanese movement from the north to reinforce Myitkyina. Moreover, they were to extend their espionage operations southward and be prepared to move their operational base in that direction.

AREA I. This area had the greatest number of guerrillas, by now about 1,500 well-armed and well-trained Kachin Rangers. Even though its location on the east side of the Irrawaddy River was such that it was unable to provide direct support to any of the orthodox military forces involved in the Myitkyina campaign, it was to make the main effort of Detachment 101. Area I was to move the bulk of its force south out of the Triangle to conduct raids on Japanese installations and to gain control of the road and trails leading into Myitkyina from the east and south, principally Bhamo. Additionally, the men of Area I were to set up fire-points or ambushes along the Irrawaddy River and its feeders, the Mali and Nmai Hkas, where they would prevent the Japanese from using these waterways to reinforce their Myitkyina garrison. They

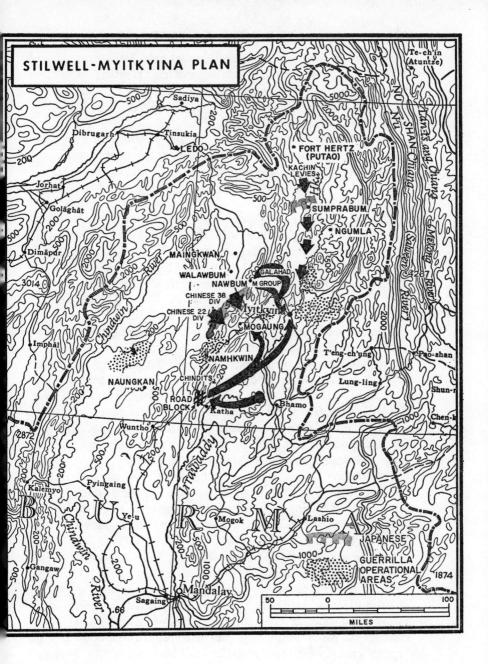

STILWELL-MYITKYINA PLAN

were also to extend their intelligence nets southward toward Bhamo to obtain advance knowledge of any Japanese movement toward Myitkyina. And, very importantly, their prime mission was to obtain a clear picture of the Japanese situation in Myitkyina prior to the movement of *Galahad*.

AREA IV. This headquarters was located at some distance from the regular combat forces participating in the operation. Consequently, it was felt that Area IV's greatest contribution would be in expanding guerrilla, sabotage and espionage operations to be ready for action upon conclusion of the Myitkyina campaign.

Colonel Kinnison's K Force led off on 28 April from Nawbum, followed by Colonel Hunter's H Force. They were preceded on the trail by a group of Kachin Rangers led by Lieutenant Bill Martin accompanied by the Marauder S-2, Captain Laffin, and a few other people from the Intelligence section. The Marauders had with them two officers from the Burma Army. They were Jack Gersham and Captain Darlington, and they knew the area.

The Kumon Range over which the K and H Forces had to proceed attains heights of 8,000 to 9,000 feet. Even the low pass through which the main body of *Galahad* was to move exceeds 6,500 feet. The pre-monsoon rains arrived early, the trail was slippery and greaselike. Progress was one step forward, two slips back. Startled mules fell off the trail to their death. Hours of hard marching wore down many American and Chinese soldiers, and they found it easier to leave all but the barest necessities alongside the trail. (So drastic was this lightening of packs that, later, a Kachin unit following the same trail collected more than 2,000 blankets.)

Meanwhile, the Kachin guerrillas were securing trails: all the advantages of having a guerrilla force completely in control of the back trails was evident as the conventional forces moved unmolested on toward their objectives.

On the east side of the Kumon Range the *Galahad* force had a brush with Japanese infantry in the area of Ritpong. Even though, in the end, K Force quickly wiped out the enemy, the engagement delayed *Galahad* by about three days; it created an air of uncertainty as to whether the movement toward Myitkyina had been discovered. Most unsettling, the place was infected with mite typhus against which the troops had not been inoculated. A plague was upon them; within a few days, Colonel Kinnison and many others were dead; large numbers of men were evacuated to hospitals where, if they recovered at all, the recoveries would be long and slow.

After Ritpong, K Force made a feint eastward toward Nsopzup and the enemy garrison there. At Tingkrukawng they overwhelmed a Japanese force of reduced battalion strength and screened the area from any possible westward movement. Meanwhile H Force had bypassed K and proceeded southward toward Arang, which was the headquarters of our Area II under Lieutenant Pat Quinn. Here *Galahad* had a liaison airfield available to evacuate sick and wounded. They also received a final airdrop and picked up a group of Kachin guerrillas under Lieutenant Hazelwood who were familiar with every trail in the area and were able to guide *Galahad* to its objective.

After leaving Arang, H Force pressed their march to reach Myitkyina as quickly as possible. The Kachin guerrillas led them over abandoned and hidden trails. Other guerrillas screened the flanks. Nau, a young Kachin guide, was bitten by a poisonous snake and, although seriously weakened, continued on, riding a local mountain pony. He led the way to the Myitkyina airstrip. After safely crossing the Myitkyina-Mogaung Road and railroad, H Force spent the night in the village of Namkwi, a Shan village. They placed cordons of troops around the town to prevent any native from slipping out to inform the Japanese. The following morning, 17 May, H Force attacked the airstrip, an attack so unexpected that before the day was over the great Myitkyina airstrip had been won. The advance carried to the bend in the Irrawaddy River to the south.

There was jubilant, almost hysterical celebration. The campaign seemed almost over. General Merrill flew in from Arang and assumed local command. K and M Forces, two to three days' march away, were notified and told to expedite their movement. On the 17th some British light anti-aircraft units were flown in by glider, and action was initiated to fly in one battalion of the Chinese 89th Regiment. General Merrill sent a message to Detachment 101 saying, "Thanks for your assistance, we could not have succeeded without the help of 101."

So far, the operation had the classic features of a stunning victory. All in the Northern Battle Area visualized the immediate fall of Myitkyina. The honor of actually capturing the city, Stilwell decided, was to be given to the Chinese.

With bugles sounding the advance, two battalions of Chinese entered the town in a supposedly coordinated attack, one battalion from the south, the other from the west. There were hardly any Japanese to stop them; the Chinese advanced with hardly a shot fired against them. At dusk, the two battalions were nearing the railway station in the center of town. Here a handful of do-or-die Japanese snipers started picking off men from both units. Then there ensued a horrible response. Possibly panic-stricken, possibly enraged, the Chinese started shooting one another. To this day, it is uncertain why. The losses were unbelievable: two Chinese battalions methodically, madly destroying each other to the point where they had to be withdrawn.

The Japanese reacted very quickly and started pouring reinforcements into Myitkyina from every direction. They came in from garrisons on the China border, from patrols and outposts east of Myitkyina, from the base and hospital at Nsopzup to the north, and from Mogaung to the west. In a week their strength approached three thousand and in a fortnight or so it was on the order of five thousand. In addition, the terrain itself aided the Japanese. Myitkyina is surrounded by paddy fields, dense jungles and fields of elephant grass; and now the monsoon rains were beginning to fall. The defenders were better off than the Allied attackers. At one point, in fact, the Japanese outnumbered the attackers, and there was a real possibility that the enemy would seize the offensive again.

The Allies, with the airfield still in their hands, brought in reinforcements from every part of the CBI Theater until there were twelve thousand men ready for the effort to break the Japanese grip. They were supported by fighters and bombers of the 10th Air Force; but it was impossible to take Myitkyina without infantry battling for every square foot of ground.

The Japanese were battle-wise and if they had kept Myitkyina, they would have had a handsome success to crow over. On the Allied side, the Marauders were spent, yet Stilwell could not spare them. Their ranks had been depleted by battle casualties; diseases and fatigue had taken a malicious toll; morale was sagging. It was at this time that acrimony between the Marauders and General Stilwell reached its highest pitch. The Chinese units, newly arrived from China and with little previous combat experience, lacked enterprising troops and leadership.

For the Japanese now there was no retreat. The odds were about even that they could hold the city and delay an Allied victory in North Burma. They meant to improve the odds. Myitkyina was foredoomed to a long, costly campaign which neither side could win with any form of distinction beyond the heroism and valor of individuals.

General Merrill suffered a third heart attack early in the siege and had to be relieved. After a number of rapid changes of command, General Wessels from the Infantry School at Fort Benning, Georgia, was appointed the new commander, and he remained in this position until the end of the campaign.

The dog-eat-dog fight for Myitkyina continued day after day: through June, through July, and into August. The monsoon heat and rain punished both sides. The Allies were able to sustain their force, but the Japanese could not replace their losses. Even so, the Japanese continued to hold; not a man among them surrendered. In late July came the first break in the battle. The Japanese began to evacuate their wounded by tying them to rafts and floating them down the Irrawaddy River. General Mizukami, the Japanese commander committed *hara-kiri*. On the night of 2 August, Colonel Maruyama led the last two hundred Japanese out of Myitkyina and across the Irrawaddy River, south toward Bhamo. The battle for Myitkyina was over.

During the siege of Myitkyina the guerrillas in Area I were particularly active. They seized Seniku, Washang, Sadon and several other Japanese-occupied towns; raided numerous Jap installations; destroyed many Japanese vehicles; ambushed several large bodies of troops trying to enter Myitkyina from the east and south; and, by the end of the campaign, controlled nearly all of the area east of the town as far as the China border. They had killed in excess of five hundred Japanese all told. They also seized and occupied a Japanese airfield at Kwitu. It was a small strip but capable of handling Japanese Zero aircraft. When Colonel Maruyama led the last Japanese force out of Myitkyina, Lieutenant Lazarski's guerrillas pursued and repeatedly ambushed them. Only a small portion of that force was to reach Bhamo.

Near the climax of the battle for Myitkyina, Lieutenant Martin and about four hundred of the Kachins who had accompanied *Galahad* moved south about thirty miles along the Irrawaddy. There they set up ambushes along the river and trails. When the Japanese attempted to escape by this route they intercepted them, killing over three hundred and taking fifty-six prisoners.

While the battle for Myitkyina Town was underway, Colonels Thrailkill and Lattin were placed in command of a small, handpicked group of Americans from Myitkyina garrison. Their orders were to contact the Chinese Nationalist Army forces in the Salween River Valley. Lieutenant Esterline and his 101 Detachment escorted the American group to Fort Harrison (Sadon), which the Kachins had captured after a frightful battle with the Japanese. From there they led the Americans to the China border and a meeting with the Chinese Army. For the first time since the fall of Burma in early 1942, a land route to China was almost open. The cost had been bitter, but a gigantic feat in the Allied war effort had been achieved. Stilwell's dream — a land route to China — was now in sight.

PART FIVE

Forcing the Kill

The Drive South

ⅬⅬⅬⅬⅬⅬⅬⅬⅬⅬⅬⅬⅬⅬⅬⅬⅬⅬⅬⅬⅬⅬⅬⅬⅬⅬ

WITH THE FALL of Myitkyina, 101's task underwent a subtle change. General Stilwell had never formally stated that he was satisfied with 101's effort to organize a three-thousand-man guerrilla force, nor did he now officially give his approval to expand the size of the force to ten thousand. It was one of those things that went without saying.

While the Myitkyina campaign was still underway we had busily engaged in extending our espionage and guerrilla operations further to the south. Two operations involving the British forces in Central Burma had a prominent part in this development.

In early 1944, the Japanese had assembled a three-division force of over 100,000 strong. In March they struck a resounding blow at the British Fourteenth Army in an attempt to drive through to India. Their maneuver was a double envelopment at Imphal and Dimapur. It was executed energetically, and only the gallant stand of the Indian and British forces at Imphal and Kohima halted the breakthrough. Shortly, the Fourteenth Army took the offensive, and was never stopped thereafter. To concentrate their troops for the drive on India, the Japanese had developed numerous small supply installations. These targets were built to order for our sabotage and guerrilla forces. Accordingly, our operations in the western area were pushed further south to deal with them.

Separate from the Fourteenth Army was General Orde Win-

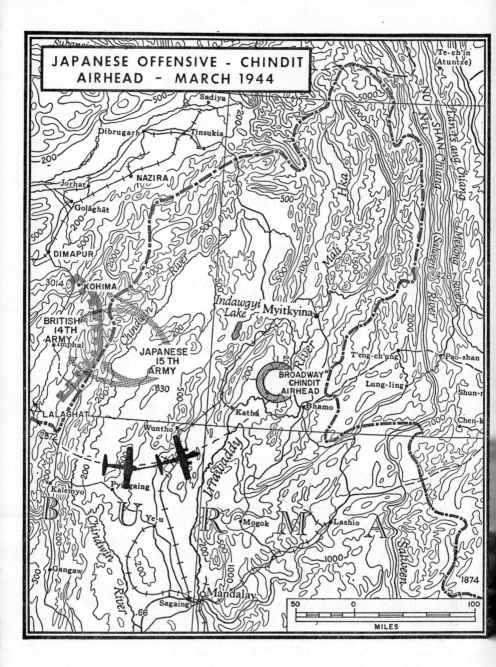

JAPANESE OFFENSIVE - CHINDIT
AIRHEAD - MARCH 1944

gate's 3rd Indian Division, better known as the "Chindits." The division aboard gliders was flown into Burma, south of Myitkyina, by the 1st American Airborne Commandos under Colonels Cochran and Alison. The principal airhead was "Broadway," located at almost the same site in the Koukkwee Valley where we had parachuted our original "A" Group.

We saw an opportunity both to be of assistance to Wingate's men and to lay the groundwork for our expansion to the south. With the Chindits we sent twelve of our best trained Kachin agents under Saw Judson, who had first visited the area with "A" Group. Judson set up listening posts along the trails and in the villages around the Chindits. When the Chindits moved out, these agents set up screens for their movements and then remained behind to continue their espionage and to serve as a nucleus for the development of guerrilla forces. To accompany the Chindits we sent along a couple of our American lieutenants, each with a radio operator and an agent or two. Their mission was to establish contact with the Kachins and start raising guerrilla forces. One of the lieutenants moved north of Katha, the other went into the Irrawaddy River Valley. Both were successful.

The Chindits had a force of their own to work with the Kachins along the China border in the area of Bhamo. The group totaled about fifty and was known as the *Dah* (or knife) Force. Captain Joost and four of our Kachins accompanied the *Dah* group across the Irrawaddy River, across the road near Bhamo, and into the mountains. Along the way they managed to put a few Jap trucks out of action. They found the Kachins friendly and desirous of working against the Japs. Oscar just happened to be there and Captain Joost used his radio to keep us advised. We wanted to get operations started near Bhamo, so we arranged with the British to have their personnel in the *Dah* Force transferred to 101.

There was a gap between the railway corridor and the British Fourteenth Army on the Imphal Front. Detachment 101 was given the mission of mobilizing its forces for fighting in this area, 200 miles wide with several north-south terrain corridors traversing it. These corridors provided ready access from the south to the Hukawng Valley and the Ledo Road (now flourishing in its constant progress) directly to the rear of the new combat troop advances. Through our intelligence, we knew the Japanese strength in the area was not very great. However, if the Japanese decided to counterattack, it would be through the gap, for it presented a clear route to the Ledo Road. A sufficient enemy force could set up roadblocks, which would require our troops to come back and clear them out. Detachment 101 had to raise troops to stop this gap — a quasi-conventional mission. Major Red Maddox, the commander of Area III, increased the guerrilla forces to approximately 2,000.

In the first corridor to the west of the railway, Lieutenant Danielewicz raised a force of about four hundred guerrillas. Defection of armed and uniformed Shans and Burmese working with local Japanese garrisons began to grow. Many of them joined Kachin guerrilla units. In the next two corridors to the west, Major Dow Grones and Captain Butch Thorlin, with several fine NCO's, organized two guerrilla units of 400 to 500 men each, with Mansi as their main base. Their camp spoke of confidence, protected as it was by row after row of *pungyis*, so numerous and planted so thickly that they served as barbed wire and would have withstood artillery fire.

From this fortress, Major Grones carried on raids and sabotage operations. On one occasion his espionage agents located a Japanese motor pool and weapons park. Dow had the target thoroughly reconnoitered by his native intelligence net. Then he planned and rehearsed the details of the operation with a small chosen group of Kachin guerrillas. They knew they would not have much time to plant demolition charges before the local Japanese force would react. Therefore, they approached the target in silence, ignoring any other enemy installations. They reached the motor park undetected, quickly set fire to vehicles, shot up the gas tanks of those they could not ignite, and shoved the artillery pieces over a bluff into a river. Protection for the saboteurs was provided by guerrillas engaging the enemy garrison. Not only the artillery pieces, but between thirty and forty sedans and trucks, were destroyed in this short action.

Further to the west Lieutenant Coussoule ("the Greek"), with a guerrilla force of about three hundred, conducted a similar operation. One evening he and a few of his guerrillas left their camp

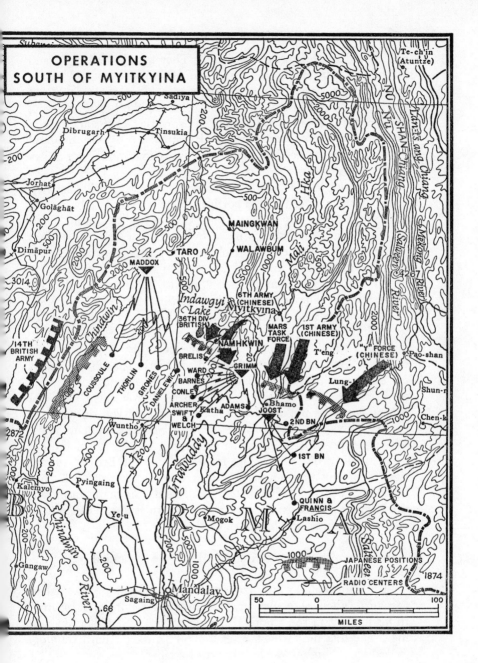

and moved south through the jungle. They marched all night and all the next day, and by midnight were fifty miles away and on the outskirts of a large Japanese supply dump. They got a couple of hours of rest and just before daybreak raided the Japanese dump, catching the enemy completely by surprise. Coussoule's men burned eleven large warehouses and destroyed over one thousand tons of critically needed supplies. Twenty-four hours later they were back in their own camp.

The enemy, with two battalions, reacted to the guerrilla activity. One battalion moved to the north in what appeared to be a feint toward the Hukawng Valley. Major Grones's and Captain Thorlin's guerrillas opposed this move by a series of delaying actions combined with numerous patrols to the Japanese rear to harass their communication lines and cut off their supplies. The Japanese lost heavily in these engagements against guerrillas whom they could not see. They eventually gave up their effort.

Another Japanese reaction was to flood the area with agents to try to find out what our people were up to. These agents were without much training and could be uncovered easily. After they were captured, some were properly trained and worked as reliable agents for our guerrillas; others were dispatched to remote villages for confinement. The occasional well-trained enemy agent captured behind the lines presented a problem. What do you do with enemy prisoners two hundred miles or more behind the enemy lines? Whenever possible, we flew liaison aircraft to pick them up and fly them to within Allied lines for delivery to the British authorities. When this was not possible, they were turned over to Kachin guards for delivery overland to Allied hands. In many instances, the Kachins after a day's march would return saying, "The prisoners tried to escape. We had to shoot them."

In the central area south of Myitkyina we expanded our operations.

Lieutenant Conley and Sergeant Aubry were among the first in the area. They were met by Saw Judson's agents and escorted to his hideout in the Hopin Hill Tract. Saw assisted them in raising a guerrilla unit which, after a short period of hard training, moved south through the hills toward Katha.

Later Lieutenant Dean Brelis joined forces with Saw. Their activities, both operationally and intelligencewise, were a model of efficiency. They seemed to know the location of every Jap in the railway corridor. When the Air Corps hit a target designated by Dean and Saw they knew everything about the target and got excellent results. Their raids and ambushes were carried out with comparable efficiency.

Captain Grimm was in charge of operations in the central area. He had six guerrilla units varying in size from one hundred to four hundred men, under Lieutenants Conley, Adams, Barnes, Archer, Swift and Welch. These converged on the Japanese center at Katha. In a short period they cleared the Japs out of the surrounding villages, put blocks on the river, roads and trails, and had effectively isolated the city. The fire fights were generally short and bitter. Japanese resistance was worn thin; when the British 36th Division arrived they entered the city of Katha almost without opposition.

In the Sinlum Hills east of Bhamo, Major Pete Joost and Major Lazum Tang of the Burma Army teamed up to develop the largest guerrilla formations ever raised by 101. Both of these men in their own way were geniuses in organization and logistics. Many ex-Burma Army soldiers resided in the Sinlumkaba (big Sinlum mountain) area, and Lazum recruited them by the hundreds. He also organized all of the nearby villages, handled distribution of food, set up an intelligence net and did many things to bolster the morale of the civilian populace.

Joost had been captain of the Yale boxing team in his college days and maintained himself in keen trim to live the life of a guerrilla head. He understood the Kachins and their psychology and they almost idolized him. 101 was extremely fortunate; a better working combination than Lazum Tang and Pete Joost could not be found. Within three months they raised, equipped and trained two battalions, of 1,000 men each, and had three more in training. Lieutenant Mudrinich took command of the 1st Battalion and moved it south, adjacent to the Burma Road. The 2nd Battalion with Lieutenants Chamales and Freudenberg moved east along the China border.

Part of the training for the guerrillas was to man the defenses, the ambushes on the trails leading into Sinlum. Although Sinlum was located less than twenty miles from the major Japanese base at Bhamo, the Japanese made no serious attempt to evict them. They made some halfhearted tries, but it would have cost them dearly, so they preferred to ignore these defenses.

Lieutenants Quinn and Francis, who had now been with 101 for over two years, also joined with Pete Joost. They set up listening posts along the Burma Road north of Lashio and produced highly reliable information until they and their agents were overtaken by the advances of the Allied forces.

The 2nd Battalion of Joost's men near the China border had an unfortunate encounter with some local Chinese in the area of Lweji. For several years the local war lords had been conducting forays into Burma, looting and pillaging as they went. On this occasion they razed nine Kachin villages. The Kachins, with American officers present, retaliated, eye for an eye, destroying nine Chinese villages. It was a situation charged with all forms of international implications.

We received word of it immediately and I took it up with NCAC Headquarters. A team composed of a United States Army Colonel and a Colonel of the First Chinese Army was appointed to investigate. Their report, in brief, was to the effect that the Chinese had been wrong in their initial action, and that our 2nd Battalion was equally as wrong in their reaction. It was tit for tat.

Much has been written about this situation in some of the more sensational periodicals. Some claimed that they had papers to prove the Chinese were under orders signed by the Generalissimo, that the agents involved were from the Chinese Intelligence Service, and the like. This to my mind is pure fantasy. I was present during the entire situation, talked with all participants, including the investigation team, yet the first I ever heard of these claims was ten years later in an American magazine.

The situation did have its bizarre aspects. A few months later I received a personal memorandum from the Generalissimo requesting payment of five hundred million CN for the damages inflicted upon the Chinese villages. This would amount to twenty-five million United States dollars, hardly payable out of the wages of a Colonel. The memorandum was turned over to CBI Theater

Headquarters, where a copy of the investigation was forwarded to the Generalissimo. This closed the matter, and nothing further was heard of the incident.

It was important to our mission that elaborate liaison arrangements be made between 101 and the combat commands involved with us. These included, besides NCAC, the British Fourteenth Army, 10th Air Force, Mars Task Force (which had replaced the Marauders), Allied Land Forces Southeast Asia, the Chinese 1st and 6th Armies, the Chindits, the British 36th Division and the Chinese 50th Division. The liaison officers were some of our best officers and represented 101 in all matters — guerrilla operations, sabotage, espionage, administration, communications, escape and deception plans.

The relief of General Stilwell as Commander of the China-Burma-India Theater took place in October, 1944. It was the end of another era. Many books have been written on this subject, so there is little to be gained in belaboring it. I can only say that I thought then, and I still believe, it was a grave error in United States military and diplomatic judgment. It greatly weakened the United States position and was one of the first steps toward the ultimate victory of the Chinese Communists.

When the CBI Theater was divided into the India-Burma and China theaters, Lieutenant General Daniel I. Sultan became India-Burma Theater Commander, and Major General Albert C. Wedemeyer took over the China Theater. We felt great concern over the future of 101. General Sultan had been Stilwell's deputy in New Delhi and had no firsthand knowledge of the battle in Northern Burma. Our fears were put to rest, however, when he visited 101. He liked what he saw, especially the Kachin guerrillas, said so, and told us to get on with the job.

Under the impetus of 101's enlarged role in the campaign, operations had expanded considerably. We were air-dropping nearly a million and a half pounds of supplies each month to the units behind Japanese lines. Radio traffic had increased, and we were handling about 10,000 messages a month. This was in excess of three hundred messages per day. All of the encoding and decoding of messages was done by hand, and as late as November, 1944 there were three cryptographic systems being used. We had been successful, at long last, with long-range intelligence activities; ten agent operations were established in locations south of Mandalay, in the Southern Shan States.

Our guerrillas no longer had to face the possibility of being wounded and left behind to die or be captured. Each guerrilla unit now had medical personnel assigned, and liaison aircraft flew the wounded to United States hospitals. The hospital food was bland to the Kachins' taste for fiery foods; they could not talk with the doctors or nurses and were not responding properly. Commander Luce supervised the construction of our own hospital at Nazira and staffed it with Burmese nurses and cooks. It worked miracles and did much to build up the morale of the guerrilla forces.

We no longer relied on a whisper of a light aircraft to keep us going. Seventeen different aircraft by now were assigned to 101, and we had a total of twenty pilots. They performed a yeoman task in evacuating the wounded; delivering radios, maps, funds and critical supplies; and moving the commanders from place to place to coordinate their operations.

There were now about two hundred and fifty United States officers and seven hundred and fifty enlisted men in 101. Included were eight officers who had requested transfer from the Marauders when that unit was inactivated. They were some of our finest. Sergeant Brough, a British subject in the United States Army serving with Seagrave Hospital Unit, and a conscientious objector, also transferred to 101. He proved a tower of strength.

Considered together, the over-all activities of 101 had become most complex. Aside from the guerrilla and espionage activities, there was a wide variety of other activities underway. To coordinate them with one another and with the operations of the combat forces kept the operations officer, Major Moore and his staff, and the communicators at their jobs around the clock seven days a week. One mock airdrop had already been carried out to assist the British Fourteenth Army in their drive on Mandalay; another was being planned. Several weather stations had been set up behind the lines to collect meteorological data for the Air Corps Weather Service. Detachment 101's X-2 (counter-intelligence personnel) were working with NCAC Headquarters to ferret out Burmese traitors and war criminals, and there were more than a few. The black propaganda operations under Lieutenant Colonel George Boldt started paying dividends: several Japanese soldiers had already surrendered, carrying leaflets supposedly printed by the Japanese high command, but which actually had been printed and distributed behind the lines by 101. And above and beyond all of this, in Southern Burma our detachment had a unit of over one hundred officers and men working with the British V Corps carrying out espionage and maritime operations — underwater swimmers and the like. There was very little going on within the combat units in Burma in which, directly or indirectly, 101 was not involved.

The role of our guerrillas had also undergone a subtle change. More and more 101 troops were battering away at the enemy with a combination of conventional as well as unconventional tactics. Nor were we bothered by the change. We were proving ourselves; and with the end of the campaign in sight, we were anxious to be present for the final kill.

XVI

Lashio and Mandalay

⊓⊔⊓⊔⊓⊔⊓⊔⊓⊔⊓⊔⊓⊔⊓⊔⊓⊔⊓⊔⊓⊔⊓⊔⊓⊔⊓⊔⊓⊔⊓⊔

WITH THE CAPTURE of Bhamo by the Chinese 1st Army, the FOR-
WARD Headquarters of 101 at Myitkyina was a long way from the
front lines and still further from the guerrilla units. NCAC had
already started moving into Bhamo proper. The 101 FORWARD
Headquarters was getting to be fairly large with several sections.
If we moved into Bhamo itself, we would be spread all over the
city. So we sent out a reconnaissance and quartering party and in-
structed them to look for a nearby village. They were most fortunate. About five miles south of the town, they located a Shan
village large enough to house the entire group. It had sufficient
housing for our needs and nearby a cattle-grazing area which could
be converted into a two-thousand-foot landing strip. We moved
into the village in late January, at the same time as the NCAC and
the 10th Air Force Headquarters completed their move into Bhamo.

Not knowing how long the operations against Lashio and Mandalay would last or what the orders to 101 would be beyond those
points, we had to plan as if the campaign would continue on toward the south. We stepped up the tempo of our espionage operations. In the next four months nineteen additional agent groups
were infiltrated into Burma, an average of about five each month.
They were put into operations by just about every means possible:
some parachuted, others were flown into one of the guerrilla units

and made overland penetrations. In one case, a helicopter was used to land the agent, the first time, to my knowledge, that a helicopter was used in clandestine operations.

"Betty" was the agent put in by helicopter. From Myitkyina, he was flown to an area north of Hsipaw; landed, and from there worked his way overland to the area of the Bawdwin mines at Namtu, near Lashio. Landing an agent by helicopter in those days was not as easy as it may sound today. The machine was an Air Rescue helicopter of the 10th Air Force, and it had definite limitations. It could not fly higher than 7,000 feet and it could not get off the ground with a passenger at elevations of over 3,000 feet. The operational area was mountainous and the plateau of the Shan States was about 4,000 feet high. Extreme care had to be taken to pick out a landing site that would be clear of obstructions, near where Betty wanted to go, and that would permit the helicopter to get back in the air. The operation went off exactly as planned and by mid-December, Betty was operating. He reported that the people were ripe for development of a guerrilla force, so we suggested to Major Joost that he move Major Lutkin into the area. Betty helped Major Lutkin recruit his guerrilla force and then was given a new mission. He went on foot through the hills to the area of Laihka and there set up operations. This area was critical. To the south lay the major road into Thailand, to the east was the route from Loilem to Lashio and in addition there were major airfield complexes at Taunggyi (Heho), Laihka and Namsang. Betty trained a group of local Shan operators, and his intelligence reports were accurate, extensive and timely. He also captured three Japanese civil administrators. One was the local governor and the other two economists. They were flown out and provided a wealth of information concerning the political, economic and military organization in Burma and in Japan.

Agent groups were successfully put into operation near Yamethin, Taunggyi, Lawksawk and Kentung. Not all agent groups were so successful. Three groups, one after the other, failed to come on the air. They were later recovered and it was found that in all cases they had been unable to locate their radio. Had we dropped a pigeon with each operator, as we later learned to do, we would have discovered the difficulty and could have dropped another radio set.

Several of the agent operations were initiated at the request of other commands. The 10th Air Force requested that agents be put into six specified areas to check on bombing and strafing targets. We had personnel capable of working in five out of the six locations. They were parachuted into operation, and four of them came on the air with their radios. One lost his communication equipment but was located later and another radio was dropped to him. The British Fourteenth Army asked that we put in some agents to check the roads in their sector. Five were requested; four were put in, and all were successful. Additionally, Z Force (which conducted clandestine operations in support of the Fourteenth Army) did not have the capability for night-drop operation, so we obliged and dropped them at their targets. They too were successful.

With the advance of the Allied Forces south of Bhamo, Major Joost moved his Area I field headquarters northwest of Lashio and began concentrating his guerrilla battalions around that city. There were now seven battalions, each at a strength of about one thousand, a formidable force.

The 3rd Battalion, under Lieutenant Joe Lazarsky, was the first to move. They crisscrossed the Burma Road north of Lashio several times, each time shooting up Japanese foot and motor columns and raising hell in general. Lazarsky was hurting the Japs, and they reacted with pressure, infantry, artillery and tanks. Joe withdrew under pressure, ambushing the enemy at every turn, until he reached his airfield. There a three-day pitched battle was fought. It was during this engagement that Sergeant Brough ceased being a conscientious objector. As a medical aid man he had three wounded guerrillas killed on his back as he attempted to carry them to safety from the far side of the strip. He said, "If that is the way they are going to fight, I am no longer an objector." He took charge of one of the companies and served with outstanding distinction. He was later given a battlefield commission in the United States Army and after the war became a medical doctor in England under the G.I. Bill of Rights.

Major Delaney's 5th Battalion, northwest of Lashio, stung the

Japs on several occasions. The Japanese, in reacting to this will-of-the-wisp threat, foolishly attempted to mount a frontal assault on some of the guerrilla outposts. The guerrillas inflicted heavy casualties on them.

One problem which faced us was in the assessing and reporting of casualties. In many of our reports to Washington and NCAC Headquarters there would be forty to sixty Japs killed and perhaps only one or two guerrillas listed as wounded. This sometimes became difficult for a commander of conventional troops to understand. In one instance Major Delaney had reported seventy-three Japs killed in an engagement on a certain hilltop with no guerrilla casualties. General Cannon at NCAC Headquarters said:

"Ray, what are you reporting stuff like that for? You know that cannot be accurate."

"Obviously I don't have firsthand knowledge, but if Bob Delaney said he killed seventy-three that is good enough for me," I replied.

General Cannon was a gentleman. I saw him a couple of days later and he said,

"Ray, I will have to apologize," and showed me a copy of a message from the Chinese 113th Regiment. When they reached the hilltop reported by Major Delaney they found not seventy-three but seventy-seven dead Japanese.

Meanwhile, the other battalions moved in to tighten the ring around the city. Lazum Tang moved the last battalion, the 6th, southwest of Lashio and Major Grones joined Captain Barnes in forming a seventh battalion of Kachins and Shans east of Lashio. The seven battalions eventually gained control of all the roads and trails leading into the city and were sitting on the ridges surrounding it. To avoid any conflict between the guerrillas and the regular troops, when the Chinese advanced on Lashio from the north, all of the guerrilla battalions were withdrawn about 15 miles to the west. The Chinese occupied the city with practically no resistance.

Further to the west in Area II under Major Maddox, the veteran but badly depleted Japanese 18th Division and some separate battalion-size units were putting up a stiff resistance to the British 36th Division and the Chinese 50th Division. The Chinese 50th

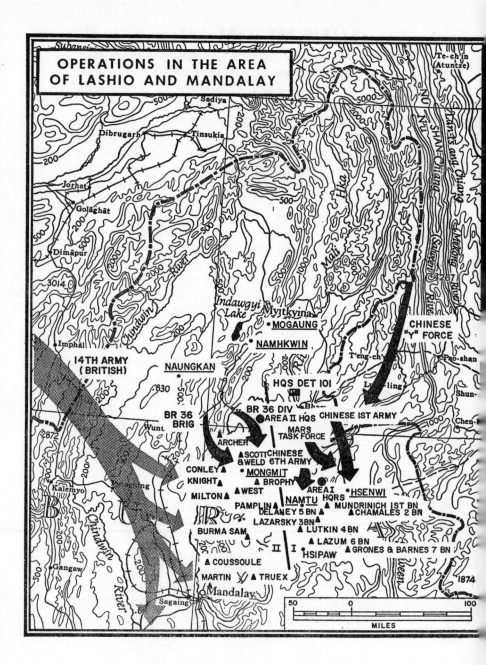

OPERATIONS IN THE AREA OF LASHIO AND MANDALAY

Division, which had relieved the 22nd in the area of Tonkwa, was given the mission of seizing the Bawdwin mines at Namtu and then occupying Hsipaw in hopes of cutting off the Japanese remaining in the Lashio area. One of its regiments decimated a Japanese company at the Shweli River after which the division crossed and proceeded on to take Namtu against light opposition in mid-February. By mid-March they had occupied Hsipaw. For no apparent reason the Japanese gave up Hsipaw without a fight, but then they severely rocked the 50th Division for a day or two with strong, sharp counterattacks. The Chinese, however, were there and they meant to stay. They were on the main road and a few days later linked up with other Chinese forces in the area of Lashio.

General Festings split the 36th British Division into two columns. One column, consisting of one brigade, was to parallel the Irrawaddy River and then turn east in the area of Twinge to attack Mongmit from the west. The other column, composed of two brigades, was to cross the Irrawaddy at Katha and advance down the trail, cross the Shweli River and attack Mongmit from the north. The western brigade advanced against almost negligible opposition. This was not so with the other two brigades; in trying to cross the Shweli in the area of Myitson, they encountered stiff resistance. Three times the Japs threw them back across the river, and they finally had to effect an envelopment to outflank and get across. In one encounter alone nearly four hundred Japs were killed.

Still further west the offensive of General Slim's Fourteenth Army was well under way. By mid-January 1945, the 19th Indian Division had reached the Irrawaddy and had joined up with the westernmost brigade of the 36th Division. Detachment 101 had provided a liaison team to work with the 19th Division. By mid-March the Fourteenth Army was knocking on the door of Mandalay. The Japanese 18th Division was sorely needed for the defense of Mandalay, so they were withdrawn from the Mongmit area except for one badly understrength regiment. Thereafter, the 36th Division had little difficulty in seizing Mongmit and, subsequently, Mogok, world-famed ruby center. By the end of March the 36th Division was also on the road, and the Allies now controlled it all the way from Mandalay to Kunming.

The activities in Area II were somewhat different from any we had ever conducted. The Japanese, with pressure on them, were retreating helter-skelter in every direction.

There were about twenty guerrilla units operating in Area II, each with one hundred to three hundred guerrillas. Some of the leaders included Lieutenants Scott, Weld, Archer, Coussoule, Conley, Martin, West, Pamplin, Hartman, Hansen, Larum, Truex, Meade, Pangborn, Powers, Poole, Romanski, Stein, Wright, Brophy, Milton and Major Saw Dhee Htu, ("Burma Sam") and Captain Brunstad. There were about thirty-five United States enlisted men with them.

Lieutenants Scott and Weld, both of whom had transferred to 101 from the Marauders, and Lieutenant Archer conducted several ambushes against the 18th Division north of Mongmit and severely stung the Japs. The Japs reacted strongly and attacked a defensive position these guerrillas had set up. The Japs had a strength of about seven hundred, and were resolved to wipe out the guerrillas, a hope they did not realize. The guerrillas finally withdrew, but not until they had inflicted heavy casualties upon the Japs. Lieutenant Scott was wounded in this action and had to be evacuated from the field.

West of Mongmit on the Thabeikkyin Road, Lieutenant Conley's guerrillas ambushed retreating Japs. In one instance they killed about sixty out of a hundred and in another they set a block on a trail and annihilated a group of forty. A few miles east of Conley's force Lieutenant "Hamp" Knight located a roadblock the Japs had set up. He attacked it with a force of about fifteen Kachins, killed two Japs and dispersed the remainder with grenades. Hamp had revenge on his mind. His younger brother, a master sergeant with the Mars Task Force, had been killed in the Namhpakka action. Posthumously he had been awarded the Congressional Medal of Honor, the only one in the CBI Theater.

From time to time Major Maddox consolidated the guerrilla forces into larger units. For example: Lieutenants Weld, West and Pamplin and Major Burma Sam all joined forces to cover the road from Mongmit to Maymyo. Lieutenant Coussoule was operating only a few miles north of Mandalay with a mixed force of Kachins and Gurkhas. He joined forces with Bill Martin's group and they began operating along the main road between Mandalay and Maymyo, blowing up a couple of large ammunition dumps, which deprived the Japs of ammunition for the defense of Mandalay at a time when they needed it most.

There was one group of Kachins in the training base which had been specially organized and was being held until the right opportunity presented itself. The unit was only about thirty strong, but every man had been selected because of his previous performance as a guerrilla; they were rough, rugged and primed for combat; they were led by Lieutenant Billy Milton, assisted by Anglo-Burmese from the O Group and a radio operator.

The proper situation finally developed along the roads leading to Mongmit and Mogok from the west. On a night drop, Billy's entire group was parachuted between the two roads so that they could operate against both arteries. The Japs in retreat before the Fourteenth Army were streaming through this area in a disorganized manner. One day Billy's unit ambushed a group of almost a hundred Japs on the Mongmit road, leaving only a few survivors. A few days later they hit the southern road and killed nearly fifty. In a two-week period this thirty-man group alone killed nearly three hundred Japs.

Further to the south beyond the Mandalay-Lashio Road Captain Larum and Lieutenant Truex each had groups of approximately three hundred guerrillas. These units conducted some effective raids, but their greatest value was the irritant effect and the threat they posed for the Japs. They also had agents and provided some excellent intelligence on Japanese activity between Maymyo and Kyaukme.

While all of these operations were underway, Area II agents were covering all the roads, railroads and trails in the Mandalay-Maymyo-Lashio area. They were keeping a close check on Japanese activity along the Irrawaddy River and its nearby roads. Their work in pinpointing targets for the 10th Air Force and the RAF was close to miraculous. We had a system of agents reporting targets from air photos, and Allied air strikes became devastatingly precise.

The Japanese had an internment camp in Maymyo. Agents of 101 were in contact with some of the prisoners, and sent messages by radio to be relayed to relatives. The internees were ill and suffering from malnutrition, so arrangements were made to drop medicine and certain concentrated foods to the agents to provide these people. We would have done it under any circumstances, but these packets gave our agents a good reputation with the local populace and greatly increased their capabilities.

A comparable arrangement was made in Mandalay. The letter from Monsignor Usher perhaps explains it more clearly.

Dear Colonel Peers: 9 May 1945

It is my pleasant duty to write on behalf of 22 missionary priests acknowledging a great debt we owe to you and your organization. During the Japanese occupation we were interned at the St. John's Leper Hospital, Mandalay. Your planes kept away most carefully from that area, so that not a single bomb fell within our enclosure.

I have been informed by Father Stuart that this was due to the special orders issued to the Air-Corps. We have the best reasons for appreciating very much your kindly action.

Will you please be so good as to convey our special thanks to Major Brown of your organization who took great pains to inform all sections of the Air Force of our whereabouts? He left nothing to chance and has thereby earned our deep gratitude.

Included among us were two American citizens, three Austrailasians, the rest Irishmen. In the same enclosure were a French Bishop, a few French priests, and nursing Sisters and other internal Sisters, in all about a hundred.

All of us shall ever remember in our prayers the success of your organization.

I am, dear Colonel Peers,
Yours very Sincerely,
P. Usher
Monsignor Patrick Usher
Catholic Bishop of Bhamo and North Burma

Not all of the intelligence operations in the Mandalay area were so successful. The HATE GROUP was the one notable failure. The reason for their failure was never determined. But from time to time the memory of this operation returns: we lost an entire group of five top-level agents. The leader and radio operator went in first. They collected some very valuable information and asked to have the other three members of the group parachuted in to them, which was done.

The group set up a base near Kyaukme and from there each man established cover for himself in towns and villages along the road. Things went well for a time, and we received some excellent intelligence reports. All of a sudden the entire net closed down. We waited and placed a special radio monitor on their frequency to pick up any signal, but could not find a trace of them. About a month later we learned they had been apprehended and assembled in Kyaukme by the Japanese. Exactly how or why they were picked up we were never able to know. Obviously, however, one must have been apprehended, broken down under interrogation, revealed the identity and location of another member and so on until the entire operation was uncovered. From Hsipaw the Japs moved them to the Lashio jail and, according to reports from other agents in the area, the prisoners were being subjected to extreme torture. One afternoon at about dusk a flight of three fighter bombers, as if by an act of providence, placed bombloads on the jail. The entire structure was levelled and the men no longer had to face prolonged torture.

General Sultan had advised 101 that, when the combat troops reached the Lashio-Mandalay line, we should take action to disband our guerrilla force. Some of the Kachins lived only a hundred miles away, but many more had come from well north of Myitkyina and had traveled nearly three hundred miles from home. They had been serving as guerrillas for over two years and were tired of fighting. They had satisfied their adventuresome, nomadic spirit and now wanted to see their families. The Area commanders prepared to inactivate their units. This involved many things such as pay, collection of weapons and equipment, awards, settlements for casualties, property damage and transportation home. Those Kachins whose homes were nearby we planned to send home on foot, while those who lived a considerable distance away, we planned to fly back to the airfield nearest their homes.

Besides the Citation for Military Assistance (CMA) which was awarded for feats of outstanding gallantry, 101 also initiated a Campaign Badge to be awarded all Kachin Rangers who had served with distinction against the enemy. It was a bar about three inches long, made of silver with BURMA CAMPAIGN engraved on its face and a lightning-slashed 101 in the center. They cost about $2.00 each to manufacture and were prized by the Kachins. We also had a shoulder patch made which was presented to them on discharge. It was red, white and blue along the lines of the CBI patch with KACHIN RANGERS embroidered across the top. The effect was tremendous. They were being treated as equals, not as mercenaries. They could hardly restrain their tears.

Everything was going well, but 101 had hardly more than begun inactivation of its guerrilla units before the situation in China became suddenly clouded with crisis. A couple of Japanese divisions started a drive which appeared headed for Chekiang and possibly Kunming. A decision was made to move the remaining Chinese divisions and the American infantry battalions to China earlier than had been planned. General Sultan called me in and informed me of the plan. He was deeply concerned because this would deprive him of his last combat soldier. He feared lest the newly opened Stilwell Road to China would be exposed to possible Japanese action north of Lashio. His main concern was the area south of Hsipaw-Maymyo where there were an estimated five to six thousand Japanese, mostly of the 56th Division. He was also concerned about the road from Taunggyi to Kengtung which the Japanese were using as an escape route to Thailand.

In the early spring of 1945 the British Fourteenth Army occupied Meiktila after a bloody battle. Part of the British thrust was then directed toward Mandalay, but even before that city was captured, General Slim turned the major portion of his Army south toward Pegu, Prome and Rangoon, the last of which was reoccupied in May. This operation cut off all Japanese forces to the west. They were sick and starved. They had to break up into small groups to try to filter through the lines and make their way to the safety of Thailand. Only a few of them succeeded.

General Sultan asked if I thought 101's ten thousand guerrillas could clear the Japs out of this area and seize the Taunggyi-Kengtung Road. Evidently, he had forgotten he had told us to disband and that it was already well in process. In addition, we had already sent a large number of our American personnel to join the

OSS unit in China. I explained to him why I thought we should go on with the inactivation, one of the main reasons being that we had told the Kachins, and they were returning home. Never once had we gone back on our word. Naturally, however, we wanted to do everything possible to achieve General Sultan's objective. With this in mind we queried each of the units and the following day I outlined what I thought we could do. Major Grones's battalion east of Lashio, and Major Lutkin's unit in the area of Hsipaw had been organized only a comparatively short time and both had done well in combat. We could retain a large percentage of these guerrillas. By obtaining volunteers from the other units we hoped to organize two additional battalions. Also, by recruiting from the local population we could obtain a sufficient number of guerrillas with previous military training to fill out all of the four battalions. We planned on deploying these battalions as independent units along a road or axis to the south to intercept the escape route to Thailand. General Sultan agreed to the plan and guaranteed all of the drop aircraft and tactical air support required to do the job.

Major Delaney took over Major Lutkin's battalion and immediately headed south through the hills. It was known as the 10th Battalion. The other three battalions were given approximately a month to reorganize, fill up, re-equip and train, prior to movement south. Major Grones retained his battalion, now known as the 1st Battalion. Lieutenant Colonel Newell Brown, who had served as the Area I intelligence officer, took command of one of the new battalions, the 2nd. Major Maddox, who had been with 101 from the first operation, took over the other battalion, the 3rd. It was both fitting and fortunate that Red took this battalion; it encountered the heaviest fighting and performed well under pressure.

XVII

The Final Mission

ᒍᒪᒍᒪᒍᒪᒍᒪᒍᒪᒍᒪᒍᒪᒍᒪᒍᒪᒍᒪᒍᒪᒍᒪᒍᒪᒍᒪᒍᒪᒍᒪᒍᒪᒍᒪᒍᒪᒍ

WE WERE TO MOVE OUT as infantry, take ground, hold ground. Our credentials were guerrilla. We knew we could whip the Japanese with guerrilla tactics, because we had done it time and time before. However, we also knew that the Kachins and other guerrillas in the unit could not stand up to the Japanese with formalized military tactics: they had not been trained for it, their equipment was not appropriate, they had seldom encountered artillery fire. With this in mind we assembled some of the more experienced guerrilla leaders to obtain their views, as well as those of the four commanders of the new battalions, to determine what type of tactics should be used. Some of the more useful principles that developed were these.

Our general tactics would have to combine the conventional and the unconventional. Straight infantry tactics would be essential at certain times, because the enemy would have to be physically ejected from his defensive positions, and because part of our mission was to comb the area so that no pockets of resistance would remain behind the guerrilla battalions. To the maximum extent, however, the guerrilla units were to remain light and mobile so that, with the heavy firepower from their light automatic weapons, they could move around the Japanese flanks to attack his defenses from the rear.

There could be no prescribed pattern of tactics for the battalions;

each unit had to develop tactics to fit its own requirements and scheme of maneuver. The 10th Battalion, for example, had a purely guerrilla mission: proceed through the hills, avoid contact with the Japs until they reached the area of Loilem, and there set up a base from which to conduct harassing, hit-and-run operations. The 3rd Battalion represented the opposite extreme. They were opposed by a vastly superior Japanese force which they were supposed to drive back to the Taunggyi area; to do so they had to use conventional tactics to a great extent. The situations of the 1st and 2nd Battalions lay somewhere between these two extremes. The fact was that their situations were all different, and 101 had to be flexible enough in its planning and logistics to meet the individual needs of these units.

From this, of course, stemmed a third important guerrilla principle. We had to place the utmost faith in the competence of the battalion commanders and in their ability to adjust the tactics to fit their own immediate situations. We gave them what are known as mission-type orders, *i.e.*, we told them what was wanted and left it up to them to determine how to do it. Each of these commanders was experienced in combat, guerrilla style. Lieutenant Colonel Brown had the least experience behind the lines (about nine months), while Red Maddox had the most, with nearly three years. Collectively, there was probably not a better group of guerrilla combat commanders any place in the world. They also had an excellent group of trained, experienced junior officers and non-commissioned officers. Likewise, the Kachin and other native guerrilla leaders were highly competent and had become accustomed to working with Americans. In the aggregate, they made a fairly awesome collection of guerrilla leaders, and anybody would have been highly pleased to have commanded them.

The final point concerned air supply. The airdrop procedures for supplying food, ammunition and sundries were satisfactory and would need no change. However, against certain Japanese strong points the guerrillas would probably need artillery support, but we did not want to encumber them with artillery and heavy loads of ammunition. In the area of Lashio, some of the battalions had encountered situations requiring artillery in which 4.2-inch mortars and ammunition had been dropped to them. This was a fine weapon, with nearly a four-mile range and the wallop of a 105mm howitzer. However, the battalions could not afford to weigh down the troops and lose mobility, so when they were through with the fire mission they blew up the weapon, its gunsight and the spare ammunition. This technique was adopted for each of the battalions; qualified mortar teams were shifted about as the situation demanded the 4.2 weapon.

The Japanese forces consisted of elements of the 18th and 56th Divisions estimated at 5,000 men scattered throughout the northern sector and a like number in the Loilem-Taunggyi-Kalaw area. These troops had artillery, tankettes and motor transport as well as the standard infantry armament. They were seasoned veterans and had adequate supplies. The paramount advantage of Detachment 101 was its intelligence network. Through this medium much was known about the Japanese strength and dispositions. The enemy, on the other hand, knew little of the activities or strength of Detachment 101.

Major Delaney's 10th Battalion started off the final mission in early April, 1945. His unit skirted Hsipaw and proceeded through the hills paralleling the road to the vicinity of Loilem. En route they encountered only one sizeable Japanese force of about sixty strong; they killed fourteen. By mid-April the battalion had established a redoubt in the hills overlooking the target — the Taunggyi-Kengtung Road — and was ready for action. During the next two months guerrilla patrols from the 10th Battalion roamed the areas far and wide and played havoc with the Japanese units. Hardly a day passed that a unit of the battalion wasn't engaged.

Toward the end of April a Japanese force of about company strength attempted to capture the guerrilla's field base camp and its light aircraft strip. The absence of many of the guerrillas, away on ambush work along the road between Loilem and Taunggyi, weakened the defenses of the field base camp. The battle for the base lasted over two days. In the end the guerrillas retained the camp with a loss of two men, while killing almost forty Japanese.

A small guerrilla force made a surprise attack on a Jap post north of Laihka. The guerrillas stole silently into the position and struck, killing seventeen, wounding many more. One truck was demolished and a warehouse burned. The enemy, thinking it was an attack in force, burned still another warehouse. The attacking guerrillas suffered no casualties.

By May, units of the battalion were striking repeatedly at the enemy lines of communication between Loilem and Taunggyi. In early May a convoy of ten trucks, loaded with about one hundred Japanese, was ambushed and attacked killing approximately fifteen Japs. Actions of this type upset the Japs so badly that they organized a force of five hundred, equipped it with artillery, and sent it north to seize the guerrilla base camp. The first encounter, on 8 May, resulted in thirty-five Japanese killed; there were no guerrilla casualties. Three days later the Japs continued the action and pushed the guerrillas back several miles, but they lost nearly thirty men while the guerrillas had only two wounded. After five costly days in which the Japs lost heavily, they learned they could not pin down the guerrillas and finally gave up their offensive.

To retaliate against the Japanese attack on his base camp, Major Delaney sent two companies of guerrillas to the Mongpawn area, where they ambushed road traffic and turned mortars on the Japanese Headquarters in the town itself. Over sixty-five Japs were reported killed in the three-day battle. A third guerrilla unit of about fifty men raided a Japanese camp west of Loilem. Of the one hundred-odd Japanese in the camp, seventy-six were killed, three trucks destroyed, and a gasoline dump burned, along with a warehouse and the entire set of barracks. A few days later near Mongpawn a Jap convoy of six trucks was caught in a double ambush, fore and aft, in which four trucks were burned and fifty-four enemy killed.

The 10th Battalion had become experts in the execution of pure guerrilla tactics. They refused to fight the enemy on his terms — the raiding of Jap camps and ambushing of motor columns were their primary tactics. These techniques proved highly successful. By mid-June the Japanese had given up completely the use of the road between Taunggyi and Mongpawn. The 10th Battalion was in complete control of this stretch of the road.

In the two and one-half months the 10th Battalion was in operation they killed three hundred and four Japs. Twenty-two vehicles were destroyed, along with numerous depots and storage areas. This battalion was nearly all Kachin. Their casualties were less than ten killed.

The 1st Battalion, under Major Dow Grones, was the first Detachment 101 unit to seize and hold a sizeable portion of the Taunggyi-Kengtung Road. This was quite an accomplishment. The battalion had only a few Kachins to serve as the nucleus, with the remainder of the unit, about seven hundred, consisting of Shans and Pidaungs, neither noted for their warlike nature. Dow worked with the smaller units, patiently and skillfully molding them into fighting formation. He had with him highly competent junior officers and NCO's such as Lieutenants Fitzhugh, Freudenberg, Hartman, Barnes and Harper. Within a period of five to six weeks they had the unit ready to move.

The battalion's mission was to move south, generally along the west bank of the Salween River, clearing out all pockets of Japanese resistance, until they reached the Taunggyi-Kengtung Road. Then they were to establish a roadblock to deny the Japanese the use of the road as an escape route to Thailand. Their first objective was Kehsi-Mansam, a state capital and a center of Shan culture. Light patrols probed the town, and a few days later the 1st Battalion struck with force to occupy it. One of the interesting highlights of this attack was that one of 101's most competent Shan agents was in the town. Before, and even during, the attack he was sending out information about the Japanese dispositions.

Patrolling by the 1st Battalion continued southward, and a few days later the road was reached. Here the battalion encountered a Japanese force of one hundred and fifty or more and drove them from a suspension bridge to the high, fortified ground to the south. Subsequent Japanese counterattacks drove the guerrillas from the bridge, but not until a considerable number of casualties had been inflicted on the enemy. A coordination of guerrilla attacks and aerial bombardment by the 10th Air Force rendered the bridge inoperable and beyond repair. Thus, the road was effectively closed. The guerrillas continued to harass the Japanese defenses on the high ground by sending patrols well south to attack them from the rear. The mobility and firepower of the guerrillas was such that there was little the Japs could do about them. In one instance a

guerrilla unit opened fire at point-blank range and killed over fifteen and wounded many more.

By the end of May the 1st Battalion had accomplished its mission and was systematically patrolling the road between the river and Namsang. In all of their engagements the 1st Battalion killed forty-eight Japanese without any of its forces being killed. The battalion had several wounded but Captain Woolington, the battalion medical officer, was always on hand, and only a few required evacuation to the Detachment hospital.

Lieutenant Colonel Newell Brown's 2nd Battalion had a rough job, one that provided little opportunity for any free maneuvering. Their mission was to advance due south along the first-class, paved road between Hsipaw and Loilem and to clear all Jap pockets of resistance as they advanced. They were also to establish some form of effective contact with the 1st Battalion on their left and the 10th on their right to insure that no Jap pockets were left behind in these adjacent areas.

Initially the 2nd Battalion encountered only scattered enemy resistance. They occupied Mongkung in early May and passed on toward Laihka. North of Laihka they captured two large dumps, one medical and the other ammunition. Both dumps were extremely well dug in and camouflaged, almost defying detection to anything but close-in ground reconnaissance. Considering the scale of the Japanese operations in Burma, these were huge depots, each spread out over a square mile or more, and they were by far the largest we had encountered in the entire Burma campaign. The hasty advance of the Battalion did not permit the Japanese to demolish the dumps, and they were seized intact. The medical supplies were surprisingly good and were an answer to 101's medical needs during the remainder of the campaign.

The town of Laihka contained three all-weather airstrips which had been constructed by the Japanese. The 2nd Battalion had expected a hot fire-fight for the town, but the Japs withdrew from it under the protection of a light covering force after setting off demolition charges on the runways. As the battalion moved south, however, they were met by increasingly stiff Japanese resistance. The guerrillas encountered several Japanese defensive positions and an ambush which stung more than hurt them. Both sides seemed willing to settle for a draw and pulled back a few miles to reorganize. The Japanese plan for the defense of the area was now becoming apparent. They had given up Laihka, which was located on an open, plain area and had withdrawn all of their troops to the tree-covered hill tracts to the south. This area offered them concealment, and they could dig in near the road leading south into Loilem and cover it with rifle and artillery fire. Loilem was the key to the Jap defenses. It was the main road junction with the Taunggyi-Kengtung Road, and there was no doubt that the Japanese intended to hold it at all costs. Major Brown's battalion contained a large percentage of experienced Kachin guerrillas. Brown's officers, Lieutenants Wright and Hansen and Captain Conklin and others, were also experienced guerrilla fighters. Some of the guerrillas were placed on extensive patrolling and they ranged far and

wide, often many miles south of Loilem. Colonel Brown accompanied one of his guerrilla patrols on the reconnaissance of a bridge.
They ran into some unexpected trouble with the result that he
was shot in the butt; however the wound was not serious, and he
remained in the field. As one of his companions jokingly put it,
"You can sure see which direction he was going." These patrols
verified the extent of the Jap defenses and in doing so also accounted for thirty-one dead Japs. Lieutenant Wright was wounded
on one of the patrols and had to be flown out to the hospital.

The situation around Loilem created a knotty paradox. On the
one hand we knew we had to occupy the town but, on the other, we
knew that if the guerrillas attacked the dug-in Japanese defenses
our defeat was likely. Certainly casualties would be high. The area
contained numerous volcanic peaks and the Japanese had dug their
defenses into the sides of the high slopes. The guerrillas tried to
attack a couple of times and had several wounded. One United
States sergeant was cut off from his patrol and killed on the slopes.
By the time the guerrillas were able to recover his body the Japs
had mutilated his arms and legs, almost dismembered him. It would
have been futile to continue the attacks; obviously a better solution had to be found.

After considerable thought, a procedure evolved which was
simple and effective. One of the Laihka airstrips would be put in
shape so that several fighter aircraft of the 10th Air Force could
be stationed there along with a few 101 liaison aircraft. These aircraft would work closely with the guerrillas to pinpoint and destroy
the Japs. General Gilkerson, commanding North Burma Air Task
Force, which had taken over in Northern Burma from the 10th Air
Force, was enthusiastic about the plan and readily agreed to make
available a flight of six P-38 aircraft with some of his best pilots.

The only problem we were then faced with was getting an airfield in condition. Major John Raiss was given the job and told to
get it done in three days. The Japanese had been thorough in their
demolition, so it presented a large assignment, especially with only
one large roller the Japs had failed to destroy and no means of
power. John employed large numbers of Shans to move rock and
dirt and he had them working night and day to get the job done.
At the end of the third day he sent in a message, "I am getting

awfully tired of pulling that damn roller. Please send me a jeep."
His request was fulfilled, and two days later the airfield was ready,
and the aircraft and their logistical support were en route to the
field.

To obtain air action on a defensive position the guerrillas would
locate the Japs and contain them in their defensive positions. A
message would be sent by radio to the airstrip, and one of the
liaison aircraft would be dispatched. By using walkie-talkie radios
the guerrillas were able to give the pilot specific instructions as to
the location of the Jap force. The guerrillas would then withdraw
under cover while the pilot dropped smoke grenades on the position. The operation was timed so that as the smoke grenade was
dropped, a P-38 loaded with napalm bombs would arrive on the
scene. Using the smoke as a marker, the pilot dropped his bombs.
After the flames had died out the guerrillas were able to occupy
the positions against light resistance. This operation was repeated
on several occasions and it was estimated that the attack aircraft
killed some four hundred Japanese.

The operation against Loilem lasted over ten days. The general
picture was of an outer ring of guerrillas probing an inner ring of
Japanese defenses while the town of Loilem itself remained almost
unoccupied. During the first four days the guerrillas cleared the
Japs east of the town and opened the road to Namsang, another,
larger airfield, which they took over and began using for supply
operations. A company of guerrillas were able to penetrate the
Japanese defenses but lacked the power to overrun a Japanese
force two to three times their size. They had to withdraw. The
guerrillas did not as yet control all their objectives, but their constant pressure, combined with the Air Corps attacks, was wearing
down the Japs.

General Sultan was greatly intrigued by the operation around
Loilem and wanted to see it firsthand. I accompanied him in his
C-47 to Laihka where he was met by Colonel Brown and Major
Raiss who reviewed the combat operations in their sector. That
afternoon the other battalion commanders, Majors Delaney, Maddox and Grones, were picked up in L-1's and flown to Laihka to
brief General Sultan on their operations. It was evident to all that
he was greatly pleased and then Major Raiss presented him with

a ten-thousand-mission Air Corps cap. It was a dirty, mangled, bedraggled thing, but the General even wore it boarding the aircraft. In returning he wanted to see Loilem, but on the edge of the town we started picking up ground fire and, since it was better to have a live theater commander than a dead hero, the pilot was directed to turn around and execute a maneuver known as getting the hell out of there.

General Sultan's trip was only the third time that a senior officer had visited the guerrillas behind the lines. The others, of course, were Donovan and Stilwell. There were strict orders against senior officers flying over or behind the lines even for reconnaissance. The obvious reason was that they were familiar with operational plans and, if the individual was captured by the Japanese, the loss of this key information would render serious damage to the Allied war effort. For the same reason those of us in 101 who were flying behind the lines every other day or so purposely learned only enough about the war plans to do our job. Additionally, when flying, a 101 officer also took along his map to assist in navigation. In the event that anything went wrong and the plane was forced down, he would know where he was and how to reach the nearest unit or how to walk out of the jungle. Moreover, to absolutely insure that the information the officer possessed did not fall into Japanese hands, such officers were drilled in what personal action they would have to take. They each carried a pistol and some also carried suicide pills to be used if necessary.

The break in the battle for Loilem came on the eighth day. The guerrillas, who had previously failed in their attack to capture a hill commanding the town, combined their assault with an extensive air attack. Although the Jap losses were comparatively small because their system of deep bunkers provided them with a high degree of protection from the napalm bombs, the pressure on them became so great that they were forced to withdraw; and the guerrillas gained control of the dominant terrain in the area. With their defenses thus penetrated, the Japanese began a general withdrawal, and within two days the guerrillas controlled the city and the surrounding area. Colonel Brown sent patrols eastward to establish contact with Major Grones's battalion and westward to contact Major Delaney. These battalions now controlled the road from

Mongpawn to the Salween River, and for all practical purposes their mission was complete. In this tough dog-eat-dog fight for control of the Hsipaw-Loilem Road, the 2nd Battalion reported only 127 Japanese killed, but the total number would have been much greater if those killed by close support air action had been taken into account.

Although each of the battalions performed most admirably, a great portion of the credit for their success must be given to the espionage agents who preceded them and provided them with a wealth of information concerning the Japanese and their activities. One of the most successful of these was Betty, who had infiltrated into the area eight or nine months previously from the area of Hsipaw.

The heaviest prolonged fighting Detachment 101 was ever engaged in and, for that matter, some of the heaviest fighting in all of Burma, took place in the 3rd Battalion area, with its hodgepodge of ethnic groups and nationalities. Kachins were the nucleus, there were also some Shans, Burmese, a platoon or more of Karens and even a few Palaung from the Inle Lake area, whose wives practice the art of stretching their necks by adding brass rings. There were also some Chinese, some Indians and, of course, British and Americans. This heterogeneous unit would have made an excellent United Nations force. Their initial strength was about seven hundred, but Red recruited as he moved south so that at times the battalion had a strength exceeding a thousand.

Red knew it was going to be a touch-and-go situation because all the agent reports had indicated strong Japanese forces in the Taunggyi region; but more were in the adjacent Heho area which had been the center of Japanese air operations in Burma; and still more had retreated into the area from Mandalay and Maymyo. To accomplish its mission, Red's unit had to head directly into the center of the Japanese strength. When the battalion had been assembled, given a rapid training course and organized into units, Red moved them south from the Burma Road and across the dangerous Namtu River. The river runs through rocky gorges and was swollen by early monsoon rains. They had a most perilous crossing. The men could only cross by use of a rope stretched taut across the river. The guerrillas knew this was the point of no return. With the increasing rains they could not expect to recross this river if forced back by the Japs. As the battalion moved south it engaged in a few local skirmishes and ambushed a few small Japanese units still retreating south from Mandalay. In these operations they killed about eighty-five Japs.

Red had a good group of junior officers, every one outstanding and experienced. A few that come to mind were Coussoule the Greek, Roger Hilsman, Hamp Knight, Ralph Truex, Bill Brough, Jim Ward, Norm Larum and a few others. Lieutenant Bill Martin was also in the area. He and eleven Kachins had parachuted in to an agent located outside Lawksawk. They later joined Red's battalion. The NCO's in Red's battalion were also a very fine group.

By the end of April the battalion had reached Lawksawk, which at the time had only about two hundred Japs in it. Red's plan was for two companies to block the road to the southwest leading to Pangtara, and two companies to block another road leading to the southeast. The remaining four companies were to assault the city from the north. The Japanese, however, had other ideas. They reinforced the city with seven hundred additional troops, and, early in the morning of 7 May, preceded by a heavy artillery barrage, moved north against the guerrilla force which numbered about four hundred. These Japs were still in a fighting mood and in all probability wanted to teach the guerrillas a lesson. The guerrillas stood up well against repeated banzai charges as the battle went on from 2 A.M. to 2 P.M. Finally, with their ammunition running low, the guerrillas withdrew in good order to the north. Nine guerrillas were killed and fifteen wounded. A conservative estimate of Japanese casualties was set at two hundred and eighty. Also, the natives reported that over eighty bullock-drawn cartloads of wounded were seen moving to the rear.

In the action around Lawksawk there were a few large, critical battles, but in addition there were numerous small engagements going on almost continuously. In one instance Lieutenant Ward's guerrilla company was in constant engagement with the Japs for eight days. Remnants of the Japanese 15th and 18th Divisions were still filtering through the area in hopes of reaching Taunggyi and an escape route. To save the maximum number of these troops and to prevent the guerrillas from seizing control of the entire area, the Taunggyi garrison was trying desperately to hold a few key points to the north, principally Lawksawk and Pangtara.

While the battle for Lawksawk was going on, Lieutenants Martin and Coussoule with their two companies attacked and occupied Pangtara, a sizeable village about twenty-five miles southwest. Pangtara was a critical point which the Japs could not afford to lose, so they assembled a force of about six hundred to re-occupy the town. The Japanese deployed their forces skillfully to the west and attacked the defensive positions set up by the guerrillas. They were stopped abruptly with numerous casualties, but sent out flanking units north and south to envelope the two-hundred-odd guerrillas. The guerrillas withdrew from the town and established a defensive position outside the town. The defensive position was so set up that it amounted to a large-scale ambush. When the Japs attacked, they were caught in a deadly cross fire from the units which had been hidden out on either flank. In this engagement, the Japs lost heavily, over one hundred. The losses of 101 were our heaviest for any engagement of the war: thirty dead, several wounded and about twenty missing.

Red's units had performed well under fire in the battles for Lawksawk and Pangtara, but they had been hurt and their supplies were all but exhausted. Consequently he withdrew the forces to hills a few miles north of Lawksawk to re-equip, reorganize and lick their wounds. A medical officer, Lieutenant Hutter, with the necessary medical supplies, was parachuted into the unit. He did an excellent job and saved numerous lives. Red built an airstrip so that light planes could pick up the wounded, and within two days the fifteen seriously wounded men had been returned to the hospital.

One key operation was conducted by a mixed company of Kachins, Burmese and Karens under Lieutenant Roger Hilsman. Red had them operating independently of the remainder of his battalion in the area between Lawksawk and Taunggyi, where they carried out several highly successful raids and ambushes against the Japanese. They were becoming most bothersome to the Japs, and an enemy unit of two hundred strong with pack animals was put on their trail. They seemed to have the guerrillas on the run and in a bad way. At this stage the guerrillas staged an ambush. It consisted of two cases of grenades, about fifty of them, connected electrically so they could be detonated simultaneously in an ambush area which was covered by Bren guns and other automatic weapons. The advance enemy guard, approximately a platoon, was allowed to pass through the ambush area, but when the main body entered, the grenades were set off and the area thoroughly sprayed with automatic fire. The guerrillas suffered no casualties, but the Japanese lost one hundred and four soldiers and eleven horses. Subsequently, Roger requested permission to move his unit south of Taunggyi into the Inle Lake area. We would have liked to have permitted this, but the orders from General Sultan were to seize and hold the road, so his request for deeper deployment to the south had to be disapproved.

As soon as the reorganization was completed, Red had the units again on the move. Many small ambushes were conducted, several bridges destroyed, and some motor transport was shot up. These and other activities severely restricted the enemy, and he chose to withdraw all of his forces into Taunggyi rather than face annihilation. Lawksawk was re-occupied 1 June, Pangtara on 8 June and, by 15 June, the unit was only five miles from Heho with patrols and demolition crews already in operation on the road. When elements of Red's battalion established contact with the British 64th Brigade pushing toward Taunggyi from the west, we ordered him to move his forces north to the area of Pangtara, for eventual disbandment.

The 3rd Battalion had done a truly remarkable job. Within a period of less than ninety days they had killed over six hundred Japs, captured five and wounded many more. They had their hard times, but they won the battle. This action completed the mission of Detachment 101 to seize the Taunggyi-Kengtung Road. On 1 July orders were issued to inactivate the unit as soon as possible.

General Sultan was greatly pleased. For its action during the period 8 May to 15 June 1945, he recommended Detachment 101 for a Presidential Distinguished Unit Citation. The award reads as follows:

GENERAL ORDERS   WAR DEPARTMENT
WASHINGTON 25, D.C., 17 JANUARY 1946
Service Unit Detachment No. 101, Office of Strategic Services, is cited for outstanding performance of duty from 8 May to 15 June 1945 in capturing the strategic enemy strong points of Lawksawk, Pangtara, and Loilem in the Central Shan States, Burma. This unit, composed of approximately 300 American officers and men, volunteered to clear the enemy from an area of 10,000 square miles. Its subsequent activities deprived the Japanese 15th Army of the only East escape route and secured the Stilwell Road against enemy counterattack. Although DETACHMENT 101 had been engaged primarily in intelligence and guerrilla activities, it set about the infantry mission of ousting a determined enemy from a sector long fortified and strategically prepared. These American officers and men recruited, organized, and trained 3,200 Burmese natives entirely within enemy territory. They then undertook and concluded successfully a coordinated 4-battalion offensive against important strategic objectives through an area containing approximately 10,000 battle-seasoned Japanese troops. Locally known as "Kachin Rangers," DETACHMENT NO. 101 and its Kachin troops became a ruthless striking force, continually on the offensive against the veterans of the Japanese 18th and 56th Divisions. Throughout the campaign, the Kachin Rangers were equipped with nothing heavier than mortars and had to rely entirely upon air-dropped supplies. Besides a numerical superiority of three to one, the enemy had the advantage of adequate supplies, artillery tankettes, carefully prepared positions, and motor transportation. Alternating frontal atacks with guerrilla tactics, the Kachin Rangers remained in constant contact with the enemy during the entire period and persistently cut him down and demoralized him. During the vicious struggle for Lawksawk, 400 Rangers met 700 Japanese veterans supported by artillery and, in a 12-hour battle, killed 281 of the enemy while suffering only 7 casualties. They took Loilem, central junction of vital roads, despite its protecting system of bunkers and pillboxes, after 10 days of unremitting assaults. Under the most hazardous jungle conditions, Americans of DETACHMENT NO. 101 displayed extraordinary heroism in leading their coordinated battalions of 3,200 natives to complete victory against an overwhelmingly superior force. They met and routed 10,000 Japanese throughout an area of 10,000 square miles, killed 1,247 while sustaining losses of 37, demolished or captured 4 large dumps, destroyed the enemy motor transport, and inflicted extensive

damage on communications and installations. The courage and fighting spirit displayed by the officers and men of SERVICE UNIT DETACHMENT NO. 101, OFFICE OF STRATEGIC SERVICES, in this successful offensive action against overwhelming enemy strength, reflect the highest traditions of the armed forces of the United States. (General Orders 278, Headquarters United States Army Forces, 16 November 1945, as approved by the Commanding General, India-Burma Theater.)

OFFICIAL: DWIGHT D. EISENHOWER
   EDWARD F. WITSELL   Chief of Staff
   Major General
   Acting the Adjutant General   (81073)

Setting a Goal

ᒐᒐᒐᒐᒐᒐᒐᒐᒐᒐᒐᒐᒐᒐᒐᒐᒐᒐᒐᒐᒐᒐ

ON 12 JULY 1945 an order was published inactivating OSS Detachment 101. We had had a life-span of approximately three and a half years, of which nearly three years involved actual guerrilla combat. Our start had been delayed because, before you can go about the business of organizing guerrillas, you need espionage agents to tell you where to begin. You never get anywhere in the guerrilla business without what might be called the "proper introductions." It's very well to say that you are going to arm so many guerrillas; but who are they to be? Espionage might not shake up an army the way a guerrilla band can, but espionage plays an important role; it leads you to the guerrillas, makes the introductions. And espionage continues as a presence after the guerrillas are formed. The espionage effort shows the guerrilla where the enemy is; and how desirable it is to strike. Any good guerrilla band must adopt the habit of good espionage.

We profited from our early mistakes. When we confined our guerrilla recruiting to the Kachins, we began to have an influence on the Myitkyina campaign.

As our guerrillas became more involved in fire-fights, raids and ambushes, the supply problem became overwhelming. The size of the 101 force was expanding rapidly and the tempo of operations was likewise increasing; hence it became essential that our aerial supply organization be further augmented and the procedures improved. Up to this point, with but few exceptions, we tried to supply the field units on an item-for-item basis, just as one would try to fill out a shopping list for a grocery or department store. This, however, was tedious, time consuming and impractical for large-scale operations. Consequently, we developed what we termed "standard drops." Such drops were pre-packaged, as it were, and included various proportions of ammunition, food and equipment. Information lists concerning the contents of these drops were supplied to the field. The field leader simply sent the number of the standard drop he required and gave the details of time and place for delivery. He used the standard list to the maximum, but was also permitted to ask for any special items he needed for operations. We made it a policy to include a bottle of bourbon now and then, books, magazines and an occasional treat such as a tin of cookies. These small luxuries tended to break up the monotony of jungle life.

In addition, the drop section also prepared what was termed "emergency drops." These were composite drops made up mostly of food and ammunition. They were all packed in aerial delivery containers with the chutes tied on and ready to go. Several of these emergency drops were assembled and retained in close proximity to a forward airfield. Then, if a guerrilla unit got into a fight and exhausted its supplies, it could send in a pre-arranged message giving the place and time for the drop. In as little as thirty minutes the emergency drop could be loaded aboard an airplane and sent on its way. Later, when our units were heavily engaged, we had to make a daily average of one to two emergency drops. In almost every drop, there was a quantity of shoes, for the Kachin guerrilla was curiously fond of a pair of shoes. Normally, the Kachins rarely wore shoes, but as a guerrilla, he was anxious to own them. Shoes meant prestige. Along the trail, the guerrillas walked barefooted, but upon approaching a village, they stopped, put on their shoes and marched through the village. On the other side, they took the shoes off, hung them around their necks, and went on their way.

For each aerial resupply drop we needed about fifteen parachutes, sometimes many more. The small broadcloth chutes we procured from the British via Lend-Lease cost about $12.00 while the larger United States rayon chute cost about $75.00. When we got up to dropping over twelve planeloads of supplies a day we were using well over two hundred chutes daily and they were difficult to obtain. Initially, we tried to have them collected in the field to be returned to the 101 airdrop station at Dinjan. This, however, proved impractical. There was no way to care for them adequately in the field; they rotted away, and there was a great deal of difficulty in getting them to places where they could be picked up by airplanes. Perhaps more important, the Kachins had been without any form of cloth for years and the material in these chutes made ideal gifts. For these reasons, we decided to let the field commander dispose of the chutes as he saw fit. By the end of the war a large percentage of the Kachin population had the mark of 101 on them: they were dressed in longies or Shan bombies made of colored parachute material.

In collecting and reporting intelligence we also refined our procedures. We found, for example, that information reported by the Kachins was generally highly accurate, but that their reports of enemy strength were almost invariably about three times the actual figures. Strength reporting was then stressed in the training program to the extent that the pendulum swung the other way, and later on the strengths given in Kachin agent reports had to be *increased* by a factor of three. It was not until the middle of 1944 that it was possible to obtain reliable strength figures from Kachin agents. Other ethnic groups were found to have comparable traits, more or less uniform within each group. The Chinese had the greatest inclination toward exaggeration. Their strength figures had to be reduced approximately ten times, and this practice remained constant to the end of the campaign.

Experience taught us that agents recruited from the Indian refugee camps could seldom operate safely in Burma. They had been away from their country and area for so long that they were no longer familiar with the day-to-day life. Consequently, it was difficult to establish plausible cover stories for them. This, in turn, caused them to be tense and to overplay their part, which too often resulted in detection by the Japanese or native informants. For this reason, we changed the entire procedure for obtaining our agents. Soon after we started operations, we began recruiting agents from inside occupied Burma, where we had sufficient guerrilla units in contact with local populations. These agents were naturally selected with an eye toward intelligence and courage. They were top people and, once chosen, were infiltrated back through the Japanese lines, either individually or as a part of a group, depending upon how they were to be used in future operations. Our underground railroad for getting these people out of Burma was never discovered by the enemy.

Safely in Nazira, the agents were put through rigorous training courses. If they were to operate alone or as part of a larger group, their training normally required three months. The training of a radio operator required about four months, at the end of which time he would be sending and receiving an average of fifteen to twenty-five words per minute; he was also capable of operating and maintaining his set. If an agent was to operate alone *and* as his own radio operator, his training took five months. When an agent's training was completed, he was put into operations as quickly as possible. Delays invariably produced lethargy, even tears. So as soon as his training was done, the agent either parachuted, walked or was air-landed behind the lines. In some cases, he operated under the Area commander, but more often, he was on his own. He, too, recruited new agents so that the cycle started all over again.

The Detachment's counterintelligence operations were purely defensive, designed to protect 101 and its field operations from infiltration by enemy agents, and were eminently successful in maintaining our security.

Somewhat more sophisticated, if not Machiavellian, was our morale operation, known as MO. Its object was black propaganda. This meant that we would make up a fake order that appeared to come from the Japanese high command, urging Jap soldiers to lay down their arms. The document was authentic enough in tone and appearance to fool a number of Japanese. Following its instructions, they surrendered. This was a subtle kind of propaganda, which, if employed properly, could cause the enemy to lose faith in his leaders and fellow soldiers. Another devilish trick which MO used on several occasions concerned quislings. A simple letter forged in a Japanese soldier's handwriting might find its way into the hands of the Kempi Tai, the occupation secret police. The forged letter purported to be an offer by the quisling to work for the Allies. It was convincing enough to make the Japanese put the unfortunate fellow out of the way.

How do you get an operation started? There are two basic methods. One is to select an area, preferably isolated, and parachute people in without benefit of a friendly group on the ground to receive them. This type of infiltration can also be accomplished by submarine or other maritime means, or by use of land routes. It is called a "blind drop" or "blind landing" and is difficult and dangerous. We tried a total of four such operations and only one was successful. In the process about fifteen well-trained agents were lost. One thing wrong with our initial blind drops was the groups: they were too large. We decided to reduce the size to two men, a chief agent and a radio operator, and to experiment with three more operations.

One group was landed by submarine north of Tavoy. They were to be picked up fifteen days later upon proper identification signals to a submarine. When the submarine returned they received improper light signals from land. The submarine waited a short while, and then received word from an accompanying destroyer that a Jap cruiser was approaching. The submarine submerged and got out of the area as quickly as possible. Our group had obviously been captured. Another group of two Burmese was dropped in the area of Bassein, outside Rangoon. They made a successful landing, buried their parachutes and a couple of days later came on the air with their radio. However, shortly thereafter they were picked up by the Japanese and made to talk. Fortunately, they knew little about 101 operations because they had been isolated in training. They were put in the Rangoon jail, where they remained for the duration.

The third group was composed of two Kachins, Tu and La. We referred to the operation as TULA. We dropped them in a remote area south of Bhamo and about thirty miles from where they were to operate. Everything went perfectly with this group. They worked slowly and, on the tenth day, came on the air as scheduled. In time they established a few sub-agents and were able to obtain reliable and timely information about Japanese activity as far away as Mandalay and Lashio.

In view of our low batting average with these blind drops, we employed them only when we absolutely had to, and we kept them limited to two men.

The other type of introduction into operations is the reception. A group already in operation selects a drop site, makes all the arrangements on the ground, is on hand to signal the drop aircraft and receive the new group when it lands. This arrangement makes possible a fast and professional job of burying the chutes, clearing the drop zone of any telltale signs, then leading the new group well away to a safe hideout until they can get started in operations. This process worked successfully innumerable times and became 101's standing operating procedure.

Hardly a Japanese force moved in Burma without 101's guerrillas or agents knowing about it. When the Japanese began to move at night to avoid detection, our guerrillas, too, took up the challenge and acted at night.

Some of our best work was done during the battle for Myitkyina. When our guerrillas suddenly appeared to strike at Japanese columns rushing to reinforce their beleaguered garrisons, our value was clear. Also there were critical moments in the final phases of the campaign when guerrillas were called upon to serve as line infantry. Detached though the guerrillas were from the conventional forces, we took few steps indeed that were not meant to aid directly the conventional forces.

Our Detachment 101 guerrillas were greatly assisted in their job because they got the best of weapons. We insisted that their firepower be infinitely superior to the enemy's. Since a guerrilla is to strike fast, it followed that he must also strike with a firepower the enemy could not match.

In jungle warfare, where the Japanese were rated high, 101's guerrillas performed even better. Our camouflage, our routes through the jungle, our vigor were superior to the Japanese, and so highly developed that Japanese prisoners willingly conceded that their confidence in themselves underwent serious strain.

The jaunty, devil-may-care attitude of some of our junior officers and NCO's, arriving fresh from the States with a gung-ho spirit, was turned, through intensive training, into effective and dependable leadership. Any man who lost this spirit in training and decided not to go into the field (every man was a volunteer) could have had numerous useful, alternative jobs at base. Yet in three years of operation only one man ever indicated he did not want to go to the field.

In trying to analyze the effects of 101 operations there are tangible results which are comparatively easy to review and comprehend. There are others, however, which are not so tangible, such as estimates concerning the volume of useful intelligence provided, the action taken on air targets which had been designated, and so on.

On the tangible side the following are some statistics taken from the Northern Combat Area Command historical account for the entire Northern and Central Burma campaigns and which can be reasonably well substantiated:

Japanese killed (known)	5,428
Japanese killed or seriously wounded (estimated)	10,000
Japanese captured	75
Bridges destroyed	51
Railroad trains derailed	9
Military vehicles destroyed	277
Supplies destroyed (estimated)	3,000 tons
Supplies captured (estimated)	700 tons
U. S. Air Force personnel rescued	232
Other Allies rescued or flown out	342

The figures above may require a brief explanation. In using the term "known" Japanese killed, it should be recognized that it represents only an educated estimate. It would be foolhardy for a group of guerrillas to remain in an ambush or raid area trying to figure out how many of the enemy were killed. This would be inviting disaster and could only lead to additional losses for the guerrillas. An enemy was classified as "killed" only if he was hit and knocked down and if the casualty was substantiated by two or more observers. Later, when checks had been made by agents, the account might be modified, if necessary. In many instances these reports corroborated the previous count; sometimes the results had to be reduced; but in a great number of cases the agent's report far exceeded the guerrilla account. Thus, the term "known" is meant to be only as accurate as was possible under the circumstances.

The question is asked, "Were all of those killed Japanese?"

A very great percentage were, but not all. In the early days particularly, a few members of the Burma Liberation Army often were mixed in with Japanese units. The guerrilla did not try to ascertain the nationality of those they killed. If the individual was in uniform and carried a weapon, that was enough proof for the guerrillas to classify him as an enemy.

With respect to the number estimated killed or wounded, many small actions took place in isolated areas and involved only one or two guerrillas. There was no way to corroborate the results, and as a consequence, they were not included in the over-all total. Also, in nearly every one of the larger guerrilla actions there were numerous borderline cases. A guerrilla might turn loose with a fully automatic submachine gun at a group of Japs at a point-blank range of ten feet, but not stay long enough even to see the results. The guerrilla's first function is his own survival and he cannot take any unnecessary risks. These actions took place in the jungle, often so thick one could only see a few feet ahead. This too obscured viewing the results, and prevented establishing any form of definite count. In almost all actions the estimation of results tended toward the conservative side. For example, in the operation along the Irrawaddy when the Japanese were trying to evacuate Myitkyina, the guerrillas accounted for many enemy dead. For nearly seven days and nights their outposts along the river were shooting the enemy off boats and rafts. They estimated only about three hundred killed, but afterward all of the backwaters were literally covered with floating dead. Their estimate easily could have been doubled and possibly trebled.

Some of the key people in 101 and of NCAC, keeping these facts in mind, were queried as to how many they would estimate were killed by 101. The consensus of opinion was about ten thousand. There is no way of either proving or disproving this figure.

Some of the other results were far more conclusive. They could be determined positively without a shadow of doubt. Of these there were the 75 Japanese captured, interrogated and turned over to the military for imprisonment. In this same category were the United States airmen who were rescued from behind enemy lines, brought by one means or another to within friendly lines, and returned to their own units. The other 342 Allied military people recovered from behind enemy lines represented a wide variety of nationalities: many of them were British, Burmese and Indian soldiers from the two Wingate expeditions. Others were Chinese from the first Burma campaign. Still others were Americans who had been wounded or otherwise incapacitated and had to be flown out. Not included in the total were large numbers of Burmese, Shans, Karens and other native personnel who were flown out from behind the Japanese lines to prevent reprisal upon them or their families. There was an almost constant flow of this type of person and no effort was made to maintain a statistical check upon them.

Some other unshakable statistics include the bridges, trains and vehicles destroyed or derailed and the tonnage of supplies and equipment destroyed or captured.

On the intelligence side, estimates were made by the agencies who used the results. The two large users were NCAC Headquarters and the 10th Air Force. The G-2 of NCAC estimated that Detachment 101 provided NCAC with between 85 and 95 per cent of all usable intelligence. Considering all of the numerous sources available to that command, including Chinese, British and American troops, prisoner of war interrogations, aerial photography and a wide variety of other sources, the magnitude of the 101 intelligence collection effort can be readily appreciated. According to the 10th Air Force, up to 85 per cent of the targets attacked by them were initially designated by 101. As they improved their own target detection capabilities, principally through aerial photography, the number of targets designated by 101 tapered off to about 60 to 65 per cent — still a very respectable figure. After a target had been attacked by the Air Corps, 101 agents surveyed it to estimate the amount of destruction. Detachment 101 would submit damage assessment reports to the 10th Air Force to assist them in determining whether or not additional air attacks would be required. Based upon the damage assessment reports, 10th Air Force estimated that they killed on the order of 11,000 Japanese. This figure is probably very conservative.

Other Statistics on Detachment 101

Americans killed	22
Native personnel killed	184
Native personnel captured or missing	86
Total agents lost	38
Greatest number native troops (Feb. 1945)	10,200
Agent groups with radio, parachuted or overland	122
Total 101 personnel in Northern Burma operation (does not include Calcutta or Southern Burma)	131 officers
	558 enlisted
Total Americans parachuted into operations	187
Total native personnel parachuted into operations	247
Total casualties from parachute jumps	0

All things taken into account, the United States, Allied and native troops of Detachment 101 suffered comparatively light losses. Only three Americans were killed in behind-the-lines combat; most of the remainder were killed as a result of aerial combat action or air crashes. On the other hand, all of the natives killed or missing were the result of enemy ground action. A large percentage of the 101 casualties were sustained during the final phase when the detachment had to combine its guerrilla tactics with conventional tactics. There are undoubtedly many explanations why Detachment 101 casualties were so light, but perhaps the outstanding reasons were our mobility and hit-and-run tactics; the Kachins' intimate knowledge of the area and of the jungles; the simple, light, rapid-fire weapons; and, of course, air supply, which gave the guerrillas a maximum of mobility and flexibility.

The important thing in guerrilla operations is not altogether how many of the enemy were killed or wounded, but what influence did guerrilla operations have upon our own friendly forces and upon those of the enemy? The United States and other Allied ground forces in Northern Burma looked upon Detachment 101 as their eyes and ears. The 101 guerrilla forces formed advance and flank patrols, set up reconnaissance screens, scouted the enemy and prevented our forces from being surprised or ambushed. This was a tremendous boost to the Allied forces. They could feel secure in the knowledge that the guerrillas were far ahead of them, on their flanks, and all about them, to prevent their being taken by surprise.

Within the Air Corps there were somewhat varied appreciations. Our intelligence reports and damage assessments were vitally important to the accomplishment of the mission of the 10th Air Force; however, from the viewpoint of the individual crewman, 101's widespread activities behind the Japanese lines provided him a hope of coming out alive in the event he was shot or forced down behind the lines. In the early days these men were frightened and they had a right to be. The dense jungles and jagged mountains of Northern Burma were in themselves frightening. The thought of being forced down in them did not make their task any easier; nor did the presence of the Japanese air and ground forces.

After the first few groups were rescued from behind the lines, there was a noticeable improvement in the morale of the Air Corps. It continued to improve with additional rescues until, finally, the crewmen took it almost as a matter of course that they would be brought out safely.

The operations of Detachment 101 and the other British and American clandestine organizations had a considerable impact upon the thinking and actions of the Burmese people.

British Force 136 operating in Central and Southern Burma, another British Intelligence Agency covering areas south of Mandalay, and Detachment 101 AFU (Arakan Field Unit) operating along the Burma west coast, must all be considered as a unit. It was the aggregate effects of all of these operations which gradually converted the Burmese people from hostility to the Allied cause to eventual armed rebellion against the Japanese.

The attitude of the Burmese did not change overnight; it was a slow process. Each guerrilla and espionage operation was proof that the Allies were coming back to Burma. Our propaganda was strong enough to counteract the Japanese propaganda. The longer the Japanese stayed the more evident it became that Burma was occupied territory and that individual liberties were far more restricted than they had been under the British government.

It was not only the presence of the clandestine organizations that caused the Burmese to make the final break with the Japanese. It was a combination of many things. One of the most important factors was that the Japanese were losing the war.

What the clandestine agencies did was to provide a rally point, a cause, a meaning for national aspirations. By the end of the war, the indigenous Burmese forces of Aung San numbered thousands, and, when Britain granted Burma its independence in 1948, the Burmese were ready for us to take over and maintain the internal security of the country. When Burma became independent as a nation, the Kachins were the backbone of the Burma Army in its fight against Communism and other dissident movements within Burma. Always steady, the Kachins were the vital force of 101 in its guerrilla operations. They were the fighters who raised the flag of freedom in the jungles of Burma. As guerrillas, they never lost a battle. It was the Kachins who wrote the splendid accomplishments of 101.

Appendix

LՐLՐLՐLՐLՐLՐLՐLՐLՐLՐLՐLՐLՐLՐLՐLՐLՐLՐLՐ

THE FOLLOWING is a list of American, British and Burmese military personnel associated with the 101 operations in Northern Burma. Every effort has been made to insure that the list is correct and any error in listing is purely one of oversight. Detachment 101 personnel who served so commendably in the Calcutta Field Office and the Arakan Field Unit in Southern Burma are not listed herein, since complete rosters of such personnel were not maintained. Also not listed are the personnel of the 71st Liaison Squadron who were not members of 101 but attached to it. To a man, they served with distinction. We could not have accomplished our mission without their help.

Detachment 101 did not have any women in its ranks; however, one of the girls (Ann Palko) from the Calcutta Office was attached to 101 for a period of about six weeks under field conditions. She worked around the clock completing the personnel records of 101's eleven thousand or so guerrillas. For her heroic and untiring efforts, she was made an honorary member of 101 and is so listed.

ROSTER OF DETACHMENT 101

Aalbu, Sigurd J.
Abbot, Delbert H.
Achelis, John
Adam, Ben
Adams, Allen G.

Adams, Robert E.
Aitken, Robert T.
Albers, George E.
Albert, Daniel L.
Alderdice, Joseph E.

Anderegg, Donald E.
Anderson, Clayton E.
Andros, Anthony M.
Archer, Elton W.
Ardinger, Joe E.
Arida, Edward
Armstrong, Howard H.
Armstrong, Jay
Asher, William B.
Aubry, Arthur S.
Aubry, Jules W.
Auerbach, Herbert

Baba, Tom T.
Babb, John E.
Bacon, Charles A.
Bailey, Thomas
Baker, James A.
Baldwin, Thomas
Baldy, Robert N.
Balfour, Francis A.
Banbury, Wesley G.
Banker, Harold J.
Barcia, Thomas
Barlet, William M.
Barnard, Jack
Barnes, Ed
Barnes, Ted U.
Barnwell, Dan
Barrett, Neil H.
Barrett, Norman W.
Barrows, Dayton S.
Barry, Mario J.
Barry, Wesley E.
Barry, William S.
Bassford, James A.
Beamish, John
Beaver, Muriel M.
Beebe, Robert
Bell, Fred
Benedict, Bruce
Berge, Walter A., Jr.
Berry, Clifford J.
Betsui, Richard K.
Bezverkov, John T.
Black, Melvin H.
Blackshear, Perry L.
Blonski, John F.
Bodgen, Wesley S.
Bodner, David
Bohny, Charles R.

Boldt, George
Bolte, Guy
Bopp, George A.
Bostwick, William F.
Bouchea, Ernest J.
Boyack, Robert T.
Boyd, Don C.
Bradley, John C.
Branch, Ross B.
Brannon, Bennie
Breen, John P.
Brelis, Constantine Dean
Brewer, Dicky T.
Brewer, Ray J.
Brickelmayer, George
Brinton, Dilworth C.
Brock, Alexander B.
Broderick, Lawrence
Brophy, Bernard
Brotman, Stanley
Brough, William
Brown, John D.
Brown, Keith J.
Brown, Newell
Bruce, Charles
Brunstad, Art
Buchanan, Jack C.
Buck, Edgar I.
Budz, Walter A.
Burchill, John J.
Burgan, John K.
Burtch, Lyman D.
Bush, Howard T.
Buto, Junichi
Byrne, John J.

Cameron, Elton
Camp, Earl C.
Camp, Roger C.
Campbell, Roger C.
Canfield, Ward L.
Cardacino, Michael
Carlson, Gus R.
Carrico, Ben F.
Carroll, William J.
Carrozzo, Vincent
Cassidy, David S.
Cate, Robert B.
Cathala, Charles
Cavanaugh, Dennis
Chadsey, Carl T.

Chamales, Theodore T.
Chambreau, William J.
Champion, Tom W.
Chang, Sukyoon
Charleston, Morton L.
Chartier, Louis Y.
Chartrand, Chester R.
Chayes, Aaron H.
Christian, Waldimar
Chun Ming, Archie
Ciezadlo, Joe V.
Clark, Vernon
Cloyd, James C.
Cocoris, Nick J.
Cody, Chester
Coffey, L. M.
Cogerian, Trayone J.
Colling, John G.
Conaughty, Charles L.
Cone, Charles W.
Conklin, Hugh R.
Conley, Ed
Connell, Orwald G.
Conrad, Louis W.
Constable, Claude K.
Cooper, Rollo W.
Cotten, Charles
Coughlin, John G.
Council, Harry G.
Coussoule, Charles
Cox, Charles W.
Crafts, Cecil
Crowley, Robert E.
Culverson, Lester E.
Cummings, William H.
Curl, Vincent
Curtis, Earle J.

Dalton, Robert A.
Dalverty, Thomas H.
Damen, Edward M.
Danielewicz, Ed. G.
Daugherty, Thomas
Davenport, John H.
Davis, Howell A.
Davis, John R.
Davis, Thomas J.
Day, Linard F.
Delaney, Robert J.
Dempsey, John D.
Denham, Archie L.

Dennhardt, Don J.
Derocker, Francis J.
Devins, Gordon D.
Devlin, Frank
DeWeese, Ralph A.
DeWeese, Robert C.
Dhee Htu, Saw
Dietz, Glenwood A.
Dinner, Richard S.
Diomandes, Damon S.
Dobberstein, Albert
Donovan, Henry P.
Donovan, John P.
Dorman, Charles J.
Downard, Robert E.
Draper, John W.
Draves, Dean S.
Drown, George
Dudley, John J.
Dumond, Eugene C.
Duncan, Joe B.
Dunlop, Richard
Dunning, Victor R.

Ebaugh, Zacharia C.
Eckhardt, Eric
Eckhoff, Oscar E.
Edwards, James W.
Ehrlich, Murray
Eichenberger, Clifford
Eifler, Carl F.
Eiseman, William E.
Eley, Randolph D.
Ellinger, Richard E.
Ellis, Alger C.
Ellis, Pierce S.
Elrod, Weldon
Emch, Harold E.
Emke, Fred A.
Eng, Donald Y.
Enos, Quentin M.
Epperson, Alex H.
Estelle, Lyle
Esterline, Jacob D.
Ettinger, Robert V.
Evans, Albert C.

Fairbairn, Don C.
Faraguna, Joe
Fate, Robert C.
Fenn, Charles H.

Fergerson, John M.
Ferrell, Thad A.
Ferry, Ed. G.
Finn, Art N.
Finnegan, John B.
Fitts, Clark D.
Fitzgerald, John T.
Fitzhugh, Robert W.
Fitzsimmons, Richard J.
Flaherty, Robert H.
Flynn, James H.
Ford, Frank J.
Fore, Clay J.
Fornes, George J.
Frake, Herbert W.
Francis, Dennis
Franklin, Robert
Frazee, Floyd R.
Fredrickson, Harold K.
Freudenberg, Alvin G.
Frye, Harold
Frye, Virgil
Furnari, Garry G.
Fussell, Bueford E.

Gabriel, Charles R.
Gabrielson, Dan A.
Gahen, George L.
Gale, Laurence
Gamble, Ralph
Gang, Julius
Garonski, Francis
Garrett, James M.
Gaston, Vestle C.
Gatto, Anthony
Gegenheimer, Eldred
Genaw, Gerald L.
Gentry, Claud D.
Geolas, Constantine
Georges, Michael P.
Georgia, Christos
Gersbeck, Gus
Geschwind, William L.
Ghizoni, George
Gibbons, Don C.
Gibbons, Don C.
Gibbons, Hoyt B.
Gildee, John J.
Gill, William G.
Gilmore, Jack
Gilmore, Martin J.

Glass, George W.
Gleason, Frank
Goarin, Tom A.
Gonzales, Diego
Goodell, Maurice L.
Goodnight, Warren E.
Gordon, Allen R.
Gore, Russell R.
Gorin, George D.
Gorman, Robert T.
Gosselin, Maurice
Grace, Ivan C.
Graham, Alex
Grakavac, Alex P.
Grangaard, Don R.
Grant, Robert L.
Green, William R.
Greenlee, Richard S.
Gremel, Norman A.
Grenci, Joe L.
Griffen, John R.
Grigg, Monroe Y.
Grimm, Laurence
Grimwood, Phillip
Grones, Dow S.
Grosso, Louis J.
Gulley, John
Gulliford, Rich D.
Gullixon, Harold R.
Guzzi, John

Haertel, Leroy W.
Haimson, Fima
Halterman, Thomas D.
Hamada, Dick S.
Hamm, Ed. B.
Hanger, Ted
Hansen, Palmer
Hanson, Frank A.
Harper, Douglas P.
Harris, Claude
Hartman, Ed. M.
Hasper, John H.
Hauge, Olaf M.
Hawkins, Roy W.
Haydu, Ed C.
Hazelwood, William F.
Head, George
Headrick, Blaine O.
Helfrich, Baird V.
Heller, Francis

Hemming, George T.
Henderson, Charles P.
Henning, Robert A.
Hess, William V.
Hibner, John H.
Higgenbottom, David G.
Hihilock, John L.
Hill, Gene
Hill, William B.
Hilsman, Roger
Hine, Milton J.
Hines, Harry C.
Hoagland, Paul V.
Hoborrow, Robert G.
Hofacker, William A.
Hoffman, John W.
Hoffman, William R.
Hollinger, Sherard F.
Honda, Robert T.
Hong, Chan
Hook, Carl
Hopiak, George A.
Hopper, Jay M.
Horner, Douglas H.
Horton, Jack E.
Houts, Marshall W.
Howell, Charles A.
Howell, John
Hubbard, Ralph H.
Huber, Carl
Huc, Harry J.
Hudgens, Robert L.
Hudson, Sam H.
Huffman, James E.
Huggins, James H.
Hughes, Dudley
Hughes, Jesse L.
Hughes, John W.
Hughes, Ken E.
Hull, Fred
Hultin, Emerick
Hungerland, Robert L.
Hunter, David A.
Hunter, David G.
Husslein, Warren
Huston, Phillip S.
Hutter, Charles C.

Ice, Ken W.
Imai, Hideo
Imbrey, Howard

Immonen, Leo
Irmiter, James F.

Jabson, Victor
Jackson, Joe
Jackson, Junior C.
Jacobs, Frank M.
Jacot, Nester E.
Jefferies, I. M.
Jendrzejzak, John C.
Jerome, John R.
Johanson, Erick O.
Johns, Harry E.
Johnson, Carlton W.
Johnson, Harry F.
Johnson, Larrabee, M.
Johnson, Olvier R.
Johnson, Robert D.
Johnson, Robert G.
Johnson, Robert J.
Johnson, Trois E.
Johnston, Graham
Jolliffe, George C.
Jones, Joe P.
Jones, Leander P.
Jones, Marion C.
Jones, Newton I.
Jones, Richard A.
Jones, Robert W.
Joost, Sherman B.
Jordan, Rudolph
Josling, Jackson R.
Judson, Saw
Julian, Luther E.
Jung, Harry G.

Kahn, Myron
Kalantzis, Anthony
Kaliff, Mendel
Karson, John C.
Katmick, Walter J.
Katwyck, Cornelius
Kazhaya, Susumue
Keber, Alex F.
Keller, T. C.
Kennedy, Howard R.
Kennedy, Ken
Kennedy, Temple
Kesler, John T.
Kevetos, James
Kidd, William A.
Kiddon, Dan F.

Kido, Fumio
Kilby, Jacks
King, Doug
King, James
King, William J.
Kirk, Elmer
Kishinami, Wilbert
Klaproth, Carl L.
Kleibert, Maurice
Klein, Jefferson
Klein, Oscar
Kloss, Frank S.
Kneal, Robert
Knight, Hale H.
Knoll, Jack
Koning, Henry I.
Kostrevic, Edward
Kramer, Charles
Kranstover, R. F.
Kreis, Bertram
Kretser, Cliff
Krey, Charles H.
Krisch, David
Krueger, Alfred C.
Kubin, Frank S.
Kurahashi, Shoichi
Kusak, Frank
Kuzmack, Jerome
Kwock, John F.

Lacomis, Ed L.
Laidlaw, Alan F.
Lajcak, Stephen W.
Lambert, Ross W.
Lang, Robert E.
Lanier, Elmer
Larsen, Gerald
Larson, Charles M.
Larue, Melvin L.
Larum, Norman R.
Lasher, Frank E.
Lawrence, Cliff
Lazarsky, Joe
Lederman, Morris Y.
Lee, Edmund
Leonard, Tom B.
Lepage, Clarence C.
Levin, Noah B.
Lewis, Kembele S.
Lewis, Robert V.
Lightstone, Harry A.

Lim, Soo W.
Lindley, Jesse O.
Litman, Sidney
Little, Harry W.
Littlefield, Joe M.
Lochner, R. P.
Loeffler, Milton
Loetterle, Francis
Logue, Asta
Longenecker, Dave R.
Loomis, William F.
Loraski, Ray C.
Lowe, Ed A.
Luce, James C.
Lucy, Sam G.
Ludwick, Philip
Lusk, Ernest
Lussier, Ed B.
Lutkin, Peter K.
Lykins, Vellie

Macauley, John P.
MacCawley, Tom G.
MacDonald, Everett
MacFarland, Wayne H.
MacGregor, Clark
MacKenzie, Malcom S.
MacLean, Marshall
Macomber, William B.
Maddox, Patrick
Magill, Orrin F.
Magistretti, William
Maharg, John D.
Maisonpierre, Robert
Malkin, Martin
Mallory, Jasper T.
Mandelbaum, David G.
Mangeng, Frank
Manousos, William
Manula, John O.
Markson, Malcom
Marling, Wayne S.
Marlow, Eldon
Marsh, Robert
Marshall, Ernest A.
Martin, Doug
Martin, Ed. F.
Martin, Elmer
Martin, Harry R.
Martin, Robert K.
Martin, William J.

Martineau, Paul V.
Martinez, Ralph
Maslowsky, Ed. S.
Mathis, Harold L.
Matsunaka, Charles Y.
Matthews, James
Matuszek, Leon J.
Maves, Floyd E.
Mavis, Arthur B.
Mazawa, Shizeto
McCabe, Ward
McCarger, John A.
McCarthy, Emmett
McCarthy, John F.
McCausland, Paul W.
McClare, William H.
McConnaughey, John N.
McCullough, James
McDerritt, Hugh A.
McDonough, John J.
McFail, John R.
McGaughy, Ed A.
McGuire, Ed J.
McGuire, William T.
McInnis, Don E.
McKinley, James S.
McKown, Ken W.
McLaughlin, Frank W.
McLeod, Francis
McMillan, Norman F.
McNally, George E.
McVicker, T. R.
Mead, Gerard
Meade, Pierre
Medlicott, Tom O.
Melchin, Harold
Melehes, Michael
Mess, Walter
Messimir, Prentice
Meyer, Milton W.
Migon, Casimir J.
Mihelich, John L.
Miller, William F.
Milligan, Wayne A.
Mills, Don A.
Milstein, George
Milton, Billy
Milton, Oliver (Oscar)
Mirbach, Walter J.
Mitchell, Earl L.
Mitsukado, Ed H.

Moehring, Glen E.
Monroe, Donald B.
Moon, Tom N.
Moore, Dan E.
Moore, Frank J.
Moore, Frank W.
Moore, Robert B.
Moore, Wallace
Moore, William B.
Moose, Virgil
Moree, Irby E.
Morgan, Joe E.
Morgan, Leon
Morgan, Tom B.
Morrissey, E. F.
Morrone, John F.
Morrow, James E.
Morse, Richard
Morwood, William G.
Moscrip, Amos D.
Mow, Chin
Mudrinich, Daniel
Mulder, Cornelius A.
Murphy, Edward
Murray, John M.
Murray, Sherwood
Myer, John C.
Mykland, Gunnar G.
Mysberg, James H.

Nardella, Ralph
Nelchin, Harold
Nelson, Herman
Nelson, Ingelo
Nelson, Isadore
Nelson, Ray A.
Newberry, Truman H.
Nickolas, Nick J.
Niemczyk, Julian
Niven, Don H.
Noble, Marshall H.
Nonni, Louis A.
Nordblom, Harold E.
Nordsieck, Carl W.
Norris, Karl
Norton, William A.
Nupen, Edly D.

Obereiner, John M.
O'Brien, Walter E.
O'Donnell, William H.

Ohn, Saw
Ong, Jo K.
O'Reagan, Samuel G.
Orlan, Joe J.
Osowski, Edward
Owen, George H.

Page, Wellman
Palko, Ann
Palmer, Quentin S.
Pamplin, Hiram
Pamplin, Jack
Pangborn, John C.
Pape, Art A.
Pappas, Anthony C.
Parker, Evan J.
Patterson, James T.
Patton, John B.
Pedrick, Richard L.
Peers, William R.
Pendergast, Ed S.
Peters, Emerson
Peterson, Roy C.
Petievich, Melvin
Pettigrew, William J.
Phee, Robert R.
Phillips, William R.
Pier, Ken M.
Pilaroscia, Albert
Pippin, Don R.
Pitman, Theodore
Pittard, Murcil
Pixley, Don
Plourde, Henry P.
Posey, Norman M.
Power, Stuart E.
Powers, George R.
Pratt, George T.
Price, Harvey C.
Provenzano, Charles
Pruett, James B.

Quinn, Patrick

Rackett, Melbourne
Raiss, John
Ramsey, Howard R.
Raposo, Manuel C.
Reach, James E.
Reardon, Francis J.
Redmond, Everett S.

Reed (Monocle)
Reese, Merlin C.
Rendulic, Stephen
Reynolds, Ray E.
Rhea, Robert
Richardson, Don C.
Richardson, James A.
Richardson, Wesley E.
Richmond, Wally G. N.
Richter, Allen R.
Rief, Herman J.
Roach, James R.
Roberts, Carl E.
Robey, Gerald W.
Robinson, John W.
Rodenberg, Robert R.
Roman, Tom
Rosenfield, John M.
Rosewick, William F.
Rost, Joe A.
Roye, Herbert F.
Rubio, Chris
Ruble, Howard L.
Rupert, Horace E.
Russell, William J.
Russo, Fred B.
Ruzick, Louie
Ryan, William C.
Ryder, Oliver A.

Saltzstein, Robert A.
Sanders, Robert H.
Saunders, Bruce E.
Sayre, Ken L.
Scharf, Ed M.
Schiefflein, William O.
Schnaps, Solomon H.
Schreiner, Sam
Schultz, Curtis C.
Scoles, Glenn R.
Scott, Charles R.
Scott, Jesse W.
Sedgwick, Thomas I.
Shaffer, Andrew W.
Shannon, Jack T.
Sharp, John B.
Shefchuck, Stephen J.
Shelby, Ray T.
Shepard, William B.
Shields, Gerald V.
Sidbury, David K.

Silver, Irwin S.
Silver, Jack M.
Silverman, Gerry S.
Singleton, Louis I.
Sipos, John J.
Skiathitis, Art A.
Skidmore, Rich C.
Slagg, William K.
Slavin, Joe W.
Slupski, Chester A.
Smith, Brooks C.
Spector, Stanley
Spegal, Bruce
Stanford, Clarence
Stanford, George W.
Starr, Roger S.
Starz, Ed A.
Stasik, Al
Steed, Ernest H.
Stein, Ken W.
Stelle, Charles C.
Stenhouse, Alex D.
Stephenson, John H.
Stern, Mike
Storm, Leroy
Straub, Joe M.
Strugis, Harry
Sturgis, Norman R.
Sussman, Harvey S.
Swadesh, Morris
Sweeney, Robert G.
Swem, John
Swift, John L.

Taheny, John J.
Tanabe, Takao
Tang, Lazum
Tate, Rudolph
Tatz, Bernard H.
Taylor, Philip W.
Techtmann, William J.
Tedeschi, Pete
Tennyson, William
Terry, Rollin
Tessari, Emil
Thomale, Robert W.
Thompson, Allen O.
Thompson, Leroy
Thorlin, Reginald
Thrailkill, Martin C.
Tillquist, Dave E.

Tilly, James L.
Timmons, Otwell
Timothy, Saw Egbert
Tindall, Francis S.
Titus, Gerald
Todd, Paul H.
Totten, Gordon K.
Tottori, Calvin A.
Trahan, Lufro
Trechter, Oliver E.
Tretheway, Burton S.
Trifletti, Vincent J.
Triska, George R.
Truex, Ralph
Tsikerdanos, Ernest
Tucker, Roger S.
Tuggle, Gaston
Tulka, Charles O.
Turner, John M.
Turrell, William A.
Tutle, Ken D.
Tutor, Everett D.
Tweed, George B.
Tweedy, John B.
Tweist, Jack W.

Van Arsdale, Albert H.
Vandervoort, John R.
Van Noppen, Leonard M.
Varalay, Theodore S.
Varnson, Thomas A.
Vella, Anthony
Vella, Walter F.
Vinson, Hal D.

Wade, Emmet M.
Wadsworth, Claude V.
Wagner, Albert
Walden, James E.
Walker, Earl
Wallace, Robert E.
Walsh, Richard T.
Walters, Robert B.
Ward, Hugh
Ward, James
Warrington, Roger
Wask, John
Waters, Martin J.
Weaver, John C.
Webb, James
Wehrum, John E.
Welch, John F.

Weld, Philip
Wentworth, Robert
Weschler, Roland
West, Lee
Wetmore, Melvin H.
Weyland, Stephen C.
White, Edwin M.
White, Woodrow W.
Wible, Charles F.
Wilcox, James K.
Wilcox, Oliver W.
Wilkinson, William C.
Williams, Alfred E.
Wilson, Lysle E.

Winkel, John C.
Wiseman, Ed C.
Wolbarst, Roger K.
Wong, Sam
Woolington, Sam S.
Wooten, Allen D.
Wrenn, Ed F.
Wright, Leroy
Wunderlich, Fred L.

Yempuku, Ralph T.

Ziino, Joe P.
Zwergel, John A.

CASUALTIES

Aganoor, B. V.
Bauman, Bernard N.
Berg, Harold J.
Bernstein, James J.
Foley, Peter F.
Fowler, Neal A.
Franklin, Guy E.
Froberg, Paul
Gallovitch, Elmer
Gibbons, Henry
Hall, Thomas F.

Krautwald, William
Meehan, Art
Orlan, Joe
Riley, Thomas R.
Rogers, Ralph T.
Seng, Lester J.
Stratis, Ralph N.
Tibbets, Robert
Tolleson, John H.
Vandervoort, Dale S.
Waldo, Maturin

Index

ꟌꟍꟌꟍꟌꟍꟌꟍꟌꟍꟌꟍꟌꟍꟌꟍꟌꟍꟌꟍꟌꟍꟌꟍꟌ

[233]

barkation, 33, 34, 35; Far East library, 34; arrives CBI, 36; and Indian food, 38; at HQ CBI, 38; and British Intelligence, 38-39; at New Delhi, 41; Burma as area of operations, 42; Stilwell meets with, 42; mission of, 43; coordinates with British XIV Corps, 43; and native labor, 61; radio equipment and design, 62-63; supply bases, 63-64; co-operation with ATC on air rescue, 70-71; first group in Burma, 77; new missions, 95; ATC cooperation, 100, 123; and air rescue, 101, 121; co-operation with 14th Air Force, 100-101, 124; acquires Gypsy Moth, 106; and Jap prisoners, 106-107; air-plane for, 111; cooperation with British, 111, 116; aids NCAC, 112; communications problems, 113; teams of, 114; commended by Gen. Davidson, 114-115; North Burma operations, 121; personnel loss, 126; expands in North Burma, 127; oper-ations, 130; Gen. Donovan visits, 130-131; Coughlin replaces Eifler, 132; liberation of North Burma, 135; field bases, 135; operational procedures, changes in, 136; bases in North Burma, 136; operations, improvement and expansion, 138; Peers commands, 138; Peers's confi-dence in, 140; V Force transferred to, 141; guerrilla tactics, 144, 146-147; supplies intelligence to Air Corps, 147-148; supports *Galahad*, 162; Gen. Merrill thanks, 165; ex-pansion to 10,000 men, 171; assists Chindits, 173; in British 14th Army sector, 173; British transfer per-sonnel to, 173; expands battalion operational groups, 176; liaison with combat commands, 179; concern of, over Gen. Sultan's appointment, 179; expansion of operations, 179; complex activities, 180; and aircraft, 180; hospital for unit, 180; Ma-rauder personnel transferred to, 180; weather stations, 180; assessing cas-ualties, 185; liaison with Indian 19th Div., 187; alerted to disband, 191; inactivation plans scrapped, 192; personnel transferred to OSS in China, 192-193; inactivation, 193; final mission, 194-209; tactics

change in, 194; battalion command ers, Peers's faith in, 195; intelligence network, 196; last mission (map), 199; security precautions, 203; mis-sion completed and unit inactivated, 207; Presidential Distinguished Unit Citation, 207; inactivated, 211; anal-yses of operations and statistics, 217, 220; casualties, 220; impact of operations, 221; indebtedness to Kachins, 222; roster of, 223-232

1st Bn., commanded by Lt. Mudrinich, 177; action during inactivation, 193; tactics, 195; Salween River mission, 198; patrolling, 198; and Taunggyi-Kentung Road, 198; at Namsang, 199

2nd Bn., under Joost, 178; move-ment east, 177; destroys Chinese villages, 178; action of, 193; tactics, 195; mission to Hsipaw-Loilem, 199; captures Jap dumps, 200; Jap casu-alties, 200

2nd Bn., crosses Burma Road, 184; action of, 193; conventional tactics, 195; prolonged fighting, 204-205; at Pangtara, 205-207; reorganized, 207

5th Bn., northwest of Lashio, 184-185
6th Bn., southwest of Lashio, 185
7th Bn., formation of, 185
10th Bn., action, 193; guerrilla mis-sion, 195; at Hsipaw-Loilem, 196; at Mongpawn, 197

Detachment 101 Arakan Field Unit, 221
DeSilva, Captain, of Kachin Levies, 94
Devlin, Capt. Frank, 27; and supply problem, 33
Dialects, Burmese, 47
Dibrugarh, parachute training at, 71
Dikoo River, 60
Dimapur, action at, 171
Dinjan airstrip, 87
Dockery, Miss, 29
Donovan, Gen. William ("Wild Bill"), Det. 101 his plan, 25; and Eifler, 26-27; Peers meets for first time, 29; visits Det. 101, 130-131; visits be-hind enemy lines, 203
Dope, use of, 69
Drown, Capt. George, 14-15

EASTERBROOK, COL. ERNEST F., 153
Eastern Air Command, 111; and air rescue, 140

Meiktila, airbase at, 100; bombing of, 109; British 14th Army occupies, 192

Merrill, Gen. Frank, mission of, 141; heart attacks, 158-159; commands *Galahad* operation, 161; thanks Det. 101, 165; assumes command of K Force and M Force, 165; versus Stilwell, 166-167; third heart attack, 167; replaced by Gen. Wessels, 167

Merrill's Marauders, 18, 19, 141-143; attacks Walabum (map), 143; Jap pressure on, 151; Japs and, 155; and 113th Chinese Reg., 155; 2nd mission, 157-160 (map), 157; Stilwell orders into bivouac, 159; dissension with Stilwell, 159; Col. Hunter commands, 159; British officers attached to, 164; exhausted by battle, 166-167; personnel transferred to Det. 101, 180

1st Bn., and Shadazup, 156; envelops Japs, 159; part of H Force, 161

2nd Bn., crosses Mogaung River, 156; at Warong, 156; at Inkangahtawng, 156; at Nphum Ga, 158; tight spot, 159; assigned to M Force, 161

3rd Bn., at Warong, 156; at Inkangahtawng, 156; at Nphum Ga, 158; envelops Japs, 159; part of K Force, 161

Miao, J Group operations at, 113

Milligan, M/Sgt. Wayne (Pop), parachute instruction by, 71; jumpmaster, 76, 89, 90; and emergency drop, 88; picks up "A" Group, 95; flies to Kunming, 100; and training, 117; on loan to ATC, 126; supply drops, 130

Milton, Capt. Oliver (Oscar), 13; maintains radio contact, 84-85; and "A" Group base camp, 87; returns to duty, 113-114; and *Dah* Force, 173

Milton, Lt. William, and guerrilla activities, 188; and night drop, 189

Mines, 147

Ming, Capt. Chun, 26, 33

Mining, 50-51

Missionaries, in Burma, 50; debt of, to Det. 101, 190

Mite typhus, 164-165

Mizukami, Gen., commits *hara-kiri*, 167

Mogaung, 19

Mogaung River, 77; Marauders cross, 156

Mogok, British 14th Army at, 187

Mongmit, British Army takes, 187

Mongols, Burmese settlers, 47

Mongpawn, attack at, 197

Monsoons, 118, 120; effect of, on operations, 19

Moore, Maj. Robert, operations officer, 180

Morale operations, 214

Moree, Sgt. Irby E., 33, and camouflage, 109

Morgan, Gen. "Butch," 101

Mortars, use of, 195-197

Moslems, 37, 49; and Hindus, 38

Moulmein, fall of, 51

Mountains, 45

Mountbatten, Lord Louis, 151

Mudrinich, Lt. Daniel, commands 1st Bn., 177

Myitkyina airstrip, capture of, 165

Myitkyina, base camp at, 12-13; a goal, 18-19; airport at, importance of, 43; Jap 18th Div. at, 56; first visual contact, 77; under observation, 92; recaptured, plans for, 135; retaking of, 147; key to Northern Burma, 159; battle for, 161-168; Jap retreat from 167; operations south of (map), 175. *See also* Galahad

Mykland, Lt. Gunnar G., 130

NAGA HILLS, 5, 45; and Ledo Road, 7; Jap activity in, 112

Nagas, 64; cooperation with, 126

Namhkwin, sabotage at, 83

Namsang, airbase at, 100; 1st Bn. at, 199; road opened to, 202

Namsang Airfield, 183

Namtu mines, 50

Namtu River, 45

Napalm bombs, 202

Nat, 49

Native labor, and building airstrips, 106

Native tribes, 47

Natives, recruiting of, 59, 63, 99; training of, 105

Nau (guide), 165

Naw, Zhing Htaw, Kachin leader, 16; aid given to "A" Group, 94; and Gen. Donovan, 131

Nawbum, Area III HQ, 156; assembly point, 161

Nazira base camp, 58-60; labor for, 60; training in, 61, 99; parachute training, 117; base radio station, 136, 138; hospital at, 180

Peirse, Air Marshal Sir Richard, 106
Pendergast, Sgt. Ed S., 130
Personnel, qualified, need for, 96
Peterson, Lt. Roy C., 110
Photography, aerial, 72-73
Pick, General, 7
Pidaung, operations at, 127-128; 1st Bn. at, 198
Pidaung Forest Preserve, base camp at, 127
Pigeons, carrier, use of, 183-184
Plant life, 46
Poison, and *pungyis*, 145
Poole, Lt. Edward, and guerrilla activity, 188
Pongyi Chaung, 49
Pongyies, 49; and fifth column, 56
Powers, Lt. George R., and guerrilla activity, 188
Presidential Distinguished Citation Unit, award given Det. 101, 207-209
Prisoners, Japanese, 13, 106-107, 217; "escaping," 176
Prome, action at, 54
Propaganda, 181, 214; Japanese and American compared, 221
PT boat, 99-100
Pungyis, 144-145, 174
Putao, 65

Quinn, Lt. Patrick, at Myitkyina, 15; sabotage by, 83, 84; missing, 89; Kachin aid to, 94; and Pidaung operation, 127-128; commands Area II, 136; and intelligence, 148; and *Galahad*, 165; and listening posts, 178
Quislings, 214

Radio equipment, 63; difficulty with, 183-184
Radio interference, Jap, 124
Radio traffic, 179; overloaded, 130; requiring elaborate network, 138
RAF, and air defense of Burma, 53; and Jap Air Force, 54; supplies plane, 106
Railroads, sabotage of, 75
Rainfall, 45
Rain forest, tropic, 46
Raiss, Maj. John, 106; gets airstrips in condition, 201-202; Gen. Sultan visits, 202
Rally points, need for, 97

Ramgarh, Indian camp at, 5; Chinese 30th Div. at, 18
Ramree Island, 115
Rangoon, 7; Jap airfield at, 51; evacuation of, 53; fall of, 54; plans for retaking, 99; first sight of, 119
Recruitment, of guerrillas, 12-13, 16, 59, 99, 138
Religion, in Burma, 49-50
Rice, 46, 50, 120
Richardson, Allan, 60
Richter, Sgt. Allen, 63
Ritpong, Jap outpost at, 128, 164
Rivers, 45
Robby (operative), leads M Group, 112
Rocky (operative), as jungle survival instructor, 124-126
Romanski, Lt. John, and guerrilla activity, 188
Royal Air Force. *See* RAF.
Royal Navy, cooperation with, 116

Sabotage, 174-176; training in, 30, 31-32; of CBI supplies, 41; "A" Group, 75; effect of, by "A" Group, 88-89; and Jap army supplies, 171
Sadon, seized by guerrillas, 167-168
Salween River, 45; as defense line, 51
Samurai philosophy, 108
San, Maj. Gen. Aung, Jap puppet, 57
Sanders, Colonel, 87
Sartz, Capt. Jake, 73-74, 77, 92, 93, 100; and 14th Air Force airdrop, 101; bombs Jap convoy, 102-103
Schreiner, Sgt. Sam, 110
Scott, Lt. Charles R., and guerrilla activity, 188
Seagrave, Col. Gordon S., 111
Seagrave Hospital Unit, 110, 180
Security precautions, 203
Seniku, seized by guerrillas, 167
Service, John S., 126
Sevareid, Eric, 126
Shadazup, action at, 156
Shan Plateau, 46
Shan States, 46
Shans, 47, 49; with 1st Bn., 108; cooperation with Japs, 124; defections of, 174; cooperation with Allies, 183
Shepard, Ens. William B., 130
Shwe Dagon, 119
Shweli River, 45
Siam. *See* Thailand
Silver Slipper, The, 50

Simla, Eifler visits, 42
Sinbo, 86
Sind Desert, 37
Sittang River, 45; Japs cross, 51
Skittles (operative), 16, 139; and L Group, 112; and KNOTHEAD, 148-149
Slim, Gen. Sir William, 19; commands British 14th Army, 151; and Mandalay offensive, 187; at Meiktila, 192
Smith, Nicol, 31-32
Smith, Sir Reginald Dorman, 42; leaves Burma, 56
Snipers, 8
Southern Burma, expansion of operations in, 115; operations in, 99, 117, 121
Starling, Lieutenant, 122
Stein, Lt. Ken, and guerrilla activity, 188
Stilwell, Col. Joseph, Jr., 4
Stilwell, Gen. Joseph, 3-4, 150-154; and Det. 101, 4; on Burmese campaign, 4-5; on retreat (1942), 6-7; urges Chinese to fight, 7; directs Chinese 22nd Div., 9; on Chinese Army, 9-10; briefed on Det. 101, 10-21; Myitkyina a goal, 18; on monsoons, 19; orders guerrilla expansion, 19; Det. 101 a plan of, 25; meets with Det. 101, 42; on Det. 101's impatience, 42; as Chief of Staff for Allied Forces, 53-54; on Allied defeat, 56; on cooperation with British, 58; opposed Lashio drop, 104; forms V Force, 110; and liberation of Northern Burma, 135; and Merrill's Marauders, 141; transfers V Force to Det. 101, 141; on poisoned *pungyis*, 145; unenviable position of, 149; and Chinese Army, 150; not appreciated, 151; commands held, 151; difficulties with British and Chinese, 151; and Chinese problem, 151-152, 153; as Chief of Staff to Chiang Kai-shek, 152; and Chennault, 152; plan for equipping Chinese Army, 152-153; and Kachins, 153-154; and ear-collecting custom, 154; health of, 154; dissension with Marauders, 159; orders Marauders into bivouac, 159; orders capture of Kamaing, 161; and taking Myitkyina, 161-168; Myitkyina plan (map), 163; versus Merrill, 166-167; tacit approval of Det.

101's expansion, 171; relieved as Theater Commander, 179; exposed to Japs, 192; visits behind enemy lines, 203
Stratemeyer, Lt. Gen. George E., 111; and air rescue, 140
Straub, Sgt. Joe M., 110
Strong, Colonel, 29
Stuart, Father James, 105; and Gen. Donovan, 131
Submarine, use of, 115-116, 215
Sultan, Lt. Gen. Daniel I., commands India-Burma Theater, 179; on Kachin guerrillas, 179; alerts Det. 101 to inactivate, 191; on Jap threat to Kunming, 192; and Det. 101's guerrillas, 192; visits Det. 101's lines, 202; behind enemy lines, 203; recommends Presidential Distinguished Unit Citation for Det. 101, 207
Sun Li Jen, Gen. 5, 150; and bamboo fortifications, 6; Stilwell urges fight with Japs, 7; maneuverability of, 9
Supply, lines, 64; drops, 72, 130; problems, 7-8, 20, 33, 34-35, 123, 129, 211
Supayalet, Queen, 48
Sumprabum, 65; Japs at, 19; action at, 161
Surprise element, 67, 116
Swift, Lt. John L., 177

TAGAP, L Group at, 112
Tang, Major Lazum; operations east of Bhamo, 177; commands 6th Bn., 185
Taro, Chinese 22nd Div. at, 9
Tarung Hka, 112
Tarung Valley, J Group in, 112
Taunggyi, espionage at, 183; Japs driven back to, 195; action at, 197
Taunggyi Airfield, 183
Taunggyi-Kentung Road, seizure of, 192-193
Taungup pass, blocking of, 115
Tavoy, 50
Teakwood, 46, 50
Temperature, 45
Tenasserim, 45; airdrop at, 117-118
Thailand, Jap Air Force in, 54; Jap escape route, 192
Thiebaw, King, 48; and Baptist missionaries, 50
Thompson, Capt. Allen O., 87-88, 90

[245]